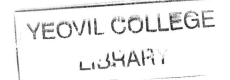
YEOVIL COLLEGE
LEARNING CENTRE

TO BE RETURNED OR RENEWED BY THE DATE
LAST STAMPED BELOW   Tel. 01935 845450

Getting Ready for
Direct Practice in
Social Work

Sara Miller McCune founded SAGE Publishing in 1965 to support the dissemination of usable knowledge and educate a global community. SAGE publishes more than 1000 journals and over 800 new books each year, spanning a wide range of subject areas. Our growing selection of library products includes archives, data, case studies and video. SAGE remains majority owned by our founder and after her lifetime will become owned by a charitable trust that secures the company's continued independence.

Los Angeles | London | New Delhi | Singapore | Washington DC | Melbourne

Getting Ready for Direct Practice in Social Work

Peter Scourfield

Learning Matters
An imprint of SAGE Publications Ltd
1 Oliver's Yard
55 City Road
London EC1Y 1SP

SAGE Publications Inc.
2455 Teller Road
Thousand Oaks, California 91320

SAGE Publications India Pvt Ltd
B 1/I 1 Mohan Cooperative Industrial Area
Mathura Road
New Delhi 110 044

SAGE Publications Asia-Pacific Pte Ltd
3 Church Street
#10-04 Samsung Hub
Singapore 049483

Editor: Kate Keers
Production controller: Chris Marke
Project management: Deer Park Productions,
Tavistock, Devon
Marketing manager: Camille Richmond
Cover design: Wendy Scott
Typeset by: C&M Digitals (P) Ltd, Chennai, India
Printed by CPI Group (UK) Ltd, Croydon, CR0 4YY

Library of Congress Control Number: 2017935032

British Library Cataloguing in Publication Data

A catalogue record for this book is available from the
British Library

ISBN 978-1-4739-8933-7 (pbk)
ISBN 978-1-4739-8932-0 (hbk)

At SAGE we take sustainability seriously. Most of our products are printed in the UK using FSC papers and boards.
When we print overseas we ensure sustainable papers are used as measured by the PREPS grading system.
We undertake an annual audit to monitor our sustainability.

Contents

About the author

Peter Scourfield first qualified as a social worker in 1984. Since then he has worked as a front-line practitioner in a variety of settings with diverse service user groups, most latterly with older and physically disabled adults. He has been involved in social work education since 2003 during which time he has been the MA Social Work Course Leader, performed the role of Practice Educator, taught a range of different modules on both the BA and MA Social Work and been both a personal tutor and a visiting practice tutor. He has also been involved in Post-Qualifying social work education. His research and writing interests, including his PhD, have predominantly been focused on older people's experiences in the social care system. Peter is currently an Honorary Visiting Fellow at Anglia Ruskin University and a freelance writer and trainer.

Series editors' preface

We have witnessed significant changes and shocks in recent years. These have resulted in numerous challenges for the wider world, and for all four countries of the UK. These include political shifts to the 'popular' Right, a growing antipathy to care and support, and dealing with lies and 'alternative truths' in our daily lives. Alongside this, is the need to address the impact of an increasingly ageing population with its attendant social care needs and working with the financial implications that such a changing demography brings. At the other end of the lifespan the need for high quality childcare, welfare and safeguarding services has been highlighted as society develops and responds to the changing complexion. As demand rises so do the costs and the unquestioned assumption that austerity measures are necessary continues to create tensions in services, policies and expectations.

Migration has developed as a global phenomenon and we now live and work with the implications of international issues in our everyday and local lives. Often these issues influence how we construct our social services and determine what services we need to offer. It is likely that as a social worker you will work with a diverse range of people throughout your career, many of whom have experienced significant, even traumatic, events that require a professional and caring response. As well as working with individuals, however, you may be required to respond to the needs of a particular community disadvantaged by world events or excluded within local communities because of assumptions made about them.

The importance of high quality social work education remains if we are adequately to address the complexities of modern life. We should continually strive for excellence in education as this allows us to focus clearly on what knowledge it is useful to engage with when learning to be a social worker. Questioning everything, especially from a position of knowledge is central to social work.

The books in this series respond to the agendas driven by changes brought about by professional bodies, governments and disciplinary reviews. They aim to build on and offer introductory texts based on up-to-date knowledge and to help communicate this in an accessible way, so preparing the ground for future study and for encouraging good practice as you develop your social work career. The books are written by people passionate about social work and social services and aim to instil that passion in others. The current text introduces you to the processes involved in beginning social work practice, setting the scene for exploring more specialised areas of practice and providing you with a grounding from which to enhance your learning.

Professor Jonathan Parker

Introduction

The background to the book: 'Readiness for Direct Practice'

Originally developed by the Social Work Reform Board and the College of Social Work, the Professional Capabilities Framework (PCF) has formed the overarching professional standards framework for professional social work in England since 2013. Now managed and delivered by the British Association of Social Workers (BASW) the PCF contains nine levels ranging from prospective student (level 1) to strategic social worker (level 9). The different levels relate to the complexity of work that someone with the identified capabilities would be able to manage (https://www.basw.co.uk/pcf/). The first four levels of the PCF relate to student social workers and, of these, the second level is called 'Readiness for Direct Practice'. The descriptor for this level explains:

> *By the point of assessment of readiness for direct practice (prior to first placement), students should demonstrate basic communication skills, ability to engage with users, capacity to work as a member of an organisation, willingness to learn from feedback and supervision, and demonstrate basic SW values, knowledge and skills in order to be able to make effective use of first practice placement.*

Consequently you need to achieve the Readiness for Direct Practice level at a relatively early point in your course. You therefore need to know enough about the domains of the PCF to be able to demonstrate to your assessors that you are knowledgeable, capable and safe enough to enter the world of social work practice and work directly with service users and carers. Reaching this standard is important because if you do not achieve the required level you cannot progress onto your first practice placement.

About the book

Getting Ready for Direct Practice in Social Work is specifically designed to enable social work students on qualifying courses in England to understand what the Professional Capabilities Framework expects of them at the Readiness for Direct Practice level. By providing the necessary knowledge, values and skills to be able to demonstrate capability at the Assessed Readiness for Direct Practice (ARDP) level, you should be sufficiently prepared to be able to progress smoothly through to your first practice placement. As well as specifically focusing on establishing capability at PCF level two, *Getting Ready for Direct Practice in Social Work* has also been written to provide a useful foundation from which to explore more deeply and more critically the range of knowledge, skills and values of professional social work required at all student levels of the Professional Capabilities Framework. As such it is most appropriately used alongside other relevant social work texts, many of which can be found in the Learning Matters Transforming Social Work Practice series.

For ease of understanding, the book devotes a chapter to each of the nine domains of the Professional Capabilities Frameworks in turn. Each chapter starts with that domain's specific descriptor as set out in the PCF and then breaks it down explaining key concepts and terminology while providing a range of interactive activities that enable you to acquire and apply the basic knowledge, skills and values required. Each chapter also finishes with a summary of its key points together with suggestions for further reading to develop your knowledge in that area. Although links between the domains are signposted throughout the book, *Getting Ready for Direct Practice in Social Work* concludes with a chapter on 'Bringing it all together' the chief aims of which are to ensure that learning across the domains is properly integrated and that you can make the transition from the Readiness for Direct Practice stage to your first practice placement as smoothly as possible.

Although there would be a certain logic in doing so, there is no requirement that you work through the chapters in numerical order. Each chapter stands on its own and can be used to underpin learning on whatever aspect of the PCF is required.

Finally, while the book is specifically structured around the current professional standards framework in England (the PCF), its basic subject matter is the core knowledge, values and skills of professional social work, most of which have been built up and have endured over time and will continue to endure and be relevant whatever framework is in place. You are therefore encouraged not only to see the book as a useful guide to the Readiness for Direct Practice level of the current regulatory framework but also as a starting point from which to reflect about what it means to be a professional social worker – regardless of the regulatory context in which you might find yourself practising. Readers should be aware that while the Professional Capabilities Framework is due to be 'refreshed' at some point it will retain the nine domains.

1: Professionalism

Achieving a Social Work Degree

This chapter will help you develop skills in the following domain of the Professional Capabilities Framework:

> **Professionalism:** *Identify and behave as a professional social worker committed to professional development.*

The Professional Capability Framework states about this domain that:

> *Social workers are members of an internationally recognised profession, a title protected in UK law. Social workers demonstrate professional commitment by taking responsibility for their conduct, practice and learning, with support through supervision. As representatives of the social work profession they safeguard its reputation and are accountable to the professional regulator.* (BASW, Professional Capability Framework – Readiness for Practice Capabilities)

This domain statement goes on to say that, at the point of going out on their first practice placement, social work students need to be able to:

- Describe the role of the social worker
- Describe the mutual roles and responsibilities in supervision
- Describe the importance of professional behaviour
- Describe the importance of personal and professional boundaries
- Demonstrate ability to learn, using a range of approaches
- Describe the importance of emotional resilience in social work

Introduction

As we saw in the Introduction, there are nine 'domains' in the Professional Capabilities Framework, all of which link and overlap with each other and all of which students must be able to evidence at different levels throughout their course. The first domain is 'Professionalism' which, in many ways, can also be seen as the overarching theme of the whole PCF and that will be the focus of this chapter.

This chapter begins with some initial exploration of what professionalism means in the context of social work. From there, it will provide opportunities for you to think about and demonstrate what each of those requirements means in practice. Following the various activities in this chapter you will also be signposted to further reading which will help further develop your understanding of each concept or theme and help you make links between the domains.

Lastly, it is important to emphasise that the ARDP assessment is not an academic or 'theory' exercise where your knowledge is assessed in an essay or some other written assignment. What will decide whether you are ready to go into direct practice will be your ability to 'be' professional and to act and behave in acceptably professional ways. However, before we engage with each of the specific requirements of the Domain Descriptors, we start off by considering the bigger picture – what does professionalism in social work mean and what does it actually look like?

Exploring professionalism

Social work in the UK has only relatively recently been regarded as a 'profession', at least in comparison to more established professions such as doctors and lawyers. 'Social worker' only became a protected occupational title in 2005. Interestingly, there are still some today that don't accept that social work either can be or should be professional in the same way as other more established occupations (Lymbery, 2005; Parker and Doel, 2013). Therefore, deciding what constitutes being 'professional' in social work terms is not always a straightforward exercise. It is something that requires a degree of thought. For example, if by saying that you are a 'professional' means that you think that you are a 'law unto yourself' in how you act or that your professional knowledge means that you are an 'expert' on other people's lives, then you are going to run into problems. For Davies and Jones (2016), 'professionalism' in the context of social work is 'not an easy subject' and 'is best understood through participation in active experiential learning' (p. 2). This is a useful starting point because it underlines that professionalism is not just something that you learn about, or that you instantly 'possess' on passing your course; it is something you have to work at constantly in order to bring it to life in your practice and make it meaningful.

Activity 1.1

Nowadays it is accepted that being 'professional' and demonstrating professionalism lies at the core of being an effective social worker. However, we need to think about what this actually means, what it requires from the worker and what it looks like to others. Consider these questions:

1. What are the benefits from social work being a profession? Are there any downsides to social work being a profession? Give reasons.

2. How do social workers demonstrate their professionalism in practice?

Share your thoughts with a colleague.

In answer to the first question, on the benefit side, you might have said that social work being a profession helps the public have confidence that it is a regulated activity and that social workers need to maintain certain standards of professional behaviour. For social workers themselves it helps to have clearly defined codes of ethics and other frameworks for practice. Looked at in a different light, you might have said that being a professional comes with certain responsibilities which, if not discharged properly, can lead to a social worker being disciplined or even deregistered. This view acknowledges that professional social workers are, therefore, accountable to a range of bodies: their employers, their profession, their regulatory body, the HCPC and, most importantly, to the public. On the downside, you might have thought that professionalising social workers enhances their status but also their power and that could lead to an unwanted 'us and them' divide opening up between social workers and those with whom they work. There are many faces of professionalism and what this means in practice will need to be thought about and debated throughout your course.

For the second question, you might have said that professional social workers need to be competent in what they do and that they need to have the appropriate knowledge, values and skills in order to do their jobs properly. This might include being knowledgeable about relevant legislation, policy and theories, being mindful of treating people with respect, being aware of the need for confidentiality and to maintain appropriate boundaries and also how to communicate with a diverse range of people. By now, you should be aware that all of these qualities – and more – are set out in the nine domains of the PCF. Therefore, one of the hallmarks of being a professional social worker is the ability to understand and integrate all of the PCF into their practice. A social worker's professionalism needs to be evident in their everyday interactions with the people with whom they come into contact: service users, carers, colleagues, managers, other professionals and the public at large.

What does professionalism require and what does it look like to service users?

Perhaps a useful starting point is to consider what expectations service users have of social workers. In 1981, Davies wrote that:

> *Client-perspective studies have greatly helped in the task of defining professionalism in social work. It is clear that the true professional is not someone who is cool, detached, career-minded or disinterested, but is the worker who can display friendliness (not necessarily friendship in the conventional sense), understanding, and a warmth of manner which convinces the client of his active interest in and concern for the client's plight. And clients are remarkably sophisticated in being able to recognise that such professionalism is part and parcel of the social worker's formal occupation. 'With lawyers it's mainly a professional job for them, they don't take a personal interest in it. They wouldn't show any feelings and not really any interest. The social worker didn't behave as though it was job, even though it was.' (p. 20)*

This is as true today as it was in 1981. Many studies have backed this up when they have asked people who use services what they expect from social workers. For example, when Peter Beresford and his colleagues launched 'The Standards We Expect' initiative (Harding and Beresford, 1996), their research indicated strongly that what service users and carers expected and wanted from social workers included qualities like treating people with courtesy, honesty and being reliable. Also highlighted as essential were being a good communicator, being up to date with knowledge about local services and possessing basic practical skills. All of these 'standards' of professionalism might seem 'obvious' and something that should be taken for granted but they are the very bedrock of professionalism in social work.

Activity 1.2

Harding and Beresford (1996) found that service users and carers expected that, as a minimum, social workers should possess certain qualities. These included the following key areas:

- to be able to listen and communicate well;
- to be able to counsel and understand people's complex emotions;
- to be knowledgeable about local services, national resources and social security entitlements;
- to be able to negotiate with rather than impose on others;
- to have basic practical skills;
- to have a realistic sense of judgement about risk;

- to be able to treat people as individuals;
- to respect others where respect means taking people's views seriously and recognising their right to be heard;
- to maintain confidentiality and privacy;
- to be able to treat people with courtesy and empathy;
- to be honest;
- to be reliable and to ensure that there is continuity of service;
- to be able to put their 'pet theories' to one side and not impose them on people or look for 'hidden' meanings that are not always there.

Task

1. Put yourself in the position of a service user and /or carer. Look through the list. Why do you think that each point is regarded as so important? Explain how you would feel if a social worker did *not* have that skill or quality in their dealings with you and your family?

2. Now put yourself in the position of a social worker. On a scale of 0 – 10, where 0 = that you do not have the ability at all and 10 = that you are completely proficient, how would you rate yourself? At this stage in your career, it might well be that some of these points prompt further questions, for example because you not fully understand what is required. If so, explain what they are. Think about what you need to do to develop this particular aspect of professionalism.

Summary

'Professionalism' in social work is a complex concept in terms of what it requires from the practitioners. It involves bringing together and demonstrating a wide range of knowledge, values and skills with diverse groups of people in diverse settings. To develop your understanding further, the texts listed below contain useful sections and chapters on this important topic.

Specific further reading

Harrison, K and Ruch, G (2007) 'Social work and the use of self', in M Lymbery and K Postle (eds), *Social Work: A Companion to Learning*. London: Sage, Chapter 5, pp. 40–9.

Horner, N (2012) *What Is Social Work?*, 4th edition. London: Learning Matters.

Oko, J (2012) *Understanding and Using Theory in Social Work*, 2nd edition. London: Learning Matters, Chapters 1 and 3.

Parker, J and Bradley, G (2014) *Social Work Practice*, 4th edition. London: Learning Matters, Chapter 1, pp. 1–18.

Wilson, K, Ruch, G, Lymbery, M and Cooper, A (2011) *Social Work: An Introduction to Contemporary Practice*. Harlow: Longman Pearson, Chapter 4, pp. 61–86.

Demonstrating Domain 1 descriptors

Earlier, it was explained that at the Readiness for Direct Practice level, certain specific capabilities were required for each domain. We now take each of these in turn for further consideration.

Describe the role of the social worker

The first thing to say about this task is that it has been recognised for a long time that social workers actually play many different roles often depending on the setting or context in which they work (Barclay, 1982; Horner, 2012; Dunk-West, 2013). As a consequence, it is not easy to find descriptions that can be expressed in just one or two concise sentences.

Social work textbooks often refer to the definition provided by the International Federation of Social Workers (IFSW) which states that:

> *Social work is a practice-based profession and an academic discipline that promotes social change and development, social cohesion, and the empowerment and liberation of people. Principles of social justice, human rights, collective responsibility and respect for diversities are central to social work. Underpinned by theories of social work, social sciences, humanities and indigenous knowledge, social work engages people and structures to address life challenges and enhance wellbeing. (IFSW website)*

This is fine as a broad, aspirational statement but is probably too abstract and too generalised to meet the requirements at the Readiness for Direct Practice stage. We need to be able to talk in terms that capture the role in ways that can be easily related to social work as it is currently practised in the UK.

Activity 1.3

Look at the following short videos about social work in different settings and identify a few (no more than four or five) broad activities that might best describe what the different social workers are saying that they do as part of their role.

1. Real social work: making the difference in West Sussex (Part One) https://www.youtube.com/watch?v=BFA4stZRB8A

2. Real social work: making the difference in West Sussex (Part Two) https://www.youtube.com/watch?v=Tp3bxRAxnKA

3. Real social work: making the difference in West Sussex (Part Three) https://www.youtube.com/watch?v=_NiDbcZPAd0

The different practitioners talk about various activities with different types of adult service user. However, your list might have included the following broad activities:

- promoting well-being and welfare;
- supporting people to get back to 'normality' or independent living;
- empowering people to take control of their own circumstances;
- advocating for people;
- assessing care and support needs;
- assessing risk;
- safeguarding people from harm;
- providing 'tailored' and personalised support and care for individuals.

For a more in-depth look at a different area of social work try a *Day in the Life of a Social Worker* at: http://www.open.edu/openlearn/body-mind/social-care/social-work/try-day-the-life-social-worker.

Did you notice any additional roles that you could add to the list?

Follow-up activity

Imagine a reporter from a local TV or radio station came to talk to you about your role as a social worker in an adult services team. Write a short script that you would use in order to explain what it consisted of.

Take turns to listen to each other's scripts. Give each other feedback on how convincing or accurate it sounds in the light of what you heard from the social workers in the video clips.

Summary

When asked about the role of the social worker, it would be reasonable to explain that the role is complex and can change depending on the exact setting. However, in general terms, we have seen that important aspects of the role usually include:

(Continued)

(Continued)

- promoting the well-being and welfare of individuals and their families;
- supporting people to live independently;
- advocacy;
- empowering people to take control of their own circumstances;
- assessing the care and support needs of individuals and their carers;
- providing 'tailored' and personalised support and care for individuals;
- assessing risk;
- safeguarding people from harm.

Specific further reading

BASW (2012) *The Code of Ethics for Social Work*. Birmingham: BASW.

Horner, N (2012) *What Is Social Work?*, 4th edition. London: Learning Matters.

Sheldon, B and MacDonald, G (2009) *A Textbook of Social Work*. London: Routledge.

Wilson, K, Ruch, G, Lymbery, M and Cooper, A (2011) *Social Work: An Introduction to Contemporary Practice*. Harlow: Longman Pearson.

Describe the mutual roles and responsibilities in supervision

In his report into the death of Victoria Climbié, Lord Laming said:

> *Supervision is the cornerstone of good social work practice and should be seen to operate effectively at all levels of the organisation. (Laming, 2003, p. 12)*

Consequently, we can see that supervision plays a very important role in ensuring that social work takes place effectively. The question is what does it actually involve? The following contribution from Beckett (2006) provides a good starting point:

> *Put at its simplest, social work supervision consists of a period of time in which a social worker, or sometimes a group of social workers, discuss their work with someone else. Typically in social work this is with the social worker's immediate line manager. (Beckett, 2006, p. 194)*

Therefore, essentially, it is a discussion about the work usually, but not always, with a line manager. However, for supervision to be effective, all parties need to be aware of their roles and responsibilities. In terms of the *supervisor's* role and responsibilities, Morrison (1993) says there are four key functions of supervision. These are:

- responsibility for managing the supervisee's work;
- providing emotional and practical support;
- helping the supervisee's professional development;
- acting as a channel of communication between frontline staff and middle and senior management.

(Morrison (1993), cited in Knott and Scragg, 2016, p. 123)

That said, in order for the supervisor to perform their role properly, the *supervisee* needs to:

- take responsibility for their own work;
- be prepared to share their thoughts and feelings about their work and any impact it might be having;
- take responsibility for their own professional development;
- identify any gaps in skills and knowledge and training needs;

An important aspect of supervision is that both parties prepare for supervision by deciding what they want to discuss and why. This requires the ability to be reflective (see Chapter 6). However, it also requires both parties to be open, truthful, trusting and mutually respectful. Careful thought needs to be given to what precisely is wanted from any particular supervision session. However, Beckett (2006) highlights an important issue with supervision arrangements that involve social workers and their managers. He points out that:

> *It has some advantages but also a number of disadvantages, in that the line manager has two distinct roles in a supervision session, and these roles can clash, just as a social worker's different roles in work with service users can clash. (Beckett, 2006, p. 194)*

Think about

Beckett raises an important point about the potentially clashing roles of the supervisor if they occupy a managerial position. What do you think the basis of that clash might be?

You might have made the point that while a manager should have the emotional well-being and the professional development of those they supervise uppermost in their mind, they will also have pressures on them to meet organisational targets, e.g. to meet certain deadlines and to get through a certain volume of work. The purposes of supervision are to ensure both the quality of work carried out and the well-being of the practitioner. However, pressures to get through a large quantity of work can easily compromise the quality of a social worker's work and impact negatively on their well-being. This is an important reason why both parties need to be clear about what their roles and responsibilities are in supervision. Another point you might have raised is that workers usually feel the need to show their managers that they are competent and capable of doing their job. This might make it difficult to 'own up' to their manager about areas of the job which they are unsure about or anxious about doing. They might fear that if they reveal too many of what might be perceived as their 'shortcomings' they will be judged negatively and even, in extreme circumstances, disciplined.

Case study/Role-play

Kirsty is a newly qualified social worker in a team for older people. She has an active caseload of twenty. Her time is mainly divided between assessing people for support packages and investigating adult safeguarding referrals. Kirsty struggles to get everything done in the hours she has, which is causing her some stress. Since she started, Kirsty has never been confident with working with cases of dementia which involve assessing mental capacity. When talking to a colleague, she discovered that she has made some mistakes in some of her assessments. Kirsty decided not to pass this onto her manager for fear of looking foolish and incompetent. However, now Kirsty is struggling with what to do in a case where she suspects that the son of a 92-year-old woman seems to be financially abusing his mother. The son is a solicitor and has already made Kirsty feel 'deskilled' and a bit silly in pointing out to her aspects of the Mental Capacity Act 2005 about which she was ignorant. In the circumstances, her inclination is to decide that there is insufficient evidence to refer the case on to a safeguarding meeting. She is aware that that is an unsatisfactory course of action but her main concern is to persuade her manager that the case can be closed at this stage.

Janine, Kirsty's manager, has often asked Kirsty how she is coping and Kirsty has always indicated that things are going satisfactorily. By the time they are next due to meet for supervision, Janine has learned that one of the team has gone off long-term sick. She wants to speak to Kirsty about taking on four new cases, three of which involve dementia and mental capacity decisions. This is her main concern as she mentally prepares for the supervision session.

Preparation for role play

In terms of roles and responsibilities, what do you think would be a professional approach for Kirsty to take in the supervision session? Give reasons.

What do you think would be a professional approach for Janine to take? Give reasons.

Role play

In pairs, one person plays Kirsty and the other Janine.

Firstly, both parties need to prepare for the supervision session by clarifying what they both need and want to get out of the session. Remember what was said earlier about being professional means social workers are accountable to their organisation, profession and, most importantly, service users. Also, remember what was said about the role of social work. What are you going to put forward as your agenda? Also, write down what your hopes and fears are about how the session will go? How can you address all of them professionally?

Secondly, armed with your plan, role-play the first five minutes.

Finally, discuss what would be an appropriate outcome for all parties. Record this in an action plan.

This activity should have highlighted that, whatever the organisational or personal context in which it takes place, supervision must focus primarily on the quality of work with service users and that, in order to do this, the practitioner must be suitably knowledgeable and skilled, but also confident, well supported and have the time and space to perform their role properly.

Follow-up activity

Read the following two articles from *Community Care* and identify at least three key points about supervision from each.

'How supervision can help social care workers improve their practice'

http://www.communitycare.co.uk/2013/02/18/how-supervision-can-help-care-workers-improve-their-practice/CC (18 February 2013)

'Why poor supervision is damaging social work'

http://www.communitycare.co.uk/blogs/social-work-blog/2012/11/why-poor-supervision-is-damagi/CC (7 November 2012)

Now, imagine that you have been invited to an interview for a social work job. The invitation letter informs you that you will be required to do a five-minute presentation covering why supervision is important in social work and what you personally expect from the supervisory relationship. Using the activities that you have done so far, draft some notes that will form the basis for your presentation and share them with a partner for feedback.

Summary

We have seen the importance of supervision in social work. If supervision does not take place or either party does not approach it professionally, problems will occur for the practitioner, for the organisation and for service users. From a practitioner's perspective, describing the roles and responsibilities in supervision should include:

- taking responsibility for your own workload;
- reflecting on your practice;
- ensuring that you receive regular supervision;
- preparing for each supervision session so that both parties are clear what the issues are and why you want to discuss them;
- maintaining your well-being;
- thinking about professional development needs;
- being honest and truthful with yourself and with your supervisor.

Specific further reading

Davies, K and Jones, R (eds) (2016) *Skills for Social Work Practice*. Basingstoke: Palgrave, pp. 145–8).

Knott, C and Scragg, T (2016) *Reflective Practice in Social Work*, 4th edition. London: Learning Matters, pp. 123–5.

McKitterick, B (2012) *Supervision*. Maidenhead: McGraw-Hill/Open University Press.

SCIE (2013) *Effective Supervision in a Variety of Settings*, SCIE Guide 50.

http://www.scie.org.uk/publications/guides/guide50/

Describe the importance of professional behaviour

Earlier it was suggested that an important aspect of professional behaviour was the ability for social workers to work to the professional and ethical standards laid down by the professional and regulatory bodies. In this section we look at what this requires and why it is important.

Currently, the Health and Care Professions Council (HCPC) is the official body that regulates the social work profession in England. It has produced both the *Standards of Proficiency for Social Workers* (HCPC, 2012a) and *Standards of Conduct, Performance and Ethics* (HCPC, 2016) and it is the body with which qualified social workers must register in order to practise. BASW is the largest professional association for social work in the UK. As well as managing and delivering the Professional Capabilities Framework (PCF) which, as we know, sets out the expectations of social workers at every stage in their professional career, BASW has also produced its own Code of Ethics for Social Work for its members. If you do not already have a copy of this code it is worth obtaining one because it sets out the commonly agreed values and principles that underpin social work practice in the UK.

Therefore the HCPC Standards, the PCF and the BASW Code not only explain the role of social work but also provide important guidance on *how* the role should be carried out ethically and according to professional social work values. This is an area that will be covered in more depth in Chapters 2 and 3. However, at this point, an extract from an article can illustrate why it is important for social workers to practise professionally and what the consequences are when they do not.

> *Social worker struck off for having second job as home care worker*
>
> *HCPC panel decided working both night and day put service users at risk.*
>
> *A social worker has been struck off the register for moonlighting as a home care worker and lying to her employer about her second job. A Health and Care Professions Council (HCPC) panel heard the social worker, who was contracted to work 37 hours for Luton council, had taken additional employment resulting in her working a total of 57 hours a week. This exposed her service users to potential harm, according to the panel.*
>
> (Adapted from *Community Care*, 6 October 2015)

Activity 1.4

Imagine you are a spokesperson for the HCPC giving a press conference. How would you explain to the conference why it was unprofessional for the social worker to act in this way on this occasion? As a follow-up, how would you explain to the public at large why it is important for social workers *generally* to act professionally? As part of your answer you should explain what the consequences of unprofessional behaviour can be both for the public and for social workers.

Summary

When describing the importance of professional behaviour, it is a good idea to demonstrate awareness of the professional and ethical frameworks that govern and guide social work practice. They are there to protect the public and practitioners by setting out clearly what is expected from the social work profession. Social workers who behave professionally, are practising:

(Continued)

(Continued)

- legally;
- ethically;
- accountably;
- in ways in which the public can have confidence;
- in ways that upholds service users' rights, protects their best interests and promotes their well-being.

When social workers do *not* practise in line with professional codes and standards they:

- place themselves and the public at risk of harm;
- erode confidence in the profession of social work;
- bring the profession of social work into disrepute;
- run the risk of being struck off the register.

Specific further reading

British Association of Social Work (BASW) (2012a) *The Code of Ethics for Social Work.* Birmingham: BASW.

British Association of Social Work (BASW) (2012b) *The Professional Capabilities Framework.* Birmingham: BASW.

Health and Care Professions Council (HCPC) (2012a) *Standards of Proficiency for Social Workers.* London: HCPC.

Health and Care Professions Council (HCPC) (2012b) *Guidance on Conduct and Ethics for Students.* London: HCPC.

Describe the importance of personal and professional boundaries

In 2011, with one in five social work misconduct cases concerning inappropriate relationships with service users, the General Social Care Council (the social work regulator at the time) produced specific guidance on professional boundaries for social workers. They began by defining a 'professional boundary' as

> the 'boundary between what is acceptable and unacceptable for a professional both at work and outside work'. The emphasis here should be placed on the word 'professional': some behaviour will always be unacceptable whether or not an individual is a professional. Professional boundaries, though, concern behaviour that is acceptable or unacceptable in light of the fact that an individual is a professional. (GSCC, 2011, p. 7)

When you consider that much of social work is about trying to build relationships with and offering support to vulnerable people, it is perhaps not surprising that, at times, deciding what is appropriate or acceptable in this context is challenging. For example, what might be considered acceptable in our personal life might not be in our professional life. Sometimes where the line is drawn is clear but often there are 'grey areas'. Whatever, the situation it is down to social workers (often using supervision) to make sure that they are on the 'right' (i.e. professional) side of the boundary line. If they are not, this can confuse, harm and disempower people in vulnerable situations making their lives more difficult. However, from the social worker's point of view establishing good professional boundaries is also important in order to avoid unnecessary emotional stress and the possibility of being compromised.

Activity 1.5 (1)

Consider the following questions and share your answers with a colleague.

You are a male social worker visiting a teenage girl in her foster home. You notice that she has had her hair restyled. Do you compliment her on how nice it looks? (You might discuss whether the gender of the social worker and young person makes a difference?)

You are a female social worker who when visiting a mentally ill male client sees him break down in tears. Do you give him a hug?

You are with a couple who are having relationship difficulties and whose teenage son is in trouble. Do you say 'when my husband and I were on the rocks we found Relate was very useful'?

A single mother is desperate for money and her benefit is not due for two days. She asks you to lend her £10 to see her through and vows she will return it as soon as her benefit comes through. Do you lend her the money?

A learning disabled young man who lives in supported housing says he is lonely most weekends. Do you invite him round to your house for Sunday lunch?

The son of an elderly person with dementia whose case you are assessing is an electrician and you need some electrical work done. Do you give them your personal number to come round and give you a quote?

Activity 1.5 (2)

Now read these questions which the GSCC proposed practitioners should ask themselves as a way of clarifying boundaries issues:

(Continued)

(Continued)

1. Would you be comfortable discussing all of your actions, and the rationale for those actions, in a supervision session with your manager?

2. Would you be uncomfortable about a colleague or your manager observing your behaviour?

3. If challenged, could you give an explanation as to how your actions are grounded in social work values?

(GSCC, 2011, p. 7)

Have your views changed at all? Explain how and give reasons.

The fact is personal and professional values cannot always be easily separated and we will return to this important area in more depth in Chapters 2 and 3. However, for new practitioners the advice would always be to err on the safe side of any boundary question. Therefore, if it is any help knowing what the best course of action is, you could follow these guidelines from an experienced social care professional who stated:

- Don't compliment a client on their looks.
- Watch your physical boundaries: don't hug or touch a client in any way that could be misconstrued.
- Don't share personal information like money or relationship problems.
- Don't lend a client money or borrow from them.
- Don't see them outside of work time.
- Don't become overly familiar, for example taking a client to your house/flat.

Blair McPherson, 'Setting the boundaries in social work', *Guardian Social Care Network*, 2 December 2011, at http://www.theguardian.com/social-care-network/2011/dec/02/setting-boundaries-social-work

Summary

In describing the importance of personal and professional boundaries, it is worth explaining that much of social work is about building relationships and reaching out to people and that, because of the nature of the work, there are bound to be times when boundary issues arise. It cannot be avoided. However, a distinction must be drawn between what might be appropriate in our personal lives and what is acceptable in our professional lives. The main reasons for this are:

- The failure to maintain professional boundaries can confuse, harm and disempower people in vulnerable situations making their lives more difficult as a consequence.
- Establishing good professional boundaries is also important in order to avoid social workers experiencing unnecessary emotional stress and the possibility of being compromised.

Specific further reading

General Social Care Council (GSCC) (2011) *Professional Boundaries Guidance for social workers.* London: GSCC.

Oko, J. (2012) *Understanding and Using Theory in Social Work*, 2nd edition. London: Learning Matters, Chapter 3.

Demonstrate ability to learn, using a range of approaches

Professionalism in social work requires that practitioners keep up to date and take responsibility for their own continuous professional development (CPD). This does not always mean that in order to do this, social workers always have to go on a course at a university or some other training facility, although that should be one approach they need to consider. There are many approaches to learning that can be used to keep up to date professionally.

Activity 1.6: Brainstorm

Quickly generate as many reasons as possible why social workers should maintain their learning, even once they have qualified.

You might have highlighted that legislation and policy change meaning that new ideas, new procedures and new approaches need to be learned. You also might have identified that researchers are always developing new ideas about what is effective in different areas of social work or what social workers need to be aware of when working within certain areas. For example, debates about how best to decide about mental capacity are continually evolving and it benefits everyone involved by keeping abreast of current thinking. You probably discussed that a failure to keep up to date with any of these developments not only compromises your ability to work professionally with service users but also means that your work might be harmful and could even leave you vulnerable to being struck off.

As discussed earlier it is not always possible, desirable or indeed necessary to sign up for a university course every time a new development comes along. This creates the challenge of how practitioners can maintain their 'up-to-dateness' in other ways. It is not simply a question of waiting for your employer to worry about this. It is the practitioner's professional responsibility to maintain their own learning.

Activity 1.7

CPD is a registration requirement by the HCPC as this video explains: http://www.hpc-uk.org/registrants/cpd/.

Claire is a social worker in a children and families team. Much of her role is about receiving referrals and carrying out safeguarding investigations. She has been qualified as a social worker for two years during which time her employer has sent her on a module on 'Assessing Risk in Child Protection' at a local university.

In small groups, discuss the range of knowledge and skills that Claire needs to continue do her job effectively and professionally. Apart from the university module, what other approaches could she take to make sure that she met HCPC requirements?

You might have come up with something like the following list:

1. Join BASW or SWAN – The Social Work Action Network http://www.socialworkfuture.org/.
2. Subscribe to or follow *Community Care* on Twitter for subject-specific articles, e.g. http://www.communitycare.co.uk/children/ or http://www.communitycare.co.uk/events-page/ for conferences and other training events.
3. Follow relevant people on Twitter such as Isabelle Trowler who is (the current) Chief Social Worker for England (Children & Families) or notable academics in the field such as Professor Harry Ferguson (Professor of Social Work at the University of Nottingham). This will help keep you up to date with debates and any new developments in policy.
4. Read textbooks or articles from relevant journals such as the *British Journal of Social Work*.
5. Organise and participate in in-house training or study groups.
6. Organise fact-finding visits to other facilities.
7. Participate in group supervisions and case discussions with colleagues.
8. Watch relevant programmes on TV, e.g. *Panorama*.

There is a range of activities that social workers can do to assist their learning. Some are more formal than others but all can help with keeping up to date and in tune with current thinking.

Extension activity: learning styles

Not only do social workers need to think critically about what knowledge and skills they need to develop, they also need to understand how they learn so that they can optimise their learning opportunities. There are different ideas about how people learn. For example, Honey and Mumford (1992) proposed that people can be put into learner categories such as activist, reflector, theorist or pragmatist. Fleming (2001) proposed 'VARK' which categorises learners into those who mainly rely on Visual, Auditory, Reading or Kinaesthetic means. There are many websites that have online tests that you can do to discover what your preferred learning style is. On a cautionary note, it is fair to say that no one 'theory' fully encompasses everybody's learning style. However, it is useful to get a better sense of what the different learning styles are and what style best suits you. The reason for this is that it can help you select learning activities that are the most effective for you and that fit into your work pattern.

Summary

- The nature of social work requires practitioners to keep up to date with changes in legislation and policy, new ideas and current ways of working.
- To undertake Continuing Professional Development (CPD) is a requirement of registration as a professional social worker.
- Social workers, through the use of supervision and other methods, need to identify their specific learning needs.
- There are many approaches to learning, some more formal and academic, others more informal and practical. These include formal courses, shadowing, reading, workshops, discussion groups and so on.
- Social workers need to reflect on how they learn best and ensure that they undertake appropriate opportunities to meet any learning needs they have identified.

Specific further reading

Fleming, ND (2006) Teaching *and Learning Styles: VARK Strategies*, 2nd edition. Christchurch, NZ: ND Fleming.

Honey, P and Mumford, A (1992) *The Manual of Learning Styles*, 3rd edition. Maidenhead: Peter Honey.

Lymbery, M and Postle, K (eds) (2007) *Social Work: A Companion to Learning*. London: Sage, Chapters 18 and 19.

Describe the importance of emotional resilience in social work

Resilience is a concept that describes people's ability to deal with stress, pressure and the demands made on them. (Howe, 2008, p. 106)

Emotional resilience is a complex topic. It is partly explained by genetics, partly by our upbringing and also by what events we have experienced and how we dealt with them. Most psychologists believe that, whatever their starting point, people can improve their resilience skills. This is particularly important in the context of social work.

Claudia Megele (2011a) offers the following tips for social workers to enhance their emotional resilience:

1. **Understand emotional states and their consequences.** Learn to recognise your emotions and their psychological and behavioural consequences.

2. **Self-regulation and change.** Developing emotional resilience is an experiential process which requires overcoming entrenched habits that are embedded deep in parts of the brain. Since emotional learning involves deeper parts of the brain, cognitive knowledge often does not suffice to modify our habits. For instance, knowing cigarettes damage one's health is usually not enough to stop the person from smoking.

3. **Express your emotions and recognise emotional toil.** Self-regulation helps you enhance your emotional resilience; however, continually suppressing your emotions and disregarding the emotional toil inherent in caring relationships can lead to long-term problems ranging from emotional bias, irritability and lack of sensitivity to psychological disorders. Therefore find the appropriate time, venue and avenue to express your emotions and let go of any negative feelings.

4. **Allocate a time and place for healing.** You are not immune from emotional toil. Allocate some time (perhaps 30 minutes) each week to your 'self' and healing. Do this at the same time and place each week.

5. **Positive regard and self-affirmation.** Positive self-affirmation enhances positive thinking and self-respect. Spend five minutes a day writing positive self-affirmations.

6. **Motivation and positive thinking.** Aspire to excellence in all that you do. Make sure you understand and can align your goals. Maintain a positive and optimistic attitude and disposition.

Case study

Joanne is on her final placement in a LAC (Looked after Children) team. In meetings with professionals she finds it very hard to hear about children that have experienced abuse or have witnessed domestic violence. This makes her very tearful and she has often had to leave meetings to regather herself emotionally. She also suffers the same reactions when reading case notes.

In pairs

Comment on Joanne's emotional resilience. Why might her emotional reactions cause problems in this line of work? What do you think the professional approach would be in such a situation?

You might have discussed that the subject matter appears too difficult for Joanne to currently cope with in a professional manner. It is distressing but social workers need to be able to put things in perspective and contain their emotions in the work environment as best they can. Joanne's reactions, while no doubt genuinely heart felt, are unsettling and disruptive and not conducive to proper information sharing and decision-making. Her emotional reactions could easily obscure the main goal of the work: promoting the best interest of the child. If she exhibited the same behaviour with service users it could well make them feel worse about their situation. In order to develop resilience in service users we need to be able to develop it in ourselves. Joanne needs to examine her reactions critically with her supervisor and work on containing and managing them using the methods highlighted by Megele. If that is not possible, Joanne should consider moving to a less personally upsetting area of social work.

Follow-up activity

Use the following link to gain a better insight into your emotional resilience. Reflect critically on what your strengths are in this area and what you need to work on:

http://psychology.about.com/library/quiz/bl-resilienceb.htm

Summary

- Emotional resilience is a complex topic but, at bottom, it is the ability to bounce back from adversity and not allow emotions overwhelm you.

(Continued)

(Continued)

- It is important in social work because often social workers are working with people whose behaviour or situation causes emotional stress and/or are very emotionally fragile themselves.
- Social workers cannot be properly effective if they are distracted or overwhelmed by strong emotions.
- Social workers who are emotionally resilient are much more effective in helping service users build their own emotional resilience,

Specific further reading

Cooper, F (2012) *Professional Boundaries in Social Work and Social Care: A Practical Guide to Understanding, Maintaining and Managing Your Professional Boundaries.* London: JKP.

Howe, D. (2008) *The Emotionally Intelligent Social Worker.* Basingstoke: Palgrave, pp. 106–9.

Howe, K and Gray, I (2013) *Effective Supervision in Social Work.* London: Learning Matters, pp. 59–60.

Lymbery, M and Postle, K (eds) (2007) *Social Work: A Companion to Learning.* London: Sage.

Megele, C (2011) 'How to . . . sustain emotional resilience', online at http://www.communitycare.co.uk/2011/02/02/how-to-sustain-emotional-resilience/

2: Values and ethics

Achieving a Social Work Degree

This chapter will help you develop skills in the following domain of the Professional Capabilities Framework:

Values and ethics: Apply social work ethical principles and values to guide professional practice.

The Professional Capability Framework states about this domain that:

Social workers have an obligation to conduct themselves ethically and to engage in ethical decision-making, including through partnership with people who use their services. Social workers are knowledgeable about the value base of their profession, its ethical standards and relevant law. (BASW, Professional Capability Framework – Readiness for Practice Capabilities)

This domain statement goes on to say that, at the point of going out on their first practice placement, social work students need to be able to:

- Understand the profession's ethical principles and their relevance to practice
- Demonstrate awareness of own personal values and how these can impact on practice

Introduction

In Chapter 1 it was highlighted that the role of the professional social worker was to practise ethically and according to professional social work values. This chapter therefore builds on many of the points discussed in the previous chapter, especially those made in respect of what constitutes professional behaviour and the different professional and ethical codes that inform and guide such behaviour.

'Values and ethics' in social work is a large and complex topic which draws on different philosophical traditions, as well being informed by notions of social justice and social and human rights. It is a topic that, quite appropriately, forms the basis for whole textbooks and has whole modules devoted to it on social work courses. Because the main purpose of this book is to focus on how social work students can demonstrate a satisfactory grasp of the domain at the readiness for practice stage, we cannot attempt to explore the topic satisfactorily in all its breadth and complexity. However, it is very important that all students engage fully in the debates around values, ethics and their application to social work. Therefore you will be signposted to a selection of relevant social work texts useful for further reading at the end of this chapter.

That said, this chapter will provide useful working definitions of what is meant by 'values and ethics' and will discuss the links between the two concepts. It will encourage you to engage actively with the different ethical frameworks that currently govern social work. It will also encourage you to think about how to 'embody' the ethical codes and commonly accepted values that underpin professional social work in your own practice in real-life situations. Here the concept of 'authenticity' is important to understand. So, for example, it is not just a question of being able to memorise a list of social work values and ethics and drop them in where we think they should go in assignments. We need to ensure that the particular values and ethics that we sign up to as social workers are translated meaningfully into practice. At an early stage we will therefore encourage reflection on the often complex relationship between values, ethics and behaviour.

As human beings we all have our own personal value systems, although seldom are they fully coherent and seldom do we make a point of making them explicit and examining them. Nevertheless, ideally, our personal and professional values and ethics should be congruent. That is they should fit together. If they do not then, in practice, it must be the professional that takes precedence over the personal, which might not always be easy. This challenge inevitably means that we need to examine closely our own personal value base. From here it will be possible to encourage how personal values might sometimes conflict with professional ethics and how this can impact on social work practice.

What do we mean by 'values and ethics'?

In social work, 'values and ethics' are nearly always bracketed together, suggesting that they are linked. But are they the same and, if so, how exactly?

In pairs discuss:

- What are values?
- What are ethics?
- Are values and ethics the same thing?
- What do you see as being the similarities and differences between the two?
- Give examples of when we might use the term values in social work and when we might use 'ethics'?

You might have discussed that the two concepts clearly link with each other but do not have quite the same meaning. Even in the social work literature it is acknowledged that definitions of both concepts can be problematic (Banks, 2012), not helped, it must be said, by the fact that the two terms are often used interchangeably (Bell and Hafford-Letchfield, 2015). However, the Social Care Institute for Excellence makes the following distinction:

> *Values are statements of belief about morally good or bad conduct. In social care and social work, ethics are typically expressed as descriptions or codes of required professional conduct, representing the active form of values. (SCIE website)*

A key phrase in this statement is that ethics represent the 'active form of values'. So this highlights that ethics are concerned with moral values when they are translated into actual behaviour or 'conduct'. The statement also describes ethics as typically expressed in codes of conduct required by professionals. Therefore, while values are the basic beliefs about life that we, as individuals, hold to be important at any particular time (e.g. 'life's a jungle, so you've got to look after number one'), ethics can be better understood as more formal guidelines or rules that are set for a professional or occupational group (e.g. doctors, lawyers, social workers and so on) rather than just for an individual. Barnard et al. (2008) explain it thus:

> *In the field of professional ethics, 'values' usually take the form of general ethical principles relating to how professionals should treat the people they work with and what sorts of actions are regarded as right or wrong. (p. 6)*

It is not hard to see that, while many people drawn to social work might share common values, they might also have some values that do not necessarily fit in with what most people might believe and they also might not always fit in with the ethical principles that the social work profession has signed up to. This strongly suggests that we should become more familiar with what the professional ethical codes of social work actually say.

Ethical codes: what they are, who they are for and what they say

In Chapter 1 two separate codes of ethics that apply to professional social work were identified. These were the *Standards of Conduct, Performance and Ethics* published by the Health and Care Professions Council (HCPC) (2016) and the *Code of Ethics for Social Work* published by the British Association of Social Work (BASW) (2012). We also listed the *Guidance on Conduct and Ethics for Students* (HCPC, 2012b).

Make sure that you have access to all three of these documents (they are available online) for the following exercise.

Activity 2.2: Part 1

Working in pairs or small groups focus on each document in turn.

Document one: *Guidance on Conduct and Ethics for Students* (HCPC, 2012b)

As its title suggests this document is directly relevant to you now. Under the heading 'Guidance on conduct and ethics' (p. 9) the HCPC sets out 13 points that they state should inform students' practice. Without referring directly to the document at this stage, write down what you think the 13 points are. To give you a start the first one is 'You should always act in the best interests of your service users.' It is worth highlighting that the list reflects the fact that it is aimed at a range of students on professional courses not just social work students. You might find that not every point is directly relevant to social work but most are.

Compare your list of points with the HCPC list. Which ones did you get? Which did you miss out? Were there any surprises? You will notice that each main point has a number of subsidiary points. Fully acquaint yourself with all of them and discuss whether you understand them all. Flag up any issues that you will need to take forward with your tutors for more discussion and clarification. At this point you must be clear what conduct is expected of you by the professional regulator both at university and in practice placement.

Activity 2.2: Part 2

Document 2: *Standards of Conduct, Performance and Ethics* (HCPC, 2016)

This document is directly relevant to those who are already registered with HCPC, those who are applying to be registered with the HCPC and also if you are a student on an HCPC-approved programme. It sets out ten 'standards'. How do the standards in this document map against the points of conduct and ethics set out in the HCPC document you looked at previously? Discuss your findings with others.

Lastly, a qualified social worker in serious breach of ethical standards can be struck off the HCPC register which would mean they could no longer practise as a social worker. Students cannot apply to join the register until they are qualified. How might a serious ethical breach affect their social work career?

Commentary

You might have highlighted how, in their own way, both documents broadly set out a framework which is based on the same professional values such as the need to work honestly and safely, communicate effectively, record accurately and practise in ways that respect others rights to confidentiality and choice and so on. Document 1 is obviously more focused on students in education and extends its guidance points to include how to manage your academic work ethically and professionally. It is important to recognise from this that improprieties in your studies (such as plagiarism) can have a knock-on effect on your being able to qualify professionally. In answer to the last question posed, if a student seriously breaches the professional code of ethics their university should not only refer this to their own 'Fitness to Practise' panel, they are also within their rights to refuse to countersign the student's HCPC registration application.

Activity 2.2: Part 3

Document 3: *The Code of Ethics for Social Work* (BASW, 2012)

BASW is the professional association for social workers run by social workers and funded largely by private subscriptions. This is in contrast to the HCPC which is the independent regulatory body set up by legislation and funded largely by registration fees. The BASW code is therefore an example of professional *self*-regulation. Its Code states that is 'binding on all social workers who are BASW members in the UK' (p. 4). Student social workers are eligible to join BASW and those who do are naturally bound by their Code of Ethics. However, given it is the code developed by the social work profession itself, it is logical and, indeed, highly desirable for *all* students to practise in accordance with both the HCPC and the BASW codes, whether BASW members or not.

Read through the BASW Code and in pairs or small groups discuss in what ways it is similar to the HCPC codes you have looked at and in what ways does it differ?

Commentary

You might have discerned a considerable degree of overlap, which should not be that surprising. It will be evident that the same values such as honesty, respect, safety, confidentiality and responsible practice underpin all three codes. However, the BASW code alerts social workers to the fact that to practise social work ethically in the fullest meaning of the word requires a deeper appreciation of the social, economic and political context in which social work takes place. As with the Professional Capability Framework, the BASW code insists that practitioners develop an understanding of ideas such as social justice, equality, social exclusion, oppression, discrimination and power in society. These all impact on questions of how to practise ethically (Banks, 2012; Parrott, 2014). That is why it is strongly recommended that students aim to work within both the HCPC and BASW codes.

Finally, while the three codes together set out a comprehensive ethical framework of values, principles and standards that informs and guides social work practice, they cannot tell practitioners what the right thing to do is in every type of specific situation. This requires careful deliberation and judgement, often made after critical reflection and in discussion with colleagues and managers. However, at this stage, at the minimum, it is important to become very familiar with what the codes say and to be prepared to develop your understanding of what they might mean in practice as your course progresses.

Summary

- Social work practice is currently governed by ethical codes published by the HCPC and BASW.
- HCPC Guidelines aimed specifically at students highlight:
  - You should always act in the best interests of your service users.
  - You should respect the confidentiality of your service users.
  - You should keep high standards of personal conduct.
  - You should provide any important information about your conduct, competence or health to your education provider.
  - You should limit your study or stop studying if your performance or judgement is affected by your health.
  - You should keep your professional knowledge and skills up to date.
  - You should act within the limits of your knowledge and skills.
  - You should communicate effectively with service users and your education provider and placement providers.
  - You should get informed consent to provide care or services (so far as possible).
  - You should keep accurate records on service users.

- o   You should deal fairly and safely with the risks of infection.
- o   You should behave honestly.
- o   You should make sure that your behaviour does not damage public confidence in your profession.

- • Serious breach of the codes by a student could lead to a referral to a Fitness to Practise panel and/or not being able to register as a qualified social worker.
- • Codes of ethics are frameworks to inform and assist with decision-making. However, they cannot make decisions for us. It is down to practitioners to weigh and decide what the ethical thing to do is taking into account all circumstances of the situation.

Values, ethics and behaviour

Because the focus of this book is 'practice' (that is to say the behaviour that service users and others actually see and experience from us as social workers), it is important to think about how our values and ethics link to our actual behaviour. This is a large topic that has both psychological and philosophical dimensions to it. But, for the sake of getting our thinking going, let us suggest that our behaviour could be represented as the observable tip of an iceberg. Below the surface (that is to say in our hearts and minds) we have all kinds of impulses, thoughts, attitudes and feelings – some of which we are more aware of than others. Not all of these find expression in behaviour.

Most adults, through their upbringing, formal education and the influence of society, generally develop ideas about what is right and wrong and what is good and bad behaviour. This 'moral' sense helps us to keep a check on and control some of our more primitive urges and anti-social thoughts in line with what we have learned is the correct or right thing to do. So, for example, if we see an older woman leave her purse full of money in the supermarket, most people would think that, even though it might provide the opportunity for 'easy money' if we quietly put it in our pocket, the 'right' thing to do would be tap her on the shoulder and give it back to her without a moment's hesitation. However, some people might struggle more than others with the thought of giving it back, others might decide to take it and hang on to it. Others might take it, notice that they are on CCTV and then, reluctantly, hand it back. For others, it might not even occur to them that this is something they should be getting involved in. The fact that the purse will not always be returned or that it will take some people longer to decide to return it than others highlights several important points about values. Firstly, not everybody shares them; secondly, if they do, they might not interpret them in the same way when it comes down to translating them into action. You might consider whether what is going through the finder's mind actually matters to the old woman, as long as they return the purse to her. However, it might affect the satisfaction the purse finder feels when returning it.

Let's take another example of a widely held value, that of charity. Most of us would like to think we are charitable towards others. However, we might have quite different interpretations of what 'charity' means in terms of appropriate behaviour. For some, this mean might giving people the benefit of the doubt, or it might mean giving money to charities like Oxfam from time to time, for others 'charity begins at home' and it means looking after those close to you. For others, just giving money to charities occasionally is not enough and they might devote their time to voluntary work in poor areas of the world. There are many ways of being charitable. Therefore a key point to recognise is that while we all might agree that a certain value is important, we might have quite differing ideas about what this means in terms of how we should behave in practice. Values do not really reveal themselves until they are translated into behaviour.

Activity 2.3: Authenticity and congruence

Don't do as I do . . .

Another key point in thinking about the relationship between values and behaviour can be illustrated by considering the following two scenarios:

Scenario 1

A colleague is always nagging others about cleaning and tidying up the kitchen area at work. They keep stressing how important it is to maintain a clean kitchen environment. On one occasion you drop by their flat and see a complete and utter mess when you look into their kitchen: dirty plates piled up in the sink, bits of old food everywhere, dirt and grime on the floor.

Question

What are your thoughts about this situation? Discuss in small groups.

You might have commented that this is a person who 'doesn't practise what they preach', someone who 'talks the talk' but doesn't 'walk the walk' or is someone who operates one standard for others and another for themselves. You might also have thought, well, that might seem a bit hypocritical of them but what does it matter because it is a good thing that the kitchen area at work is kept clean and tidy. What they do in their private life is another thing altogether.

Here is another case to consider based on a real-life example.

Scenario 2

Ex vicar escapes jail

A former Langdale vicar has escaped jail after being found guilty of a sex attack on a teenage girl. Rev Martin Carroll, who was the vicar of St Andrew's Church, in Coaldale Road, until September 2014, also admitted beating a second girl and assaulting his wife. Carroll, 59, was told by the judge at the Crown Court last week that his offences were so serious they merited a lengthy prison term.

The court had heard how, between May and June 2012, Carroll touched the legs and private parts of a 16-year-old girl he had encountered in a park in Boroughvale. He also admitted two offences which occurred last year, an assault by beating a 15-year-old girl, and common assault on his wife, Janice Cozens. (Langdale Gazette, 23 April 2016; actual names changed)

Questions

In the context of thinking about the relationship between values, ethics and behaviour, what are your thoughts on reading this case? Should the vicar have been allowed to keep his job? Discuss in small groups.

You might have commented that this is another case of hypocrisy, a case of someone who professes to uphold certain (in this case Christian) values but behaves quite differently. If you linked this case with the previous one you might have said that this is more serious because actual harm was done to other people. It would be hard to argue that your colleague should be sacked for their hypocrisy, but in the case of the vicar his disrespect not only for the law but also for other people and for the values of his church (his hypocrisy), make him unsuitable to hold that office. You might have commented that it would be difficult to take him seriously or trust him again. The gap between what he preached and what he did was too big. It is not just the fact of being hypocritical – we all are at some time or another – it is the impact that our hypocrisy has on others that is the important thing.

These two cases highlight important points about the links between values, ethics and behaviour that need to be considered. Both cases raise issues of 'congruence' and 'authenticity' in our practice. Authenticity means that someone is 'genuine'. In other words, they are not pretending to be something that they are not. The values they say they hold are the values they really do hold. They don't think or say one thing and do another. Congruence means that there is consistency or a close fit between our values, the code of ethics by which we are bound and our actual behaviour. Apart from the ethical case, there are obvious benefits to congruent practice. For example, Cormier et al. (2009) observe that 'when personal values of helpers are consistent with professional standards of conduct, helpers are more likely to interact genuinely and credibly with clients and other professionals' (p. 32). It is also worth highlighting that authenticity and congruence are rated highly as part of the standards of behaviour that service users expect from social workers (Harding and Beresford, 1996).

Now, hardly anyone's behaviour is congruent and authentic all the time. The first case illustrates that while you might think slightly less of someone for acting one way at home and another way at work, it might not be a great significance if no one is harmed. In fact, ironically, it might even be beneficial for the workplace if their nagging helps keep it tidy. The second case is more serious and illustrates, among other things, that someone's failure to uphold and act consistently within the values and ethics of their profession not only harms the victims, it harms the reputation of the offender him or herself and also harms the reputation of the church for which he is working. It erodes trust which makes it harder for others working in the same institution.

There is plenty more than could be said about these cases and the ethical and moral issues arising. However, at this stage, we summarise what we need to be mindful of as we move forward.

Summary

- Values and ethical codes are open to different interpretations in terms of what actual behaviour one might expect to follow from them. We saw that with our discussion of honesty and charity.
- Just learning and reciting a list of social work values or a set of ethical principles is not the same as practising ethically.
- People are not always authentic. They might claim to sign up fully to a set of professional values and ethics but they might not genuinely subscribe to them. This will almost certainly come out in their behaviour at some point.
- When our personal values are at odds with professional ethics this will cause conflict and difficult dilemmas which can have harmful consequences for all parties concerned.

How personal values can impact on practice

We live in a diverse society and either consciously or unconsciously our personal values, may, from time to time, conflict with those of the profession. Therefore, it is important for social workers to develop self-awareness about their own values and recognise their own biases.

Activity 2.4

Firstly, bearing in mind the points that have been made in the chapter so far, read the following article from *Community Care* magazine from April 2016.

Anti-gay marriage social work student loses appeal against removal from course

Sheffield University stands by its decision to expel Felix Ngole from its social work Masters course for anti-gay marriage Facebook post.

A social work student who posted anti-gay marriage views on Facebook has lost his appeal against being expelled from his course.

Felix Ngole, who was a second-year social work masters student at Sheffield University, was excluded from the course in February after making a Facebook post in support of Kim Davis, a US county clerk who was jailed after refusing to give marriage licences to same-sex couples.

Ngole said his views were a part of his Christian faith. He had also published quotes from Leviticus on his private Facebook account, which described homosexuality as an 'abomination'.

The appeals office at Sheffield University said his social media posts were 'inappropriate' in light of the professional conduct set by the Health and Care Professions Council (HCPC). He had been told he did not offer insight or reflection into the potential impact of his postings, or how the profession might be perceived as a result of what he posted.

Fitness-to-practise

In response, Ngole said it should not be a university's decision to 'arbitrarily "vet" who should enter a chosen career' and that it should be up to the professional body to decide.

However, the university said this was a fitness-to-practice issue judged using the guidance all social workers are held to, and that he had not been excluded from studying at Sheffield, only from studying social work.

Ngole said: 'I did not say that everyone has to agree with me. However, I was reported to the university for these views and they unilaterally decided to end my course. In so doing, they ended my training for my chosen vocation.

'All students would expect every professional body to have their own set of codes and practises when the time comes, and each student would decide whether they felt comfortable in applying to that profession, given those codes.'

(Continued)

(Continued)

He said he will take further action over the 'legal questions' his case has raised, such as whether Christians with "traditional biblical and moral beliefs" can still enter professions like social work.

Split opinion

A spokesperson for Sheffield University said: 'The committee came to its conclusions based on the professional standards of conduct, performance and ethics and guidance on conduct and ethics for students set out by the [HCPC].

'He now has the option to register on an alternative course of study at the University of Sheffield.'

The story split opinion among *Community Care* readers. Some argued his views were 'not compatible with the job', while others said his ability to be a social worker should have been tested on his behaviour in the profession rather than his thoughts.

Andrea Williams, barrister and founder of the Christian Legal Centre, which is supporting Ngole, said this is the first case of a Christian student being stopped from entering a vocation.

She added there was 'no evidence' his biblical views would have negatively impacted his work.

'Mr Ngole has worked with those who identify as homosexual in the past and has always treated them with respect, never discriminating against them,' Williams said.

(Luke Stevenson, *Community Care*, 8 April 2016, at http://www. communitycare.co.uk/2016/04/08/anti-gay-marriage-social-work-student-loses-appeal-removal-course/)

Task 1

In pairs or small groups discuss:

1. Your overall reactions to this story. Do you agree with the decision? Give reasons. What issues in terms of values, ethics and behaviour does it raise for you?

2. From your knowledge of the HCPC codes of conduct where do you think the student might have found themselves in potential breach

3. Where specifically in the two codes we looked at, i.e. HCPC (2012b) and BASW (2012), might the student's behaviour on Facebook have possibly placed them in conflict with professional social work ethics?

4. The article mentions that the HCPC decision had 'split opinion'. Of the two views expressed, which do you have most sympathy with and why?

Commentary

In the question about the codes, you might have discussed that, from the HCPC (2012b) code, the student's 'conduct outside the programme (p. 7)' affected their being allowed to complete the course. Their behaviour on Facebook might well have contravened the code in that their behaviour did not 'treat everyone equally (p. 9)'. Also, arguably, their behaviour was such that it might have damaged 'public confidence' in the profession of social work. This, in turn, 'may affect the trust that the public has (p. 12)' in professional social work. It is also arguable that by describing homosexuality as an 'abomination' the student was making a discriminatory comment putting them in breach of the HCPC codes and in obvious conflict with the BASW (2012) code which states that 'its values are based on respect for the equality, worth, and dignity of all people' (p. 5). However, this case does raise questions about the extent to which someone's activities outside of their social work role – especially when they might have occurred sometime in the past – can reasonably be taken into account when assessing their conduct as a professional.

Activity 2.4 cont'd

Task 2

Individually:

1. Reflect on what this case means for you in terms of your use of social media and your behaviour, generally, outside of the course?

2. Could you see yourself in a similar position of conflict over personal values that you hold, for example on religion, animal rights, abortion, veganism or politics generally?

3. How will you manage this in a way that ensures that you remain within professional social work ethical frameworks? Share with another if you want to.

Commentary

The case described in the article highlights that even though we might think our professional world and personal world are separate, becoming a professional social worker means that we need to be aware that our personal values and the behaviour that might result from these could affect our ability to practise professionally. Conflicts are bound to occur for all of us so we should not deny this. If conflicts go unrecognised and unresolved, our practice with service users will be affected. However, Comartin and González-Prendes (2011) argue that when these conflicts are acknowledged, explored and resolved, there is potential for personal and professional growth. Therefore it is not necessarily a problem having some values that might be at odds with social work codes of ethics. The key is dealing with it honestly and professionally. Trying to live a 'double life' will not work. Potential conflicts are best shared with line managers and supervisors.

Summary

- We live in a diverse society where we all have our personal value systems. Usually such systems are seldom fully consistent, coherent or well-articulated. However, our values inevitably affect our behaviour – particularly if they are strongly held.
- It is not always possible to disconnect completely the personal values that we hold from our practice when in our role of professional social worker. This can lead to conflicts and dilemmas.
- It is our choice if we choose to allow personal values prevail over professional social work ethical principles. However, we have to accept that there could be harmful consequences for all parties involved if we make that choice. Service users could be harmed, the reputations of our employing organisation (or university if we are a student) and the profession could be harmed and we ourselves might be harmed by facing disciplinary proceedings and even being required to stop practising.
- In order to avoid any conflicts or dilemmas causing harm, we need to practise reflexively and use professional supervision to talk through any issues that we might be experiencing. Ignoring or attempting to conceal any conflicts or dilemmas is unprofessional.

Further reading

Beckett, C and Maynard, A (2013) *Values and Ethics in Social Work: An Introduction*, 2nd edition. London: Sage.

Gray, M and Webb, S (eds) (2010) *Ethics and Value Perspectives*. Basingstoke: Palgrave.

HCPC (2012a) *Standards of Proficiency for Social Workers in England*. London: HCPC.

3: Diversity

Achieving a Social Work Degree

This chapter will help you develop skills in the following domain of the Professional Capabilities Framework:

Diversity: *Recognise diversity and apply anti-discriminatory and anti-oppressive principles in practice.*

The Professional Capability Framework states about this domain that:

Social workers understand that diversity characterises and shapes human experience and is critical to the formation of identity. Diversity is multi-dimensional and includes race, disability, class, economic status, age, sexuality, gender and transgender, faith and belief. Social workers appreciate that, as a consequence of difference, a person's life experience may include oppression, marginalisation and alienation as well as privilege, power and acclaim, and are able to challenge appropriately. (BASW, Professional Capability Framework – Readiness for Practice Capabilities)

This domain statement goes on to say that, at the point of going out on their first practice placement, social work students need to be able to:

- Recognise the importance of diversity in human identity and experience, and the application of anti-discriminatory and anti-oppressive principles in social work practice

Introduction

This domain – as with many of the others – involves understanding a range of complex and often contested concepts such as 'identity', 'human diversity', 'discrimination' and 'oppression'. Nevertheless, we will provide a grounding which will be sufficient to meet the requirements of the Readiness for Direct Practice level. However, it is strongly suggested that, to improve your understanding in this area, you undertake further reading as signposted in this chapter and that you also link the discussions here to those you will be having elsewhere in your course modules around topics such as Human Growth and Development, Well-Being and Rights. This is a domain that repays reading widely, making connections and also looking at your own values and 'world-view' honestly and critically. In this respect it links closely with the discussions around values and ethics covered in Chapter 2 and those around Rights, Justice and Economic Well-being that we will look at in Chapter 4. We begin the chapter by unpacking the key terms and concepts included in the domain title and descriptor and as the Chapter progresses you will be encouraged to undertake activities that will enable you to demonstrate your ability to put your understanding of these key concepts into practice in social work situations.

Understanding diversity

The fact that the domain descriptor requires us to 'recognise diversity' suggests that it might be asking us to do something that isn't as straightforward as we think. In order to recognise 'diversity', first we need to have some sense of what it means and why it is important.

Activity 3.1: Defining diversity

Think about these questions and discuss your answers with another colleague.

1. In the context of social work, what does 'diversity' mean to you?
2. Why do you think it is important the social workers 'recognise diversity'?

Commentary

In your answer to the first question you might have talked about how social workers work with people who come into all kinds of diverse categories. This could be in terms of characteristics such as gender, ethnic group, culture, sexuality, disability, age or religion. However, your ideas about diversity could have also included people in different states of health (physical and mental), people with different levels of cognitive ability, with different levels of income or of different social class. Your discussion might have concluded that the concept of 'diversity' covers a wide range of differences that can exist between us as human beings. However, it might have occurred to you that while people can be different from each other in many ways, they can be similar to each other in many other ways. This brings us to a very important point. However positively we might do it, if we focus too much on 'difference' to the exclusion of everything else we might unintentionally raise barriers between people rather than lower them.

In response to the second question, you might have discussed that 'recognise' can have at least two meanings in this context. In the first sense it means that you are able to identify someone from having encountered them or someone similar to them before. In other words, you might be able to 'recognise' a male or a female, a traveller or a Sikh is because you have encountered people in that category before. However, in this sense of recognise you might have discussed that it is not always that easy to identify (or recognise) every kind of human diversity. People do not come with labels attached to them listing all their identity characteristics.

In the second sense 'recognise' means that you acknowledge the existence, worth or status of someone. When we say that we recognise someone's contribution, for example, this is the second sense of the word. Although the first sense is important, it is this sense of 'recognise' that is probably more what the descriptor wants us to focus on. In this respect, you might have discussed that it is important that social workers treat the people with whom they work with equal respect, whatever categories they might come into or whichever characteristics they might have.

Defining diversity

Cocker and Hafford-Letchfield (2014) provide a definition of diversity which makes the point that, in social work, it is more than just acknowledging the fairly obvious fact that people are different, it involves the process of active and deliberate recognition. They state that:

> Diversity is a concept which encompasses acceptance and respect rather than just people being diverse. It means understanding that each individual is unique and actively recognises differences along the dimensions of race, ethnicity, gender, sexual orientation, socioeconomic status, age, physical abilities, religious beliefs, political beliefs and other ideologies. Diversity intends to move beyond simple tolerance to embracing and celebrating its rich dimensions. (p. 227)

Gaine (2010) is recommended reading on this topic for any social work student. He makes the point that:

> Human diversity is a concept with lots of layers. It can just refer to differences, like height, hair colour, whether you have freckles or the kind of food you like, but the kind of diversity that matters to social workers is diversity with social significance, diversity that makes real differences to people's lives, (p. 2)

In policy and in law 'diversity' mainly focuses on what Gaine describes as diversity with social significance. For example, the Equality and Human Rights Commission (2015) states that diversity:

> *tends to be used to refer to a group of people with many different types of protected characteristic, e.g. people of all ages, religions, ethnic background etc. (p. 76)*

The Equality Act 2010 sets out the personal characteristics that are protected by the law and the behaviour that is unlawful in respect of people with those characteristics. The full list of 'protected characteristics' under the Equality Act 2010 is:

- age;
- disability;
- gender reassignment;
- marriage and civil partnership;
- pregnancy and maternity;
- race;
- religion and belief;
- sex;
- sexual orientation.

The fact that a law has been introduced to protect people who share certain characteristics underlines the point made by Gaine that, for some, aspects of their 'diversity' can make a difference to their lives and not always a positive one.

Activity 3.2: The social significance of diversity

In pairs or small groups:

Read the example below based on 'age'. Then, using the list of protected characteristics, think about why the government has decided that people with these characteristics might need to be protected in the UK and link this to Gaine's idea about diversity with social significance. Think about the various ways in which these characteristics can be significant for people in today's society.

Example: 'Age'

Age can be socially significant for a variety of reasons. It can be, for example, for legal reasons because there are certain things like voting that you are not allowed to do until you are 18. You also have to be a certain age before you can qualify for a state pension. But there are cultural and attitudinal reasons (often ageist) that can make age significant as well. For example, being a certain age can mean that you are regarded less favourably in the jobs market or if you are of pensionable age you might be more likely to be stereotyped as a hard of hearing, denture wearing, grumpy, 'oldie' and so on. Such stereotyping can lead to older people experiencing a lower sense of self-worth.

Commentary

The social significance of age can also be related to commercial, institutional and organisational practices. For example, younger males generally get charged more for their car insurance, but if you are 75+ it can be harder to get travel insurance. People aged over 65 are not always treated as younger people would be in the NHS. An example here was a report revealed that when people in the 65+ age group had falls and other accidents they were not being transferred to specialist trauma centres in the same way that people under 65 were (Smith, 2014). These and other 'facts' about life in the UK generally show that there are many ways that age is socially significant and that its significance – especially old age – can often (but not always) be negative in terms of the impact on opportunities. When old age is socially significant in a negative way it can contribute towards feelings of marginalisation, exclusion and lowered self-esteem.

Activity 3.2: cont'd

Back to the task

Using the example above on 'age' as a guide, work your way down the list of protected characteristics thinking about the various ways the characteristic might have social significance.

Commentary

In doing the exercise you might have discussed that having a protected characteristic need not always be significant for any particular individual. Not everyone with that characteristic is necessarily treated the same. However, often we can identify general trends that might affect many people with a particular characteristic, at least at some point in their lives. Therefore, your discussion might have highlighted how, despite equality legislation, having a disability might impair someone's chances of getting a job and increase their chances of being in poverty. People who have undergone gender reassignment can attract negative comments and experience social isolation and its consequences such as loneliness and depression.

Marriage is usually regarded positively in Britain; however, it's debatable whether civil partnerships have yet achieved the same status in society. Women who are pregnant can often be socially celebrated but might also find it difficult to maintain employment. Younger pregnant teenagers can still face social condemnation and problems balancing becoming pregnant and continuing their education. You might have also discussed how black and other minority ethnic groups still face discrimination in many areas of life. Some people can be mocked for their religious beliefs or for being gay. Lastly, you might have discussed how, despite decades of equal pay legislation, there is still a pay gap between men and women's average earnings. There is clearly much more that could be said about the various consequences that difference has for people but, hopefully, undertaking this activity has stimulated some initial thoughts about diversity and how it has social significance on many levels and in many areas of life. Sometimes consequences are positive but they can often be negative.

Diversity and identity

In your discussions, you might well have said something along the lines of 'Hold on, some people fall into more than one category – they are not defined by one characteristic alone. You can be old and gay, you can be young, female, black and disabled. We are not defined by one label. That is not who we are.' These questions highlight that our sense of who we are – our identity – cannot simply be 'read off' from one or two 'characteristics'. It is more complex than that.

Activity 3.3: Can we choose our identity?

The story of Rachel Dolezal which emerged in July 2015 brings out some of the complexities of 'identity'. Read the story, answer the questions for yourself and discuss your answers with another. (If you search using her name on Google you will find numerous images of her, including those published alongside the *Guardian* article mentioned below.)

Rachel Dolezal: the world may be confused about who I am, but I'm not

Dolezal identified as a black woman and was president of the National Association for the Advancement of Colored People (NAACP) chapter in Spokane, Washington, until her estranged biological parents revealed last year that her heritage is white. She subsequently resigned from the NAACP and lost her position teaching Africana Studies at Eastern Washington University, while facing a wave of anger from African Americans. {. . .}

In December 2015, Dolezal told the Guardian that she still identified as black. 'For me, how I feel is more powerful than how I was born,' she said. 'I mean that not in the sense of having some easy way out. This has been a lifelong journey. This is not something that I cash in, cash out, change up, do at a convenience level or to freak people out or to make people happy. If somebody asked me how I identify, I identify as black. Nothing about whiteness describes who I am.'

Source: Guardian, 13 April 2016

Questions

1. What are your reactions to this story? Do you have any sympathies with Dolezal's position?

2. What about your own 'identity'? To what extent do you think your sense of who you are is a question of how you feel inside rather than being defined by the circumstances of your birth or other factors beyond your immediate control that might occur during your lifetime?

Commentary

It might be that you discussed that our identity is not a fixed entity. Our sense of identity (our sense of who we are) is inevitably shaped to a significant degree by the social categories into which we fall – male/female, black/white, upper class/working class, nationality and so on. However, not only are many of these categories not fixed permanently, it is also the case that we have an element of 'agency' (choice) about what we emphasise in who we are. That said, it could be argued that the choices that we have available are constrained by circumstances that we have little or control over. So, for example, some might say that while Rachel Dolezal might 'identify as black', others (including black people) might not share that view, not just because her biological 'heritage' is white but also because she doesn't really know what it is to experience being black in America. However, that still doesn't alter the fact that, subjectively, Dolezal feels herself to be black.

Activity 3.4: Factors that form our identity

Try this 'social identity exercise':

1. Think about a group or social category you belong to and with which you identify. Describe what the group means to you and list some examples that demonstrate your high level of identification.

(Continued)

(Continued)

2. Think about a group or social category you belong to but with which you don't identify. Describe what the group means (or doesn't mean) to you and list some examples that demonstrate your lack of identification.

3. Think about a group or social category you belong to but with which you actively disidentify. Describe what the group means to you and list some examples that demonstrate your disidentification.

4. What kinds of factors influence the level of identification with a group? What kinds of factors make a category or group membership irrelevant?

Commentary

Completing the activity should have underlined the fact that how our 'identity' is formed is complex. More traditional 'common-sense' views about identity such as 'you are what you are, or 'a leopard can't change its spots' are clearly too simplistic and reductionist. For most of us our identity develops from a range of interrelated subjective and objective factors. Smith (2008) captures the situation well when he states:

> Structural factors such as race, class and gender may be factors in identity formation, but they are not crucial in determining specific individual personalities. However, such characteristics may act as reference points, according to how people define themselves and how others may also define them. In this way, there is a degree of coherence and continuity in the maintenance of identity, which may provide some sense of consistency even in changing situations. Identity is thus negotiable without being completely arbitrary in character. (p. 55)

For social workers it underlines that while we need to be mindful of the structural factors that help form people's identities because factors such as our age, class, gender or race have social significance, we also need to avoid jumping to conclusions or stereotyping on the basis of structural factors or general categories alone. To understand people fully as individuals we also need to understand what they themselves feel is important about what makes them who they are. To establish how someone identifies themselves social workers need to ask questions such as 'What's important to you?' and 'What's meaningful to you in your life?'

To pursue this interesting but complex topic, you might want to read the article by Younge (2005) 'We can choose our identity, but sometimes it also chooses us', available at:

https://www.theguardian.com/uk/2005/jan/21/islamandbritain.comment7.

Activity 3.5: The importance of understanding identity for social workers

Read the article 'Culturally sensitive social work is about more than meeting social care needs', available at: http://www.communitycare.co.uk/2015/11/06/culturally-sensitive-care-just-someones-social-care-needs/.

Questions

Why does the author suggest that social workers need to concern themselves with service users' personal identities? How do they suggest that social workers do this?

Lastly, this article was written in the context of adult social care. Think of other areas of social work. Give examples of where getting a fuller sense of a service user's personal identity might lead to better outcomes for them. Give reasons.

Summary

- There are many dimensions to human diversity.
- People can differ from each other in many ways. However, they can also have much in common with each other at the same time.
- Social workers need to recognise human diversity actively and positively.
- To have a 'protected characteristic' can be socially significant but it must not be assumed that everyone with that characteristic is socially disadvantaged.
- Social workers need to understand the ways in which diversity can have social significance and be prepared to combat the negative effects where possible.
- Our identities are shaped by structural factors such as gender, the class or the ethnic group we are born into and life experiences. However, those factors in themselves do not determine who we are, we can also exercise agency in how we see and define ourselves. However, our choices are not without limits. As Smith (2008) said, identity is 'negotiable'.
- Social workers need to tread carefully in matters of identity. They should not make any assumptions about people's identities based upon the broad social categories that they appear to fall into. Social workers need to ask questions that seek to discover how an individual identifies him or herself rather jump to conclusions.

The consequences of difference

It was highlighted in the domain descriptor that social workers must be able to appreciate that:

> *as a consequence of difference, a person's life experience may include oppression, marginalisation and alienation as well as privilege, power and acclaim, and are able to challenge appropriately.*

Activity 3.2 started off the process of thinking about the consequences of difference. These can be positive or negative. However, we will now explore further the various negative consequences that people can experience of being different.

Prejudice, discrimination, harassment and victimisation

The difference between prejudice and discrimination is that prejudice refers to the thoughts and attitudes that we might hold toward a group of people, whereas discrimination refers to actual actions or behaviour against such a group. The act of discrimination in itself isn't necessarily negative in its intent or its consequences. We can discriminate in *favour of* something or someone for positive reasons and with positive outcomes (Gaine, 2010). However, this section is focused on forms of discrimination that mean that people end up being treated *less* favourably. That is when they are discriminated *against* because they are different. As we saw earlier, in terms of legislation, the Equality Act 2010 made it unlawful to discriminate against, harass or victimise someone because they have or are perceived to have a 'protected characteristic' or are associated with someone who has a protected characteristic. It is useful to have a better understanding of what these unlawful activities are and how they affect people.

Harassment as defined in the Equality Act 2010 is:

> *Unwanted conduct related to a relevant protected characteristic, which has the purpose or effect of violating an individual's dignity or creating an intimidating, hostile, degrading, humiliating or offensive environment for that individual.*

Examples could be name calling, continually laughing behind someone's back, mocking, ostracising or even communicating hostility through looks and gestures.

Victimisation is when someone treats someone badly or puts them at a disadvantage because they complain about discrimination or help someone who has been the victim of discrimination.

A classic example of victimisation is to respond to someone who has complained about negative treatment by accusing them of 'having a chip on their shoulder' and subjecting them to further negative treatment 'to put them in their place'.

In everyday terms harassment and victimisation are forms of bullying behaviour – they are abuses of power. Discrimination is also an abuse of power and it can take several forms.

Activity 3.6: Discrimination

Guidance related to the Equality Act 2010 such as that produced by ACAS (2014) and the Equality and Human Rights Commission (2015) identifies four types of discrimination that occur:

- direct discrimination;
- indirect discrimination;
- perception discrimination; and
- discrimination by association.

Imagine you had to provide a leaflet to give to new employees of a care agency explaining what the different types of discrimination are. Write a brief description of each and provide appropriate examples. Use the Guidance cited for help if necessary, but remember to put the leaflet in your own words and provide your own examples.

Commentary

Hopefully, your leaflet made it clear that 'direct discrimination' occurs when someone is treated less favourably than another person because of a protected characteristic they have or are thought to have, or because they associate with someone who has a protected characteristic (this is discrimination by association – see below). Direct discrimination tends to be the most obvious form of discrimination. For example, in the world of employment this might be paying women less than men even though they do exactly the same job. Or it might be that a female job candidate with the best qualifications and the most experience does not get an interview for a job whereas a male candidate with lesser qualifications does get an interview. Similarly, if a female employee is ignored for a promotion and the job is given to a male worker with fewer qualifications. In a care setting it might involve a situation where gay, lesbian or transgender people are not moved up the waiting list for places because the management or staff do not want them in the home. Or at a day centre, non-Muslims might get better treatment than Muslim service users or vice versa.

Indirect discrimination occurs when an organisation's practices, policies or procedures have the effect of disadvantaging people who share certain protected characteristics. So this might occur when a rule or policy is introduced that applies to everyone but particularly disadvantages people who share a protected characteristic. Examples where indirect discrimination occurs on the grounds of religion or belief would be where a workplace or education provider failed to provide a choice of religiously appropriate food as part of their catering arrangements. This would also be the case if services were only offered at a limited time which conflicted with various religious observances. An example of indirect discrimination on the grounds of gender would be the failure by a service provider or employer to provide gender appropriate services, an obvious but unlikely example being if there were only male toilets on the premises. Disabled people might experience indirect discrimination if providers of public services did not think through how their facilities (such as revolving doors) might prevent certain groups of people gaining access.

Discrimination by perception occurs when someone thinks a person has a particular protected characteristic, even if they do not. For example, a care home manager might reject an application to their home from a white person whom they wrongly believe is black because they have an African-sounding name.

Discrimination by association occurs where a person is associated with someone who has a particular protected characteristic. This could be, for example, when a female employee gives birth to a disabled child. On her return to work after maternity leave, she applies for a promotion. She is turned down and a less qualified colleague (a mother whose children are *not* disabled) is given the job because the employer thinks that the mother of the disabled child will need more time off and be less reliable because her child is disabled.

Anti-discriminatory practice is when social workers use their knowledge of the law around discrimination to challenge and address unfairness. However, it cannot be done effectively unless social workers are aware of the groups that legislation is designed to protect and knowledgeable about the different types of discrimination to which the law refers. In Chapter 4 we will extend the coverage of international and national legislation and policy that protects the rights of all of us as citizens and human beings.

Extension task

Read the article 'Social workers should use Equality Act to embed anti-discriminatory practice', available at: http://www.communitycare.co.uk/2013/01/09/social-workers-should-use-equality-act-to-embed-anti-discriminatory-practice/, for more useful information on this topic.

Oppression

What harassment, victimisation and the various forms of discrimination all have in common is that they all represent abuses of power that come out of unequal power relationships.

They can also be regarded as forms of 'oppressive behaviour'. Oppression is defined by Thompson (1993) as:

> Inhuman or degrading treatment of individuals or groups; hardship and injustice brought about by the dominance of one group over another; the negative and demeaning exercise of power. Oppression often involves disregarding the rights of an individual or group and is thus the denial of citizenship. (p. 3)

Burke (2013) goes further, saying:

> Oppression is not simply the absence of justice but the consistent denial of individuals' or social groups' humanity. It is reproduced and sustained by conscious and unconscious actions of individuals and groups through routine institutional practices, policies and procedures. (p. 414)

The concept of oppression, then, covers a wide range of abuses of power that can occur in different ways and at different levels. Social work practice therefore needs to recognise how and where power imbalances exist, to be prepared to challenge any abuses of power and to help empower those on the receiving end. In order to combat the full range of power abuses, social workers' practice needs to be not only anti-discriminatory but also anti-oppressive.

Before we examine more closely what such practice looks like, we need to briefly define and think about two other states of relative powerlessness referred to in the domain descriptor: marginalisation and alienation.

Marginalisation

Thompson (2011) defines marginalisation as 'the ways in which certain groups of people are pushed to the margins of society, and thus excluded from the mainstream' (p. 92). He goes on to say that the process of marginalisation is 'broadly the experience of all oppressed groups, as it is a characteristic of oppression that the people so affected are excluded from decision-making processes and the operations of power in general' (p. 93).

Activity 3.7: Marginalisation and its impact

In pairs:

Read the *Guardian* (2010) article 'Scope warns cuts will further marginalise disabled people', available at: https://www.theguardian.com/society/2010/sep/01/scope-warns-cuts-disabled-people. Using this as a starting-off point, think about the various ways that disabled people as a group can be marginalised in society.

Commentary

You should have highlighted the points from the article that disabled people risk being marginalised by cuts in financial and other forms of support that help them participate in everyday life. However, there are other factors to take into account over and above cut backs in government support. These can include attitudinal, social or environmental factors. Thompson (2011) argued that disabled people tend to be marginalised by:

- social attitudes that patronise, infantilise and devalue disabled people;

- physical barriers that deny access to certain buildings or areas;

- a lack of positive steps to enable disabled people to participate fully in social, political and economic activities.

(pp. 92–3)

You should be able to extend the points made in this example to other groups at risk of marginalisation in society and think of additional factors that might be more specific to that group. For example, a lack of facility with the English language can be a contributory factor in some people becoming marginalised. Others might be marginalised by being negatively stereotyped and labelled as dangerous, risky or 'deviant' in other ways.

This activity should have prompted thinking about the range of strategies needed to combat marginalisation. Some can be dealt with at the individual level; others require social change and political action.

Alienation

Alienation is possibly a more complex concept. It has its origins in Marxist philosophy (Cunningham and Cunningham, 2008). Marx argued that the process of industrialisation in the nineteenth century meant that workers in factories and other places of mass production were reduced to being mere cogs in the machine doing highly repetitive tasks on a production line moving at a speed they could not control. Under such conditions they become estranged from the work they were doing and became dehumanised. He contrasted this with craft workers who had a much great degree of control over their work and a much greater sense of creativity and feeling of job satisfaction as a result. Since then, the concept of alienation has generally come to mean a state where people feel isolated, not only from society but also from their true selves – their sense of who they are. In the broader sense, alienation means that people do not feel that they are part of everyday society. They experience a strong sense of powerlessness and feel a lack of control. Such feelings emanate from being excluded from decision-making, being given the message that no one is interested in or values their opinion and being constructed as a burden or threat rather than an asset to society. You can therefore see the common links in concepts such as alienation; marginalisation, discrimination and oppression are about a lack of control, powerlessness, and unfair and often demeaning unequal treatment. Social workers therefore need to understand the different ways in which certain groups of people are rendered powerless – at both the individual and societal level – in order to be able to challenge effectively.

Summary

- Oppression, discrimination, harassment and victimisation are all abuses of power that are possible when there are unequal power relationships.
- Power can be exercised in many ways and at different levels, some more subtle then others.
- Oppressed groups of people run the risk of being marginalised and alienated in society.

Challenging appropriately: anti-discriminatory and anti-oppressive practice

Professional codes and guidance require social workers to celebrate diversity but also to recognise that it can have negative consequences for certain groups in society. Guidance also requires social workers to understand the ways in which unequal power relations at a societal as well as an individual level can lead to a range of different types of abuses of power occurring. However, most importantly, guidance directs social workers to challenge any such abuses of power they encounter requiring them to apply anti-discriminatory and anti-oppressive principles to their practice.

Activity 3.8: Challenging discrimination and oppression

Corinne is a first-year social work student. It is week five of the course and she has just started a short observation placement in a day centre for people with learning disabilities. She has been assigned to shadow one of the more experienced workers Margaret. Margaret takes Corinne along to meet the day centre manager Antony. While they are in the office, Corinne witnesses the following conversation:

Antony to By the way that new Asian chappie from the Boundfield estate, was he
Margaret: on the transport today, you know, Jamal or Jamelia, whatever his name is?'

(Continued)

(Continued)

Margaret: You mean Jamal Alhadi?

Antony: Yes, that's the fella. Alhadi, or was it jihadi? It's something like that. Let's hope he's not wearing one of those suicide belts. That's all we need on a Monday morning.' (He keeps glancing at Corinne to see whether she's getting 'the joke'.)

Margaret: I'll check. I think he was going to start in the cooking group.

Antony: Well if he is, make sure it's not pork sausages or else we'll never hear the end of it. (More smiling and looking at Corinne.)

Margaret: (Clearly finding this distasteful.) OK anyway, I need to continue my tour with Corinne.

Antony: Nice to meet you Corinne. You look like a quiet one. We all like to have a laugh here. We love our banter, don't we Margaret? I say 'we' I mean the staff, half the service users wouldn't get a joke if you hit them over the head with it. I was with Barry in the transport group the other day. We were both cracking up they were just sitting there. I think they thought we were mad. Still, keeps us in a job.

As they leave the office, Margaret tells Corinne 'sorry about Antony, you'll have to ignore him, he's a bit of dinosaur but his heart's mainly in the right place. Anyway he retires in two years.'

In pairs:

1.   What are your reactions to this scenario? Has Corinne witnessed anything of concern?

2.   Should she challenge or do anything about what she has witnessed or should she try to fit in with the banter culture that Antony seems to say exists at the centre?

Commentary

Corinne has witnessed unprofessional behaviour from Antony. He has singled out and mocked a service user of Asian heritage and made a very poor taste and discriminatory 'joke' at his expense, based on his name. He also has made disrespectful and demeaning comments about the day centre service users generally. He has passed this off as 'banter' and tried to entice Corinne to play along with it. Concern is increased because Antony is the manager and is in a position of power and responsibility. Antony's behaviour suggests that the abuse witnessed should not just be understood in terms of someone's professionally inappropriate personal values, because a casual disrespect towards service users seems to have become embedded ('institutionalised') in the culture of the organisation. This might be a reason why Margaret puts up with his offensive behaviour. However, even though as social work student, Corinne is, herself, relatively powerless, this episode should not be ignored and 'shrugged off'. Just because no one is actually observed to be hurt, abuses of power like this should always be challenged in some way. Not to do so will mean that problematic behaviour is likely to be perpetuated and service users will not be given the respect they deserve. An inappropriate, unprofessional, oppressive culture will persist. Corinne should therefore not go along with it and try to fit in with a 'banter' culture which appears to be racist and disablist in some of what is said.

On occasions such as these students or members of the workforce might fear that they may be victimised or harassed if they report inappropriate behaviour. Again, this would be a consequence of an imbalance in power relations. Therefore, it is important that, on this occasion, Corinne speaks to her university tutor or placement supervisor about this. It will be the university's responsibility to protect their student and to bring the matter up with the placement provider. The most important thing is that, even if it feels difficult to do anything personally, you should not feel pressure to collude with practices that are discriminatory or abusive. Always report them to the relevant authority who should take the necessary action. In the unlikely situation that the university did not take any action, the matter could be reported to the Care Quality Commission, the regulator of care providers.

With the case of Corinne we have seen how abuses of power over people with protected characteristics must be challenged, even if it is passed off as 'banter'. We have suggested that, in this case, the matter is reported to a supervisor or tutor. However, there are many other ways in which individual social workers and social work students can challenge different forms of discrimination and oppression. The key is to understand how power imbalances can occur and affect relationships.

Activity 3.9: Disempowerment and oppression explored

Firstly, you need to think of an occasion when you (or someone close to you) felt you were 'disempowered' or discriminated against by an organisation either as an employee, customer or in some other relationship. For example, this might be because you were not treated with sufficient respect, you were not treated as an individual, your rights were ignored, you were not given a fair hearing, you were being pre-judged, you were not being taken seriously, you were patronised or you were simply communicated with very badly. In other words, think of an occasion where the interactions between you and the other people left you feeling diminished, frustrated and powerless.

(Continued)

(Continued)

- Identify the different factors that contributed to your feeling disempowered. Explain more about how that made you feel.
- What would have helped on that occasion to make you feel better and more powerful?
- Discuss your experiences with another.

Commentary

You might have identified situations where no one took the time to find out exactly what the situation was and to ask you what you wanted to happen (or even if they did, they did not listen). Or it might have been that people were using terminology or language that you couldn't grasp. It might be that you were 'pigeon-holed', pre-judged or labelled in a way that was not helpful. People might have used a very patronising tone towards you. There are lots of ways that organisations (and the people working in them) can disempower people either intentionally or unintentionally.

There might have been several different ways in which you could have been helped to feel more respected, in control or empowered. They could have included having a supporter or advocate to help you though the process and interpret things that you didn't understand, or being given information that explained the process in language that you understood which included clear details of your rights and how to complain if not happy. Additionally, you might have said that things would have been better if you had been treated as an equal and you worked 'in partnership'. That would include if someone had taken the time to get to know you properly as an individual, to ask your views about decisions that affected you and treated you as a person of worth equal to anyone else. Part of that would be to become more familiar with your personal context including your culture.

Working anti-oppressively

The activity was designed to demonstrate that there is no mystique to working anti-oppressively at an individual level. If we are aware of the various ways in which people can be disempowered, for example by discriminatory practices, by stereotyping, by lack of linguistic ability or by other factors that impair their voices being heard effectively, there are basic things that we can do to address this. Working in partnership, working in a culturally sensitive way, concentrating on communicating effectively and engaging the input of advocates or interpreters as appropriate can all help equalise power imbalances and enhance the chances of a fair, respectful and satisfactory outcome. These practices would be in line with the standards of professionalism and values discussed in the first two chapters. Dalrymple and Burke (2006) say that that anti-oppressive practice requires the following:

- an empowering approach which aims to overcome barriers for service users in taking more control of their lives;

- working in partnership so that as far as possible service users are included in decision-making processes about their lives;

- minimal intervention to reduce the oppressive and disempowering potential of social work intervention;

- critical reflection and reflexivity. This involves a continual consideration of self in practice in order to understand how our values and our biographies impact on our practice relationships.

(p. 20)

Anti-oppressive practice does not limit itself to understanding power imbalances at the interpersonal level. As discussed earlier, it sees the bases of oppression as being present in institutions, organisations and, ultimately, in social structures. Challenging oppression in the broadest sense is about working to combat social inequalities and to work for social justice. These are big, complex tasks which require social workers to work collectively to promote social change (Dalrymple and Burke, 2006; Gaine, 2010). At the readiness for direct practice stage the important thing is to know what anti-oppressive practice looks like at the interpersonal level. However, as the course progresses, you will need to engage with debates that broaden the focus to how social workers should address social issues like inequality, poverty, racism and sexism at the societal and structural level. A range of useful texts on the subject are listed below.

Summary

- Social workers must be able to recognise all forms of discrimination and oppression and to be able to understand why certain groups are more vulnerable than others to such abuses of power.
- However powerless they might feel social work students must not collude with any discriminatory or oppressive behaviour they observe.
- It is important that social work students adopt a critically reflective attitude to power imbalances, discrimination and oppression and share any concerns with their tutor or supervisor at the university. This will enable the most appropriate course of action to be taken.
- There are a range of things that can be done at the personal level to help combat and challenge discrimination and oppression and to empower service users. Among these are working in partnership, using advocacy, critical reflection and reflexivity.
- The causes of oppression can run deep in society and can require collective and political action to bring about social justice.

Further reading

Burke, B (2013) 'Anti-oppressive practice', in M Davies (ed.), *The Blackwell Companion to Social Work*, 4th edition. Oxford: Wiley-Blackwell, pp. 414–16.

Cocker, C and Hafford-Letchfield, T (eds) (2014) *Rethinking Anti-Discriminatory and Anti-Oppressive Theories for Social Work Practice*. Basingstoke: Palgrave.

Community Care (2013) 'Social workers should use Equality Act to embed anti-discriminatory practice', 9 January 2013. Online at: http://www.communitycare.co.uk/2013/01/09/social-workers-should-use-equality-act-to-embed-anti-discriminatory-practice/.

Community Care (2015) 'Culturally sensitive social work is about more than meeting social care needs', 6 November 2015. Online at: http://www.communitycare.co.uk/2015/11/06/culturally-sensitive-care-just-someones-social-care-needs/.

Dalrymple, J and Burke, B (2006) *Anti-oppressive Practice*, 2nd edition. New York: McGraw-Hill Education.

Dominelli, L (2002) *Anti-oppressive Social Work Theory and Practice*. Basingstoke: Palgrave Macmillan.

Hugman, R (2013) *Culture, Values and Ethics in Social Work: Embracing Diversity*. London: Routledge.

Thompson, N (2011) *Promoting Equality: Working with Diversity and Difference*, 3rd edition. Basingstoke: Palgrave.

Thompson, N (2012) *Anti-discriminatory Practice*, 5th edition. London: Macmillan.

Williams, P and Nzira, V (2008) *Anti-Oppressive Practice in Health and Social Care*. London: Sage.

4: Rights, justice and economic well-being

Introduction

In Chapter 3 we looked at how social workers need to be aware of legislation such as the Equality Act 2010 in order to be able to safeguard the rights of those with protected characteristics to be free from discrimination. In this chapter we will extend the scope of the discussion to include a broader range of rights about which social workers need to be knowledgeable in order to practise professionally. This will require learning about the most important pieces of legislation, conventions and policies in which such rights are embedded. As part of this discussion you will be encouraged to think about the very notion of what a 'right' actually is. This will not only highlight that there are different types of rights with different status in law, but also that rights are open to interpretation about what they mean in practice. Social workers therefore need to be thoughtful about rights and to be able to negotiate their way through such complexities if they are to promote the interests of service users. Beyond rights, we will also look at the key concepts of social justice and economic well-being in terms of what they mean and how they relate to each other.

Considering the breadth and complexity of the topics under discussion, coverage here cannot claim to be comprehensive or exhaustive. Nevertheless, this chapter will provide sufficient activities, commentaries and signposting to further reading to enable you to have a basic grounding upon which to build and to be ready for practice in your first placement.

Rights

The Oxford English Dictionary (2016a) defines a right as 'a moral or legal entitlement to have or do something'. This definition captures an important point about rights. Not all rights are laid out in or backed up by law. Rights can be reflections of what we think *ought* to be the case. For example, we might make 'rights' statements such as:

1. 'It is a fundamental right to be free from the fear of poverty.'
2. 'It is everybody's right to be accepted for who they are.'
3. 'Everyone has the right to a job.'
4. 'All women should have the right to feel safe walking home on their own at night.'
5. 'We have a right to die the death that we choose.'

In all the statements cited above, there is no obvious legal course of action available to back up those 'rights', however worthy or socially desirable we feel they are. In addition, such statements suggest that questions about what rights actually mean in practice are not always easily settled. For example, for the first statement, you should be aware that definitions of poverty differ. Therefore what that right means in practice is contestable, as will be the means of enabling it.

The first four statements also prompt the question of if a right is not enshrined in law does it mean that we cannot or should not take action to promote it? In many cases people are driven by their values to advocate for a particular right. For example, in the case of the statement about the right to feel safe walking home at night, that is a moral stance rather than a legal one. Campaigners for such a right might want it underpinned by law but that raises the question of how exactly to put it into law. 'Rights' therefore, can have different meanings and require interpretation to make sense and to be put into action. Social workers need to be clear about what sort of rights they are talking about and whether they exist in law or not.

In the case of statement 5 (the right to die) it is obvious that what, for some, should be a fundamental human right might not enjoy universal agreement. Therefore to talk about rights is complex and social workers need to learn at an early stage that knowing about the rights laid down in law, conventions and policies is important but thinking about how these rights are interpreted and enabled in any specific context is possibly even more important.

Activity 4.1: Rights

1. Individually write down your own personal top ten fundamental rights that should be universal to human beings.

2. Compare your list with another. What are the similarities and differences? Discuss how your ideas about rights might have developed?

3. Of the rights on your lists, how many of them do you believe are protected by law, convention or policy?

Commentary

It would be hard to guess everyone's top ten. However, it is highly probable that 'the right to life' would feature highly on all lists. Thereafter, lists might differ according to personal values, education and upbringing, our social context and cultural beliefs. This underlines that human rights were not handed down, immutable, to human beings at the dawn of time. In fact, although the concept of rights has a long history (think about the Magna Carta, for example) the idea of universal human rights as conceived today is a relatively recent phenomenon. Visit http://www.humanrights.com/ for a broad historical overview. Both Ife (2001) and Seymour and Seymour (2013) provide an informative discussion of rights in the context of social work.

Ife (2001) provides a wide framework to understand the rights we think of as relevant today. He talks about there being 'three generations' of rights (see Table 4.1 below). Originating in the seventeenth and eighteenth centuries, the first generation would include civil and political rights such as the right to equality before the law, the rights to privacy, self-expression and so on.

Table 4.1 The three generations of human rights

	First generation	Second generation	Third generation
Name	Civil and political rights	Economic, social and cultural rights	Collective rights
Origin	Liberalism	Socialism; social democracy	Economics; development studies; green ideology
Examples	Rights to vote, free speech, fair trial; freedom from torture, abuse; protection of the law; freedom from discrimination	Rights to education housing, health, employment, adequate income, social security, etc.	Rights to economic development and prosperity; benefit from economic growth; social harmony; healthy environment, clean air, etc.
Agency	Legal clinic; Amnesty International; Human Rights Watch; refugee work	Welfare state; third sector; private market welfare	Economic development agencies; community projects; Greenpeace, etc.
Dominant professional	Law	Social work	Community development
Social work	Advocacy; refugee work; asylum seekers; prison reform, etc.	Direct service; management of the welfare state; policy development and advocacy; research	Community development: social economic, political, cultural, environmental, personal/spiritual

Source: Ife (200), p. 42.

About first generation rights Ife says that they:

> *are sometimes also referred to as negative rights; they are rights which need to be protected rather than realised, rights which people are seen as somehow 'possessing', and the state is required to ensure that they are not threatened or violated. (p. 25)*

Developing more in the nineteenth and twentieth centuries, second-generation rights include social rights and economic rights such as the right to education and to social security. About these rights Ife (2001) says:

> *Second-generation rights are referred to as positive rights because they imply a much more active and positive role for the state. Rather than simply protecting rights, the state is required to take a stronger role in actually ensuring that these rights are realised, through various forms of social provision. (p. 26)*

Finally, Ife identifies third-generation rights which, unlike first- and second-generation rights, only make sense if defined at a collective level. He gives examples such as the right to clean air or the right to live in an economically prosperous and harmonious society. For these rights to be realised obviously requires actions at the collective level within and between countries. You can see in Table 4.1 that Ife sets out where and how social work has a role to play in enabling the three generations of rights. The most obvious role is in promoting second-generation rights such as access to services but is not just confined to this area.

Currently the role of social work in the UK is more focused on protecting people's first-generation rights and 'realising' people's second-generation rights. However, both in the UK and in the wider world, it is now proposed that the role of social work needs to change to think more about third-generation rights. This is particularly the case if we are seriously interested in promoting social justice and economic well-being, as will be discussed later in the chapter.

Activity 4.2: Debate – is it the role of social workers to change society?

Read the article 'What's the role of social work: to change society or to help individuals?', online at

https://www.theguardian.com/social-care-network/2016/jun/29/whats-the-role-of-social-work-to-help-individuals-or-change-society?CMP=ema-1696&CMP=.

Divide the group into two.

One side needs to think about and propose arguments for:

'Social work can only promote rights, social justice and economic well-being by concentrating on working with individuals.'

The other side needs to think about and propose arguments against:

'Social work can only promote rights, social justice and economic well-being by concentrating more on promoting social change.'

Commentary

There is no obvious right or wrong side in this debate. Such questions have engaged and divided social workers for many years. The aim at this stage was to encourage you to think more about what it means for social workers to promote rights, social justice and economic well-being in practice. While there is much that can be done at the individual level, there are limits to how far just working individually can achieve the desired change. It would be fair to say that most social workers are employed by organisations who expect them to work primarily with individuals and their families. Therefore the challenge for social work is how to find an effective and legitimate way to address problems of social injustice and inequality at a social level. We will return to this theme when we discuss social justice and economic well-being later in the chapter.

Rights in national and international law, conventions and policies

There are several pieces of legislation, conventions and associated policies which set out fundamental first and second generation rights important to social work and about which social workers need to be knowledgeable. The main ones are:

- The European Convention on Human Rights

- The Human Rights Act 1998

- The UN Convention on the Rights of the Child (UN General Assembly, 1989)

- The Children Act 1989

- The Adoption and Children Act 2002

- Every Child Matters

- The Children Act 2004

- The Mental Capacity Act 2005

- The Equality Act 2010

- The Care Act 2014

Space does not permit adequate coverage of all of their contents and provisions. However, each of these laws, conventions and policy documents can easily be found on the Internet and you should take the time to find them and read them either in the original or in summary form. It would be also be useful for you to be aware of the United Nations Convention on the Rights of Persons with Disabilities and (for the time being) the European Social Charter.

Activity 4.3: Rights quiz

The answers to the following questions can all be found in the documents listed above. Make sure that you can answer all of them correctly – even if that requires some research.

1. How many Articles relating to rights and freedoms are there in the European Convention on Human Rights (ECHR)?

2. What does Article 8 of the ECHR say?

3. What is the relationship between the European Convention on Human Rights and the Human Rights Act 1998?

4. Which Act sets out a carer's legal right to assessment and support?

5. What right does Article 12 of the Human Rights Act 1998 give?

6. Which Act is mainly concerned with giving people with protected characteristic rights freedom from discrimination?

7. What are Articles 3 and 4 of the UN Convention on the Rights of the Child (expressed in child friendly language)?

8. In which laws are children given the right to advocacy and under what circumstances?

9. In which piece of legislation will you find the principle stated that every adult has the right to make his or her own decisions and must be assumed to have capacity to do so unless it is proved otherwise?

10. Where can we find the 'Right to liberty and security' laid down?

11. What are the five outcomes for children set out in Every Child Matters?

12. What was the relationship between Every Child Matters and the Children Act 2004?

Note: The answers to the quiz and some accompanying commentary can be found at the end of the chapter.

Overall commentary

While all social work students should familiarise themselves with the Articles of the Human Rights Act 1998, the quiz has hopefully made it clear that there are other important laws, conventions and policies that establish rights which are important for social workers to know about. Some of these are specifically focused on universal human rights (in other words rights that apply to everyone); others are more specifically focused on establishing rights to services to people who come into certain categories – for example rights for carers to have an assessment and support. In some policy and legislation rights are implicit rather than explicit. For example, Every Child Matters and the Children Act 2004 expect agencies to work together to provide specific outcomes for children as if they were rights. In addition, as we have seen, the Equality Act 2010 aims to ensure that people that have certain protected characteristics have the right to be protected from discrimination in its many forms.

The other important point that emerges from the quiz is that knowing about what rights there are is one thing; it is another to be able to interpret a particular right and enable it in practice. For example, what does 'the right to respect for a private and family life' actually mean for someone who is sleeping rough on the street? Similarly, a child can have the right that adults will always make decisions in that child's best interests, but who decides what is in any particular child's best interests, how do they come to that decision and who is to say they are right? Putting rights into practice always requires more than just knowledge of the law; it requires careful interpretation, weighing of evidence and judgement. Often previous cases are used to help with difficult decision-making (see, for example, Braye and Preston-Shoot, 2010; Dalrymple and Burke, 2006; Johns, 2014; Preston-Shoot, 2014 and Seymour and Seymour, 2013). When social workers take legal advice on matters of rights previous 'case law' can be very useful in deciding what to do.

Activity 4.4: Case study – Ken

Ken is an 80-year-old widower with Parkinson's disease who, because he could no longer live at home, moved into a private care home with the help of his local social services. He is often confused because of the medication that he takes and is prone to falling. On visiting, his daughter Carol was most unhappy to find that Ken was sharing another room with another male resident with just a curtain to create a partition between them. Ken wasn't too happy with this arrangement, particularly since he uses a catheter and the care staff not only change the bag in full view of the Ken's room-mate but also they sometimes leave the door to the room open. Carol is also concerned that in the home, all the rooms have CCTV cameras installed in them. The care home management say that this 'is a way to enhance the security and safety of the premises and property, and to protect the safety of people.' Ken is finding it very hard to settle but indicates that he doesn't want to make a fuss. Carol wants to know what she can do as the care home is refusing to change anything saying that Ken will need to adjust to the ways of the home. She has contacted the local social services but they have failed to get back to her after several calls and emails.

Questions

1. How might knowledge of human rights help resolve this situation?

2. What rights and which pieces of legislation might be relevant in this case?

Commentary

Ken's dignity and well-being are clearly being threatened by the lack of privacy in his care and living arrangements. The human rights applicable to Ken's situation are Articles 3 and 8 of the Human Rights Act 1998: Article 3 'right to freedom from inhuman and degrading treatment' and Article 8 'right to respect for private and family life'. In all cases of this nature, the best approach in the first instance is to talk to the management and try to resolve the matter informally. However, if, as seems the case with Ken, the management do not want to change their practices, then the next step would be to make a formal complaint about the poor quality of care being delivered. This would involve contacting the local authority who commissioned the care for Ken.

Under relevant legislation such as the Care Act 2014 service users and carers have the 'right' to complain about services and the local authority has the legal duty to act lawfully and to respond reasonably and fairly towards service users and carers making complaints. If it does not, it can be challenged in court by a legal procedure known as judicial review. If no change for the better was forthcoming from the complaints procedure then there would be a good case for Carol escalating the matter further by seeking legal advice about the breach of Ken's human rights under Articles 3 and 8. In cases like this the knowledge of rights in care legislation and human rights generally is useful because it provides a clear justification and process for action and means that if more informal steps do not provide satisfactory outcomes, as a last resort legal action is possible that can resolve the situation.

Summary

- Rights can be defined as a moral or legal entitlement to have or do something.
- Rights can be categorised in 'generations' where, currently, the role of social work in the UK is more focused on protecting people's first-generation rights and 'realising' people's second-generation rights.
- There are several pieces of legislation, conventions and associated policies which set out rights important to social work and about which social workers need to be knowledgeable.
- However, knowing about what rights there are is one thing; it is another thing to be able to interpret a particular right and enable it in practice

Social justice

In Chapter 1 we saw that the definition of social work provided by the International Federation of Social Workers (IFSW) included the statement that:

> *Principles of social justice, human rights, collective responsibility and respect for diversities are central to social work.*

This is also reflected in the BASW Code of Ethics (2012) which states that:

> *Social workers have a responsibility to promote social justice, in relation to society generally, and in relation to the people with whom they work. (p. 9)*

Unfortunately, neither the IFSW nor BASW explain what the principles of social justice are. Like many of the concepts that we have looked at, the definition of social justice is open to debate. For some people, it is concerned with bringing about a fairer society; for others it is concerned with bringing about a more equal society. These two views are not necessarily seeking the same outcomes and, even if they were, there might not be agreement on *how* to achieve those outcomes. Nevertheless, at this point we need a working definition. Thompson and Thompson (2008) provide a reasoned and realistic view which would appear to make sense in the light of the professional social work values, ethical codes, principles and domains that we have reviewed thus far. They say:

1. *A commitment to social justice is {. . .} a commitment to making sure that we are tackling inequalities as far as we reasonably can rather than adding to them. This involves recognizing the inherent injustices in a social system characterized by poverty and deprivation, racism, sexism, ageism, disablism, heterosexism and other such forms of discrimination.*

2. *It is important to recognize that, while full social justice in the short term may be an unachievable goal, social work can make a positive and valuable contribution to moving in the right direction in the longer term. We can be part of the solution, rather than part of the problem. This is an important point to emphasize, as some people have rejected social justice as a Value, on the grounds that it is unrealistic. Social justice is an idealistic notion, in the sense of an ideal to work towards, rather than something that can be dismissed as 'utopian' or out of touch with reality.*

3. *The term social justice is used rather than simply justice to show that it is more than a matter of individual fairness (although that too is very important); rather, it is a matter of understanding how social processes and institutions systematically combine to produce unfair outcomes. Social justice is therefore a socio-political matter, rather than simply an issue of personal ethics. It reflects the social nature of social work and its links with wider social and political issues.*

Adapted from Thompson and Thompson (2008, p. 214)

Activity 4.5: Working towards social justice

Questions to discuss in groups:

1. We have already looked at the ways in which inequality can be caused and sustained by different forms of discrimination. How might social work add to inequalities (albeit unintentionally)?

2. Is working towards social justice simply 'idealistic'? Should social work abandon the idea as simply 'utopian'?

3. Why would Thompson and Thompson propose social justice for social workers is more than a matter of ensuring that we deal with individuals fairly?

Commentary

Social workers can add to inequalities in several different ways. They can limit people's choices and life opportunities by having (often unacknowledged) stereotyped ideas about certain groups of people in society, for example that people with learning disabilities cannot work or are unable to form intimate relationships, that black men make unreliable fathers or that older people with complex needs can only be looked after in residential care. Social workers can also disempower people by being paternalistic – usually with good intentions – by doing things *for* people rather than allowing them to learn the skills and acquire the knowledge and confidence to do more for themselves. Stereotyping and paternalistic practices can help to maintain people in disempowered positions. The best way to keep a check on this sort of disempowering practice is through being critically reflective.

Other ways in which social workers can add to inequalities are by passively accepting cutbacks in resources and reductions in services, managing their service users' expectations downwards and assisting them to adjust to their disadvantaged situation. While it might be unethical to create false expectations among service users, especially in a context of cutbacks (Beckett and Maynard, 2005), that does not mean that social workers should simply accept an unfair status quo and encourage their service users to do the same. Service managers, commissioners, local and national politicians can all be lobbied. Service users can be put in touch with campaigning groups and others in the same position.

In response to the second question, you could argue that to think we can have a society without poverty, without inequality, without oppression and discrimination is a pure fantasy. You could make the pragmatic argument that social workers should concentrate on performing the core tasks that their employing organisation pays them to do, for example carrying out assessments, putting together support and safeguarding plans, carrying out reviews and so on. A cynic might add they don't always manage to do that properly, let alone taking time to campaign for social justice. However, as Thompson and Thompson (2008) indicate, just because achieving the ultimate goal of social justice might seem a long way off, that does not mean that, either individually or collectively, social workers cannot do their bit to fight poverty, inequality, oppression and discrimination in society. Whether it's through consciousness-raising, campaigning, lobbying or in a range of other practical ways, history tells us that social action can make a difference in producing changes that bring about socially just outcomes.

Lastly, the point that Thompson and Thompson make in the third point recognises the importance of the social and economic context in which social work takes place. Yes, social workers need to be fair and just in their interpersonal practice with individuals and families, but we must also acknowledge that many of the people who require social work services face issues that have organisational, institutional, social and economic origins. Their lives will not improve as much as possible and their potential will not be fully realised if we just focus on the individual rather than on the wider causes.

Summary

1. Social justice is a contested concept which has several dimensions to it both in terms of what it looks like and also in how to achieve it. Nevertheless, most would agree that a commitment to social justice involves recognising the inherent injustices in a social system characterised by poverty and deprivation, racism, sexism, ageism, disablism, heterosexism and other forms of discrimination.
2. Social workers can unintentionally add to social injustice by not working in a critically reflective way and being led by unchecked stereotyped and paternalistic thinking.
3. Even though the perfect, socially just society is unattainable, this does not mean that either individually or collectively social workers cannot take steps to improve current social injustices.
4. Working with individuals in a just way is important but social justice is more likely to be achieved by people joining together and working collectively to change society.

Economic well-being

In Activity 4.3 (the rights quiz) we saw that the government Green Paper *Every Child Matters* made 'economic well-being' one of the five outcomes for all children. The Green Paper goes on to say that children should 'not be prevented by economic disadvantage from achieving their full potential in life' (HM Treasury, 2003: 9). Guidance to the Care Act 2014 (Department of Health, 2014) also makes promoting 'social and economic well-being' a goal for local authorities 'when carrying out any of their care and support functions' in respect of adults (p. 7). The need to promote economic well-being across all service user groups is therefore well established in policy. However, as with all the concepts we have studied, in order to put something into practice, we need to have a clearer sense of what it is we are trying to achieve.

Activity 4.6: Economic well-being

Questions to discuss in small groups:

1. How would you define economic well-being?
2. What helps create economic well-being?
3. What gets in the way of economic well-being?
4. What can be the physical and mental effects of a lack of economic well-being?

Commentary

Economic well-being is a person's or family's standard of living based primarily on how well they are doing financially. There is a numerical or financial dimension to this in that it depends on how much money someone has either in income, savings or other material assets. However, there is also a subjective or psychological dimension to it in that we all have our individual sense of what we think is enough to live on, what we think are necessities and what are luxuries and so on. Partly this is to do with what people consider 'normal' in society at any given time. So, for example, while having a television or a fridge was considered a luxury in the 1950s, these days not only are these goods considered to be 'basics' but so, in many people's eyes, too are computers, mobile phones, DVD players and many other electrical goods. When talking about matters of economic well-being and poverty, sociologists are less likely to talk of 'absolute poverty', where you have nothing at all, but are more likely to talk of 'relative poverty' where one is poor in relation to the norms of society and therefore are likely to face social exclusion as a consequence. For a fuller discussion of this topic see Cunningham and Cunningham (2008) and Backwith (2015).

As far as what creates economic well-being, it is having enough income, savings or assets to feel confident that you have enough to lead a satisfactory lifestyle. It might not just be a question of being in work and earning a good salary. Two people could be on the same salary but have vastly different outgoings. A single person with low housing costs and no commuting costs will have more disposable income than someone with dependents, higher housing costs and huge commuting costs. Their actual economic well-being will be different. Students, for example, might be living off a loan but for some their parents could be well enough off to make sure that their economic well-being is taken care off. Others might need to take part-time jobs just to keep out of debt. People on benefits are, by definition, only just above the poverty line. The fact that some disabled people or families might get hundreds of pound a week from different benefits might make them seem well off to a student trying to manage on a loan. However, their economic well-being could be affected by their outgoings and other circumstances such as not having a family to support them financially, the need to buy special equipment or to pay back loans. Research has shown that living in poverty means that life is more costly (*Guardian*, 2015).

Economic well-being can be affected by many factors and all the more so when they occur in combination with each other. They would include:

- being unable to work;
- having no qualifications and being unable to find permanent, well-paid work;
- the need to live on a fixed income such as a benefit at a time when prices are rising;
- having disproportionately high housing and utility costs;
- being unaware of all of one's benefit entitlements and other potential concessions;
- getting into trouble with loan sharks;
- having an expensive addiction.

The impact of a lack of economic well-being can be mental stress, anxiety, physical ill health and social exclusion (see, for example, Payne, 2012). This is particularly the case if the lack of well-being has lasted a long time.

Activity 4.7: What can social workers do to help people achieve economic well-being?

Below is an extract from *Community Care* which you should read and then answer the questions.

> When Nassima heard a knock on her door, earlier harassment from bailiffs had left her too scared to open it. This time, however, it was a social worker calling. Struggling to cope after the birth of her son and unable to return to work due to mental ill health, her bathroom was in disrepair and the debts had mounted. 'I'd been living off credit cards,' Nassima recalls. Her social

worker, Jo Turberville, persisted, leaving notes for her client 'checking if she was OK', until she finally opened her door.

It emerged that Nassima was not receiving benefit entitlements because she was unaware of her rights, so Turberville arranged appointments with an adviser and a debt support agency. She also helped her access emergency grants to buy essential household goods and repair the bathroom, which improved the family's health and hygiene. Now, Nassima is repaying her debts and receiving the range of benefits to which she is entitled.

'Without Jo's intervention I don't know where I'd be,' Nassima says. 'She's been such a help — supporting me to claim for benefits and get my finances on track and under control. No one was willing to practically help me apply for benefits before I spoke to Jo. She sat down with me and helped sort everything out. Life's easier now I don't have to worry about money as much.'

For Turberville, who works for the Building Bridges project with Family Action in Lewisham, south London, cases like Nassima's illustrate the multiple challenges of promoting social justice, rights and tackling poverty. 'I have to work within the limits set by welfare policy,' she says, citing the 'negative impact' on families of the cap placed recently on housing benefit. 'I don't think this is fair or right but feel disempowered by having to work within this flawed framework,' she adds.

Another challenge has been finding support for families as local authority cuts result in service closures or reduced support. 'Many of my families are housebound due to panic disorder and social phobia and find it difficult to access services,' Turberville says. 'I had real difficulty in finding Nassima debt advice because none of the services were prepared to visit her at home and she was not at a point where she was able to cope with leaving the safety of her home.'

The impact of poverty on children is also often overlooked in many children's support services, she says. 'In many of the meetings I have attended this is not mentioned or discussed. In Nassima's case, I felt it was left to me constantly to raise this during meetings and push to ensure it was addressed.'

Source: 'Social work reform: promoting rights, justice and economic well-being', *Community Care*, 10 March 2011.

1. In what ways does the social worker advance Nassima's economic well-being in this case?

2. Generally, what sort of activities can social workers undertake to ensure that their service users' economic-well-being is promoted? Make a bullet-pointed list, share lists among groups and develop a 'mega-list' of strategies that are possible.

Commentary

In the first question, Nassima's social worker was aware that Nassima was not receiving all the benefits to which she was entitled. She therefore made Nassima aware of her welfare rights. She then did practical things like helping her with applications and referring Nassima to a debt support agency which helped her get her debts under control.

For the second question, apart from the important activities above such as signposting and providing practical support, social workers can give service users who are able to work the encouragement to look for jobs together with any information about specific schemes that might be directed at that particular group – for example, people with disabilities of different kinds. Beyond the official benefits system, sometimes social workers are able to apply to local or national charitable funds set up to help certain groups of people, for example people with certain illnesses or former service personnel. For service users with debts social workers also need to be aware of credit unions. These are non-profit financial organisations usually set up on a mutual basis by members for the benefit of their local community. They lend at much lower rates than private institutions and very much lower than 'same-day cash' lenders and unregulated loan sharks.

Nassima's social worker also raised the issue of debt among other professionals by talking to colleagues at meetings. These latter activities are important as the more people are aware of benefits entitlements and debt advice services the better. Organisations can come together to help problem-solve matters of debt and poverty locally. Also, organisations are more effective at lobbying for change than individuals, and the more organisations the better. Therefore raising the importance of economic well-being for the overall well-being of service users as much as possible is a positive activity.

You might have thought of more strategies. Make sure that you share them. There is no single way of helping people achieve economic well-being.

Further reading

Suggested further reading on poverty, economic well-being and social work:

Backwith, D (2015) *Social Work, Poverty and Social Exclusion*. Maidenhead: Open University Press.

Summary

- The need to promote the economic well-being of service users is embedded in policies aimed at both adults and children.
- Economic well-being can be defined as a person's or family's standard of living based primarily on how well they are doing financially.

- Economic well-being can be affected by many factors. These can include: unemployment, low wages, a lack of savings personally or in the wider family and high levels of costs and outgoings.
- The impact of a lack of economic well-being can be mental stress, anxiety, physical ill health and social exclusion.
- Social workers can promote economic well-being by being aware of welfare entitlements and encouraging service users to claim what they are due. They can signpost welfare rights agencies, credit unions and debt advice centres as appropriate. They can promote employment and training schemes. They can also take collective lobbying action such as campaigning against cuts in benefits and employment schemes and against low wages.

Activity 4.3: Answers and commentary

1. The ECHR contains 17 key articles relating to rights and freedoms.
2. Article 8 concerns 'the right to respect for private and family life'.
3. The Human Rights Act 1998 incorporates the rights set out in the European Convention on Human Rights (ECHR) into domestic British law.

Commentary

You will therefore see that Article 8 of the Human Rights Act 1998 is the same as Article 8 of the ECHR - 'the right to respect for private and family life'.

4. The Care Act 2014.
5. Article 12 of the Human Rights Act 1998 establishes the 'right to marry and start a family'.

Commentary

Not only does this apply to gay couples, the Equality and Human Rights Commission clarifies that 'the European Court of Human Rights ruled in 2002 that this right extends to transsexual people'.

6. The Equality Act 2010
7. Article 3: All adults should do what is best for them. When adults make decisions, they should think about how their decisions will affect children.

   Article 4: The government has a responsibility to make sure your rights are protected. They must help your family to protect your rights and create an environment where you can grow and reach your potential.

Source: http://www.unicef.org/rightsite/files/uncrcchilldfriendlylanguage.pdf

Commentary

It is always important to think about how you would explain someone's rights to them whatever their age, disability or language.

8. The Children Act 1989 as amended by the Adoption and Children Act 2002 gave the right to advocacy services for a looked after child, a child in need or care leaver directly making or intending to make a complaint on their own behalf.

9. The Mental Capacity Act 2005.

10. The 'right to liberty and security' is set out in Article 5 of the Human Rights Act 1998.

11. Every Child Matters identified the five outcomes that are most important to children and young people. They are:

- Be healthy
- Stay safe
- Enjoy and achieve
- Make a positive contribution
- Achieve economic well-being.

12. Every Child Matters (ECM) was a policy document (Green Paper) that laid the foundations for the Children Act 2004 which had as its guiding principles:

- To allow children to be healthy
- Allowing children to remain safe in their environments
- Helping children to enjoy life
- Assist children in their quest to succeed
- Help make a contribution – a positive contribution – to the lives of children
- Help achieve economic stability for our children's futures.

Commentary

Questions 11 and 12 illustrate that ideas for legislation are often first presented to professionals and the public in policy documents such as Green and White Papers. Neither ECM nor the Children Act 2004 talk about conferring legal rights as such. The outcomes are presented as ambitions that local authorities and service providers must meet on behalf of children. However, social workers and other professionals are encouraged to practise as if they were actual rights.

Further reading

Brammer, A (2015) *Social Work Law*, 4th edition. Harlow: Pearson.

5: Knowledge

Achieving a Social Work Degree

This chapter will help you develop skills in the following domain of the Professional Capabilities Framework:

> **Knowledge:** *Apply knowledge of social sciences, law and social work practice theory*

The Professional Capability Framework states about this domain that:

> *Social workers understand psychological, social, cultural, spiritual and physical influences on people, human development throughout the life span and the legal framework for practice. They apply this knowledge in their work with individuals, families and communities. They know and use theories and methods of social work practice. (BASW, Professional Capability Framework – Readiness for Practice Capabilities)*

This domain statement goes on to say that, at the point of going out on their first practice placement, social work students need to be able to:

- Demonstrate an initial understanding of the application of research, theory and knowledge from sociology, social policy, psychology, health and human growth and development to social work
- Demonstrate an initial understanding of the legal and policy frameworks and guidance that inform and mandate social work practice
- Demonstrate an initial understanding of the range of theories and models for social work intervention

Introduction

As the domain descriptor indicates, this chapter covers a very broad range of content indeed. That said, it states that, at this stage, you are only required to demonstrate an 'initial understanding' of this considerable range of knowledge. Even so, it is a lot to cover satisfactorily in a single chapter. Therefore, even more than has been the case with previous chapters, you are strongly urged to develop your knowledge and understanding of this domain by further reading and linking to other related modules on your course.

The chapter begins by using a case study activity based on children's safeguarding to illustrate why social workers need to have the range of knowledge indicated. This leads on to a discussion about the different types of knowledge used in social work generally. You will be introduced to the five types of knowledge proposed by the Social Care Institute of Excellence (SCIE) (Pawson et al., 2003) together with the TAPUPA framework suggested by SCIE as an effective means with which to assess the quality of any sources of knowledge used.

Using the case study, activities will be used to explore the range of theories and models for social work intervention. You will also be signposted to specific further reading to expand your knowledge in this core area of the social work curriculum. A further case study based on an older person is used to provide further coverage of the domain, particular in terms of knowledge of human growth and development and legislation and policy around adult safeguarding. Again, suggestions are made for relevant further reading.

Lastly, to ensure that coverage of the domain is complete, we discuss the relevance of the important but seldom discussed concept of spirituality in social work. The chapter concludes with a summary of the key points.

Case study: The Vasiliauskas family

Thinking about why knowledge of social sciences, law and social work practice theory is important

The Vasiliauskas family:

- Henrikas (29) – father

- Jolanta (26) – mother

- Lėja (7) – daughter (from another relationship)

- Jonas (4) – son

- Petras (10 months) – son

→

Henrikas and Jolanta Vasiliauskas are originally from Lithuania. They have lived in rural East Anglia for four years. The father Henrikas has been working much of the time as an agricultural worker. The work is hard and involves long hours. The pay is low. Because it is mainly seasonal it can involve periods of unemployment and to supplement his income Henrikas is involved in drug-dealing activity. He has a drink and drugs habit himself. He also suffers from mental illness, mainly depression. He has significant mood swings. He first met Jolanta five years ago through Lithuanian contacts in Britain. She already had a daughter, Léja, from a previous relationship. They decided to get married and set up home on their own. Subsequently they had two children together, the most recent, Petras, who is just ten months old.

Jolanta also takes drugs and has an alcohol problem. She currently doesn't do any paid work but has worked in the sex industry in the past. This was against her will. She was trafficked from Lithuania to another part of Britain and forced to participate in pornographic films and other sex acts for money. Her meeting and then marrying Henrikas helped her to escape the clutches of the gang exploiting her. Jolanta suffers with depression and anxiety. Like Henrikas her verbal English is only very basic. At home the family all speak Lithuanian. For various reasons there is occasional domestic abuse in the household. From time to time, Henrikas screams at and hits Jolanta. Jolanta puts up with it. She feels trapped and has not made any plans to leave. She does not want to return to her family in Lithuania and does not have any friends in England.

Léja is in Year 3 at the local primary school. She is said by her teachers to be mainly well turned out, a little on the thin side, a pleasant girl but quiet and withdrawn. She doesn't like to talk about her home life.

Jonas has just started in reception class on a half-day basis. He, too, is reported to be mainly well dressed and quite thin for his age. His mother often brings him in late and can be quite late at collecting him at times. His teachers have noticed that his language is quite delayed. They notice that he can get frustrated when playing with the others and occasionally hits out. The school has found it difficult to engage with Jolanta about both children.

According to the Health Visitor, Petras is reasonably physically healthy for his age but rather under-stimulated mentally. He has no age-appropriate toys for example and is left for long periods in his chair staring at the TV. The Health Visitor has also noticed that he gets nappy rash quite often because Jolanta leaves him unchanged for longer than she should. Because of this and also because of suspicions that Jolanta might be abusing drugs and alcohol based on circumstantial evidence, the Health Visitor has continued to keep in contact with the family and visits quite frequently. Jolanta does not always open the door when the Health Visitor calls and, when she does, she often looks quite 'out of it'. The Health Visitor, as with the school staff, feel that Jolanta has lots of issues and needs on many scores but will not open up about her problems. This not helped by the fact that her knowledge of English is so limited.

$\longrightarrow$

Referral

On one occasion Jolanta completely forgot to collect Lèja from school. After trying to contact Jolanta with no success, a member of staff took Lèja home. When they arrived, Jolanta was clearly under the influence of drugs, alcohol or both and could not make it to the front door meaning that Lèja had to let them in through the back door. The teacher could see Jolanta lying on the sofa and Jonas was sat on the floor watching something on the television in the same room. The house was very sparsely furnished. Petras was crying in his cot in the corner of the same room. Later that day, with the information given to them by their member of staff, the head teacher made a referral to Children's Social Care.

Questions:

1. In the scenario above what range of knowledge would a social worker need in order to understand fully what is going on with this family? That is to say what would they need to know about in order to make a proper assessment and then formulate ideas about what should be done next? Make a list of the different areas of knowledge.

2. From the list you have generated for question 1, try to group the different areas of knowledge into broader headings.

Commentary

From the details provided in the case study, it is clear that, like many situations that social workers have to work with, it is complex with many elements to it. To make full sense of this situation a social worker would therefore need to have knowledge about:

*   families, family relationships and family systems;
*   child development;
*   mental illness: its causes, effects and possible treatments;
*   understanding life transitions and loss;
*   the experience of immigration and of being an immigrant in the UK;
*   what it is like to live on the poverty line;
*   alcohol and drug misuse: causes and treatments;
*   domestic abuse and what can be done about it, including the effects on children in the household;
*   sexual exploitation and its effects;
*   policy and legislation relevant to child safeguarding, mental health, drug abuse and domestic violence;
*   inter-agency, inter-professional working and knowledge of local services, e.g. what agencies provide which services and who does what;

- methods of assessment;
- how to communicate with people with limited use of English;
- working with interpreters;
- how to work directly with children;
- how to improve parenting capacity and family relationships;
- knowledge of the local community;
- a grasp of Lithuanian culture.

The list could go on. However, for the second question you might have grouped the various areas of knowledge under this type of heading:

- 'knowledge that helps us understand human behaviour' (social and human sciences);
- 'knowledge which sets out what social workers and others are required to do in such situations' (legislation and policy);
- 'knowledge that enables social workers to intervene appropriately and change situations' (social work theories); and
- 'knowledge of what services are available either locally or from outside the area' (practical knowledge).

You might have also felt that it is important that social workers get a better sense of the family culture and what the experience of living in that situation is actually like for those involved. In this case, we refer to understanding the perspectives of Henrikas, Jolanta, Lėja and Jonas (service user and carer knowledge).

Types of knowledge

Complex situations such as the one outlined therefore require a range of different types of knowledge. Knowledge disciplines such as psychology, sociology, child and human development all help with understanding human and group behaviour and why people and social situations develop the way they do. They also help identify what can be considered 'normal' and 'abnormal' development. However, social workers also need to know what the law and policy requires in such situations, that is to say what should be done, what can be done and what cannot be done. In addition, social workers not only need to understand what is going on they also need to be able to bring about change and ensure, as we saw in Chapter 4, that rights are protected and that well-being is promoted. This requires knowledge of a wide range of different theories, models and approaches which inform social work interventions. Added to this social workers need to have knowledge of what other services and which other professionals are available to help any particular situation. Social workers alone cannot sort out all the problems experienced by a family such as the Vasiliauskas. No single agency can.

Therefore, as well as knowing what other services are available, social workers need to know how to work effectively in partnership with other agencies and professionals.

Lastly, but most importantly, social workers need to gain knowledge of what the family members themselves understand the issues to be. 'Solutions' which are not informed by and take into account the perspectives of the service users themselves are unlikely to be successful. This knowledge is not always straightforward to gather for a variety of reasons. In this case there are challenges presented by language, the age of the children and probably a lack of trust.

SCIE knowledge review: types of knowledge, TAPUPAS and 'research mindedness'

The Social Care Institute for Excellence (SCIE) has published a useful guide written by Pawson et al. (2003) which identifies the different types and quality of knowledge used in social care. From research carried out, they identified the following five types of knowledge:

- **Organisational knowledge** – this refers to the formal and informal knowledge that has been accumulated over the years within specific organisations about how to work with certain cases
- **Practitioner knowledge** – this is largely informal knowledge (sometimes referred to as 'practice wisdom' (Sheppard, 1995)) which social workers develop with experience. Some of it comes from training, some of it from what they have picked up in the workplace and from experience generally. It is often intuitive.
- **Knowledge from the policy community** – for example *Working Together to Safeguard Children* (HM Government, 2015) would be a good example of policy guidance relevant to the scenario above.
- **Research knowledge** – this is knowledge gathered systematically with a planned design and is mostly published in academic journals or by academics in official reports. A relevant piece of research applicable to the Vasiliauskas family scenario would be a study commissioned by the government and carried out by Cleaver et al. (2006) titled *The Response of Child Protection Practices and Procedures to Children Exposed to Domestic Violence or Parental Substance Misuse*. This would be a useful study for you to track down and read.
- **Service users and carer knowledge** – this form of knowledge has taken on increasing importance in recent years as social workers realise that people are often 'experts by experience' in their own lives.

Because the different sources and types of knowledge used in social work can vary in how reliable or relevant they are, Pawson et al. (2003) developed a set of criteria under the acronym of TAPUPAS against which the quality of knowledge should be judged fit for purpose. TAPUPAS stands for:

- **Transparency** – are the reasons for it clear?
- **Accuracy** – is it honestly based on relevant evidence?
- **Purposivity** – is the method used suitable for the aims of the work?
- **Utility** – does it provide answers to the questions it set?
- **Propriety** – is it legal and ethical?
- **Accessibility** – can you understand it?
- **Specificity** – does it meet the quality standards already used for this type of knowledge?

Now, it is not suggested here that every time a social worker applies a piece of knowledge in their work – whether it be from child development, psychology, legislation, service user or some other source – that they dutifully apply each of the TAPUPAS criteria. However, the framework should at least alert us to consider questions such as where the knowledge we use comes from, whether it is actually relevant or trustworthy and so on. Many studies have shown that decision-making in social work is often flawed because it is based on flawed assumptions or inaccurate knowledge.

Research mindedness

The Social Care Institute for Excellence (2016) also talk about the need for social workers to be 'research minded'. This means that social workers need to possess:

- a faculty for critical reflection informed by knowledge and research;
- an ability to use research to inform practice which counters unfair discrimination, racism, poverty, disadvantage and injustice, consistent with core social work values;
- an understanding of the process of research, and the use of research to theorise from practice.

Therefore, being able to critically assess research and to apply knowledge and evidence to practice appropriately is considered a core social work skill. To do this effectively requires both a good understanding of the principles of research and of research methods. We will return to discuss this in more detail in Chapter 9.

Theories and models of social work intervention

The case of the Vasiliauskas family provides us with the opportunity to think more about what can be done in such cases. We know that legislation such as the Children Act 1989 guides social workers and others to promote the best interests of children and to protect them from harm but this leaves the important question of *how* to actually do this effectively. Because it is a complex situation there are many points to take into consideration if positive outcomes for all concerned are to be achieved, especially for the children.

Activity 5.1

In small groups firstly discuss what you think are the main problems or issues to be tackled in the Vasiliauskas case. Then brainstorm what you think could be done to improve the situation.

Commentary

There are several issues or problems that need to be tackled. In no order of priority these include:

- Henrikas and Jolanta's drug and alcohol abuse;
- Henrikas' drug dealing;
- domestic abuse;
- low pay and poverty (especially rural poverty);
- Henrikas and Jolanta's mental ill health;
- Jolanta's social isolation;
- suspected neglect of all three children;
- children being in the same household where domestic abuse is taking place;
- Jonas' language delay, his behaviour at school and educational progress.

In terms of what can be done, because most of the issues appear to be interlinked, it would make sense to take a 'joined up' approach, that is to say to take a multi-agency (or 'partnership') approach where all relevant services – for example education, health, social care, the police and domestic abuse and mental health organisations – communicate, share information and work closely with each other. However, 'joined up' working also requires a 'systemic' approach in thinking about the problems. For example, the reason why the children's needs are being neglected by their parents are probably connected to their mother's mental health which, in turn, is possibly connected to her relationship with her husband which, in turn, could be connected to his work patterns and his frustration with his work situation and also connected to both of their alcohol and drug habits. There are many interconnected issues to take into account.

Taking a systemic approach means recognising that simply giving advice to Jolanta about, say, how to avoid Petras getting nappy rash or how to get Jonas to school on time would not really deal with the multiple causes of the problems. Even trying to do this would be hampered by possible language problems or other reasons why Jolanta might not be able to fully process the information. A systems approach would recognise that to produce the necessary change, because they are interconnected, the whole range of contributory factors needs to be tackled in some way or else there is every likelihood that the problems will recur. Therefore we have highlighted at least one model for social work intervention – **a multi-agency approach**, which, in turn, links to an important theory widely used in social work – **'systems'**. These two approaches form the bedrock of much social work practice.

However, alongside these common approaches there are other theories and models for social work intervention that could be useful in producing positive outcomes. If we return to the list of 'issues' these might include the following:

- **Henrikas and Jolanta's drug and alcohol abuse.** These problems might benefit from a referral to the NHS or other support groups. Theories such **motivational interviewing** can assist people who are reluctant to or ambivalent towards taking the responsibility to seek and use help with this kind of problem. Also, when problems appear to be too big to be dealt with, often **a task-centred approach** can help to break them down into manageable chunks.

- **Henrikas' drug dealing.** This is obviously criminal behaviour and, whatever you think about the impact on the family of doing so, it needs to be reported to the police. However, if it is in some way linked to the need to supplement low wages (see below) then the family can be given **welfare rights advice** to ensure that they are getting all the benefits to which they are entitled.

- **Low pay and poverty.** This links to the discussion about rights, social justice and economic well-being in the previous chapter in the sense that there are obvious limits to how far an individual social worker can positively affect socio-economic problems. Issues such as rural poverty, low pay and the exploitation of immigrant workers need to be tackled collectively at the political level. This could be an example of a **radical social work** approach but it also fits in with **anti-discriminatory** and **anti-oppressive practice**.

- **Domestic abuse.** Much of the work with abused women is informed by **feminist theories**. Jolanta could be referred to a domestic abuse support organisation and/ or a domestic violence programme such as the Freedom Programme (http://www. freedomprogramme.co.uk). This would be on the basis of the **'empowerment'** model which would be designed to provide Jolanta with real options about how to get control back over her life – which might even mean making the choice to leave Henrikas.

   However, were the family to stay together, Henrikas could be offered anger management sessions as part of a child protection plan. Such courses are commonly based on **behavioural modification** techniques derived from **rational emotive behaviour** theory.

- **Henrikas and Jolanta's mental ill health.** These problems would benefit from a referral to specialist mental health services within the NHS. This might lead to a course of medication or talking therapies such as **cognitive behavioural therapy** or both. But their mental ill health might also improve if the causes of the mental ill health were mitigated or removed, such as the stress of being socially isolated, living on low pay and so on. Considering the bigger picture in this way and thinking about how different factors interact and combine with each other to maintain problems is an example of taking a **systemic** approach.

- **Jolanta's social isolation.** It could help if Jolanta was linked up to other mothers in the area. To do this might require doing some work with Jolanta to improve her English and to boost her social confidence. There could be community classes or groups for this. Social work in this area could reflect a **community work** or **narrative** approach. Simply to advise Jolanta to 'meet people' would probably not work, even if this was accompanied by leaving leaflets. Taking a **strengths** or **solution-focused approach** would allow Jolanta herself to take the lead in generating solutions that are acceptable to her rather than just doing this for her.

- **Suspected neglect of all three children.** Provided it was decided that the risk to the children was such that they could remain at home, referral to a parenting programme could be helpful in educating the parents learn how to look after their children properly. Many of these programmes are based on **social learning theory.**

- **Children being in the same household where domestic abuse is taking place.** Taking a **family therapy** approach could help with the dynamics between the parents. However, the children might benefit from appropriate interventions in their own right such as **counselling** or **play therapy** or more **practical help** in meeting their basic developmental needs, such as access to safe play spaces, having fun, getting into school, making friends, maintaining safe contact with the wider community and having stability in their lives.

- **Jonas' language delay, his behaviour at school and educational progress.** This suggests that referral to **educational psychology and/or language therapy** might be an appropriate course of action.

Summary

The set of suggestions made above as to what might help improve the situation in the Vasiliauskas family was not exhaustive by any means. However, it was designed to highlight that there is a large range of theories and models for social work intervention available. Many are compatible with each other but some are not. Also, some would be carried out directly by social workers, others would be provided by different professionals and services working in partnership with social workers. However, the range of approaches that can be used reflects not only the complexity of the situations that social workers face but also that there is no 'single magic bullet' that can bring about change. Social workers need to assess and then work out the best fit between what outcome they are trying to achieve and which theory, model or approach will most likely bring about that outcome. This will almost certainly vary from individual to individual and from situation to situation. With so many approaches available it is important to avoid unthinkingly 'throwing the kitchen sink' at problems which will only lead to an incoherent and confusing set of interventions. Fewer interventions more thoughtfully carried out are more likely to be effective and also easier to evaluate.

Activity 5.2: Theories, models and in approaches – a five-minute introduction

In pairs or small groups choose one of the following theories or models which were mentioned above:

- systems approach;
- task-centred approach;
- social learning theory;
- strengths perspective;
- solution focused;
- motivational interviewing;
- narrative approach;
- community social work.

Conduct research and be prepared to do a five-minute presentation to the rest of the group that:

1. defines that model theory or approach in no more than two or three sentences;

2. explains in which situations (or with which service users) in social work it is most appropriate to use that model/theory/approach;

3. explains when this model/theory/approach is not considered to be that appropriate to use;

4. provides references for further reading.

(Continued)

(Continued)

Suggestions for further reading

Beckett, C and Horner, N (2015) *Essential Theory for Social Work Practice*, 2nd edition. London: Sage.

Healy, K (2005) *Social Work Theories in Context*. Basingstoke: Palgrave.

Howe, D (2009) *A Brief Introduction to Social Work Theory*. Basingstoke: Palgrave Macmillan.

Oko, J (2011) *Understanding and Using Theory in Social Work*, 2nd edition. Exeter: Learning Matters.

Payne, M (2014) *Modern Social Work Theory*, 4th edition. Basingstoke: Palgrave Macmillan.

Teater, B (2014) *Applying Social Work Theories and Methods*, 2nd edition. Maidenhead: Open University Press.

Although it contained elements of adult mental health, substance misuse and domestic abuse, the Vasiliauskas family was primarily a children's safeguarding case. The main legislation and policy that would have informed and mandated practice in that case was the Children Act 1989 and the *Working Together to Safeguard Children* document (HM Government, 2015). However, it is recommended that you check out the NSPCC website for a full list of legislation, policy and guidance relevant to children's safeguarding/child protection in England: https://www.nspcc.org.uk/preventing-abuse/child-protection-system/england/legislation-policy-guidance/.

We will next look at the case study of an older Vietnamese man. This will highlight the need for a different set of knowledge in order to meet his needs and promote his well-being.

Activity 5.3: Nguyen Thanh Binh

Nguyen Thanh Binh (78) and his wife came to live in Leeds as Vietnamese 'boat people' in 1976. He worked as a cobbler until he retired ten years ago. His wife died three years ago which was around about the time that Thanh Binh started to show signs of having a form of dementia. What is left of his family is still in Vietnam and he has had no contact with them for many years. He lives in a block of flats linked to a mobile warden via a call care system. As his dementia has advanced Thanh Binh's short-term memory has been greatly affected and he is prone to confusion. This means that while he can just about attend to his personal care, he can no longer shop or cook for himself. He has left the gas on in his oven with empty saucepans catching fire on more than one occasion. He also has lost his use of English which means he is very socially isolated, there being no other Vietnamese speakers in the immediate neighbourhood. On several occasions the warden has needed to be called as Thanh Binh has been found walking confused several streets away. The warden feels that Thanh Binh is at risk, needs safeguarding and probably needs to be moved to a residential care home. She makes a referral to her local adult social care team.

Task

In the scenario above what range of knowledge would a social worker need to make a comprehensive assessment of Nguyen Thanh Binh so that he could be safeguarded from harm, his needs met, his well-being advanced and his rights protected?

Structure your thoughts and ideas under the following three headings:

1. Relevant knowledge from social sciences such as sociology, social policy, psychology, health and human growth and development.

2. Knowledge of the legal and policy frameworks and guidance.

3. Theories and models for social work intervention.

Commentary

In your answer under the first heading you could have highlighted that Thanh Binh's situation would be better understood by knowledge of life course theories, theories of loss and life transition. Thanh Binh has endured many losses and transitions over the years. For example, he has experienced the loss of his homeland and all that means in terms of his job, family connections, identity and so on. He has experienced the loss of his wife and now he is losing his memory and his ability to communicate in English. The world must be quite a confusing and frightening place at times for Thanh Binh and it is not clear to him where he can turn to for support when facing the challenges of ageing and of living with dementia. Despite the various losses he has experienced, this need not be seen purely in negative terms; knowledge of the psychology of resilience will be important because it is evident that Thanh Binh is a survivor. He has strengths that need to be identified and built on. A social worker would also clearly benefit from knowledge of mental illness in old age, particularly dementia and depression. Many old people with dementia also suffer from depression and this does not always get picked up.

Legal and policy frameworks

Under the second heading it would be vital to have knowledge of the Care Act 2014. However, given the suggestion from the warden that she feels Thanh Binh should be moved on to residential care and, given what you know about Thanh Binh's mental state, knowledge of the Mental Capacity Act 2005 (MCA) and the Human Rights Act 1998 (HRA) would be very important. The MCA would require you to establish whether Thanh Binh understands what the warden's suggestion means in terms of whether he would really want to move from his current home and whether he understands the risks both associated with living where he is and of moving. The HRA would bring up his right to respect for private and family life which could be infringed if he was moved against his will. Relevant policy guidance would certainly include knowledge of *Putting People First* (HM Government, 2007) in which it is explained that care should be person-centred and offer older people choice. Here it is advocated that personal budgets can be used to ensure that the system can respond to individual circumstances and preferences as far as possible. (See Gardner, 2014, for a fuller explanation of the 'personalisation' agenda in social work.) It would also be useful to have knowledge of what services were available locally, whether there was a Vietnamese community anywhere nearby and what they could offer. Social workers would also need to know how to work in partnership with health and other services such as interpreters.

Under the third heading we can refer back to many of the suggestions made for the Vasiliauskas family. Many social work theories and models are applicable across diverse service groups. For example, systemic thinking and a multi-agency approach would be good starting points as well a commitment to anti-oppressive and anti-discriminatory practice.

However, possibly some of the other approaches that were featured in Activity 5.4 earlier might not be so appropriate, partly because the nature of the task is different but also because of Thanh Binh's dementia. It would, however, be appropriate to take a person-centred approach (Hall and Scragg, 2012) and to consider advocacy and empowerment as ways of ensuring that Thanh Binh's rights to choice are protected. Taking a strengths perspective would ensure that Thanh Binh was not seen as a passive 'victim' but as someone who can still do various things for himself. A community approach could possibly help him get in touch with other Vietnamese people. As with Activity 5.3 we can see that social workers cannot take a 'one size fits all' approach to the cases with which they work. They need to be prepared to use different interventions depending on what they and the service user are trying to achieve. This is a case where Thanh Binh clearly needs to be safeguarded but this concern needs to be balanced with protecting his rights to choice and his human rights generally. The approaches adopted should reflect this. Below suggestions are made for further reading about this area of social work. Each of the books will encompass all three of the headings discussed here.

Further reading relevant to this activity*

Crawford, K and Walker, J (2008) *Social Work with Older People*. Exeter: Learning Matters.

Gardner, A (2014) *Personalisation in Social Work*, 2nd edition. Exeter: Learning Matters.

Hall, B and Scragg, T (2012) *Social Work with Older People: Approaches to Person-centred Practice*. Maidenhead: Open University Press.

Lymbery, M (2005) *Social Work with Older People*. London: Sage.

* Remember that these books were published before the introduction of the Care Act 2014.

Spirituality in social work

The domain descriptor requires social workers to understand 'spiritual' influences on people. It might not have occurred to you that the cases that we have studied in this chapter had any obvious 'spiritual' dimension to them. However, they almost certainly did and it is important that this dimension to our lives is better understood. Therefore before we conclude the chapter the activity below will help you reflect upon areas where an understanding of spirituality can be useful in social work.

Activity 5.4

1. What does the word spiritual mean to you?

2. Why is it important for social workers to engage with and understand spiritual matters?

3. How might an understanding of spirituality help in the two case studies studied in this chapter?

Commentary

You might well have struggled to provide a straightforward explanation of what spirituality means. It can be a difficult concept to pin down. Many of you might have mentioned religion, but the two concepts, while similar, are not exactly the same. You can feel spiritual feelings without being religious. However, where the two concepts overlap is the connection to the search for meaning in life, and the belief that there is something bigger than ourselves (although not necessarily a God). Spiritual feelings can be sparked by, for example, when something that you see or experience gives you a sense of wonder or makes you think deeply about the meaning of life. This might be when you first see Stonehenge looming in the distance as the sun rises, when you listen to music that touches you, or events like witnessing the birth of a child. Spirituality is an important way in which we make sense of the world and our place in the universe. It therefore shapes our sense of who we are (our identity). It is not necessarily scientific or rational but is bound up with our personal values and intuitions about the world. In its own way our spiritual well-being is as important for our overall well-being as our physical and mental health. In fact all three are connected.

This brings us on to the answer to question 2. If social work seeks to be holistic and person-centred in both the assessments that are made and the services that are provided, then someone's spirituality and spiritual needs must be taken into account where appropriate. Mathews (2009) makes the point that service users often want to have their spiritual needs recognised and sometimes feel this does not happen. This might arise because social workers (and their employing organisations) believe that the subject is too difficult to deal with. Nonetheless it is important element in shaping who we are. Suggestions for further reading on this topic are provided below.

As far as question 3 is concerned, we could imagine that all members of the Vasiliauskas family are struggling to cope with the various losses and changes in life they have experienced. Because of her experiences Jolanta, in particular, might well have lost a sense of who she is. The children also might be faced with difficult questions in relation to their self-concept and their sense of identity and how to make sense of the situation they are in. For example, why are things so difficult at home? Who are they? Are they Lithuanian or British? Do they belong in this society? Useful as they are, there are limits to how far these fundamental but complex questions can be dealt with by referring to health or psychologically based services. Consequently, a social worker would need to create opportunities for them to find answers, to discover hope and to find direction in life in ways that are meaningful to them as individuals. People need to be given the time and space to explore these issues in ways which help and sustain them personally. This might involve an established religion, it might be something more individual or it might be a combination of both.

Equally, Nguyen Thanh Binh has experienced many losses and changes in his life. He also has to cope with the effects of ageing and illness in old age. While it is also true for Thanh Binh that health, social and other services would be useful, he too might need something both to give him hope and sustain him through these many challenges that has a spiritual dimension. In both these scenarios it is important that this dimension is not left unexplored.

Further reading: spirituality and social work

Holloway, M and Moss, B (2010) *Spirituality and Social Work.* Basingstoke: Palgrave Macmillan.

Mathews, I (2009) *Social Work and Spirituality.* Exeter: Learning Matters.

Summary

- Most social work situations are complex and therefore require a range of different types of knowledge in order to fully comprehend what is going on and to decide what actions should be taken and what forms of intervention will be most effective.
- Understanding human behaviour and human situations fully requires knowledge from across the range of social sciences: sociology, psychology, health and human growth and development. Increasingly it is recognised that social workers must consider matters of spirituality and people's spiritual needs in their assessments.

- Social workers' actions are bound and guided by legislation and policy. They therefore must know the provisions of relevant legislation and policy guidance in order to practise legally and professionally.
- There are a range of theories, models and approaches available for social workers to use in order to make effective interventions. However, not all approaches are compatible with each other and social workers must avoid using approaches thoughtlessly and incoherently. Commonly in the UK today, social workers are urged to use systemic thinking and to work collaboratively with other partner agencies.
- SCIE propose that there are five main types of knowledge that social workers use: organisations, practitioners, research gathered systematically with planned design, the policy community, that is knowledge gained from the wider policy context, and service users and carers.
- Social workers must be able to assess and evaluate the quality of the knowledge they apply to their work. This requires a degree of 'research mindedness' and the ability to decide what counts as evidence and knowledge in any particular case.

Further reading

Cunningham, J and Cunningham, S (2008) *Sociology and Social Work*. Exeter: Learning Matters.

Ingleby, E (2010) *Applied Psychology for Social Work*, 2nd edition. Exeter: Learning Matters.

Mathews, I and Crawford, K (2010) *Evidence-based Practice in Social Work*. Exeter: Learning Matters.

Walker, J. and Crawford, K. (2014) *Social Work and Human Development*, 4th edition. Exeter: Learning Matters.

Whittaker, A (2010) *Research Skills for Social Work*. Exeter: Learning Matters.

6: Critical reflection and analysis

Introduction

In Chapter 1 we explained that critical reflection is a core skill required in professional social work. In this chapter we return to this key topic and explore it in more depth. We discuss the purpose of critical reflection and its importance in the context of social work. We explain the basic skills and attributes required to reflect critically, making suggestions about helpful tools that can assist with reflection. We also provide for discussion models of reflection that are commonly used.

The different sources of knowledge used in social work were introduced in the previous chapter. We return to this topic and explore the similarities and differences between what constitutes knowledge and evidence. The chapter uses a case study to help you learn how to identify, distinguish, evaluate and integrate different sources of evidence and knowledge. From here we discuss how social workers need to be able to construct and test hypotheses as part of making professional practice decisions. The chapter concludes with a summary of key points and suggestions for further reading.

Domain descriptor terminology

The domain descriptor refers at different points to 'critical reflection', 'critical thinking', 'reasoned discernment' and also 'reflective practice'. For the purposes of this discussion we are going to bracket together 'critical reflection' and 'critical thinking'. Throughout the chapter we will mainly use the term critical reflection. 'Reasoned discernment' is not a term commonly used in social work practice. It refers to the ability to use critical thinking to make practice decisions that are both properly analysed and evidence-based. To avoid unnecessary confusion and repetition we will not refer to this term again; however, both 'analysis' and 'evidence' are defined and discussed in this chapter.

There is some debate about the exact nature of the relationship between critical reflection and reflective practice (Jones, 2013). However, for the purposes of this chapter it is proposed that critical reflection forms the basis of 'reflective practice'. Critical reflection and critical thinking are cognitive (mental) activities; reflective practice is the behaviour (for example, practice decisions) that follows from such activities.

Why is critical reflection so important in social work?

In previous chapters we have seen how social workers often have to deal with complex issues and problems. They also need to work ethically and draw on and utilise a whole array of different knowledge. Social workers are presented with situations which are unique to the people concerned; where there are multiple factors involved; where there is often no single obvious straightforward answer; where there are multiple (sometimes conflicting) perspectives to take into account; where there are often risks and dilemmas to be considered in any possible solutions; and where a diverse range of knowledge and skills are required. In short, deciding what the 'right thing' to do under these circumstances is tough. Appropriate solutions do not usually simply present themselves. As a matter of course, information needs to be gathered and analysed, different perspectives sought and other professionals consulted. Each situation needs to be thought through, options worked out and the law and policy needs to be followed at all times. All of this requires the ability to think clearly and critically. Not to do so can easily lead to ill-informed, biased and sub-optimal decision-making.

How does critical reflection differ from everyday thinking and reflecting?

There are lots of words and phrases for the 'thinking' activity that we undertake when making tricky decisions. We might say that we are 'turning things over in our mind', 'ruminating', 'reflecting', 'mulling over', 'musing', 'cogitating', 'dwelling on', 'contemplating', 'meditating upon', 'chewing over', even 'agonising over'. Most human beings are naturally reflective. The more tricky or complex the decision, the more thinking activity this is likely to generate.

The concept of 'critical reflection' is not dissimilar to these everyday activities – in fact it shares many of their characteristics. However, the 'critical' part of it implies a better *quality* of thinking rather than just doing more and more of it (i.e. increasing *quantity*) which can often involve turning the same thoughts over and over unimaginatively and unconstructively. Critical reflection is not a 'magic bullet'. It cannot guarantee 'perfect' decisions, if such decisions can ever be said to exist in social work. However, it is a process that should not only lead to better outcomes but also outcomes that can be better justified. The activity below invites you to think about what critical reflection might involve.

Activity 6.1: Thinking about thinking

1. If 'critical reflection' represents a better quality of thinking, in what ways do you think it might be different from the everyday 'mulling' or chewing over' that we do when we have a problem or a decision to make?

2. What do you think might be some of the challenges involved in reflection critically?

3. What do you think might be needed in order to be make critically refection as effective as possible?

Commentary

Question 1

Whatever language we use to describe it most human beings reflect. Many things cause us to reflect – decisions we need to take, problems we need to solve, the things that happen to us – it could be anything. Reflection is an important part of making sense of the world around us. To be clear, the use of the word 'critical' in this context does not mean being negative or fault-finding. The term critical suggests our reflection is a more consciously *analytical* activity. According to Jones (2013, p. 5), analysis means being able to:

> Be *discerning about how you gather information and recognise the significance of its structure and constituent parts.*

That is to say, being able to break information down for what is important and to see how it fits together to make proper sense. However, reflecting critically also means being mindful about the act of reflecting itself. The critical part can be seen as a kind of 'quality control' process on the very act of thinking.

Ultimately, how any individual reflects is personal to them (Rutter and Brown, 2015). However, there are some generally agreed points about the range of skills and qualities that social workers need. These include:

- The ability to develop a good 'background knowledge' of the issue under consideration (Rutter and Brown, 2015). This refers to the ability to put things in their correct context. To do this effectively not only do you need to gather together all that you know about the situation, but also be aware that they are things that you do *not* know. Remain open to the possibility of new (and conflicting) information emerging.

- Being aware of and understanding your feelings (i.e. be emotionally intelligent). Much research indicates that our emotions affect our decision-making, often in ways that we are unaware of. Many studies also show that most of our decisions are not made on the basis of 'rational' analysis but on what our intuitions tell us (O'Sullivan, 2011; Rutter and Brown, 2015). That is not necessarily a bad thing and we cannot always do anything about it anyway. But it means we need to be better at examining our intuitions and 'gut' feelings.

- Understanding that being under stress limits our ability to reflect effectively. We need therefore to be able to recognise and manage stress (Knott and Scragg, 2016).

- Developing 'habits of mind' (Rutter and Brown, 2015). That is to say establishing a professional mindset that is open, curious, analytical and ethical. A good starting point is always to ask oneself basic questions such as 'How do we actually know this?' and 'How can I be certain that it is true?' On the subject of professional habits of mind, Epstein and Hundert (2002) have added the ability to 'observe' one's own thinking and emotions; to be attentive; to recognise and respond to cognitive and emotional biases; and to have a willingness to acknowledge and correct errors. A valuable habit of mind is to be able to recognise and challenge the 'taken for granted' assumptions that we are all prone to make. For example 'She's a heroin addict, she'll never be able to look after that child.'

- Communicating effectively (Knott and Scragg, 2016). This is particularly important in how information is gathered, and also in how a situation is shared, discussed and explained with colleagues and supervisors. Be careful not to pre-judge situations and bias what other people think by providing less than full or distorted information. But also be careful not to always take someone else's account at face value. Look for supporting evidence, but also look for any contradictory evidence.

- Lastly, being aware that critical thinking is hard work and uses a lot of mental energy – therefore to be aware of our tendency to avoid it wherever possible (Wilkins and Boahen, 2013). Often what we believe is a genuinely thoughtful and analytical is the rationalisation of an intuitive decision based on first impressions.

Much has been written about what critical reflection is and what it involves. For example Schön (1983) distinguishes between reflection-*on*-action and reflection-*in*-action, arguing that how practitioners 'think on their feet' is not the same as when they think about what has happened after the event. Unfortunately, space does not permit anything other than an introduction to the subject here. However, suggestions for further reading are provided at the end of the chapter. Texts such as those by Knott and Scragg (2016), Jones (2013) and Rutter and Brown (2015) in particular provide an accessible introduction to this key social work topic.

Question 2

There are several factors that can get in the way of critical reflection. The time and effort involved cannot be underestimated. In a highly pressurised work environment and working in stressful conditions it is likely that many poorly considered and ill-informed decisions might be made. Other obstructive factors can include unprofessional 'habits of mind' both individually and as a team. So, for example, people can be quick to form opinions based on stereotypes or because it is the sort of case or situation of which they have prior experience and assume that they know all about. First impressions and snap decisions can be shored up by the use of 'confirmation bias' (Rutter and Brown, 2015) or a team might succumb to 'group think' (Taylor, 2013). Often, once an initial judgement has been made, we are often reluctant to revise it – even in the face of contradictory evidence. We find it difficult to let go of first impressions, possibly because, to do so, might make us feel less competent in our judgements in some way. We might think we would come across as dithering or lacking conviction if we changed our minds.

Question 3

There are several things that practitioners can do to assist with critical reflection. Firstly, it is important to be able to manage things so that you can find the time and space to reflect. Beyond this, there are several tools one can use. These include using reflective logs or diaries or participating in practice discussions with colleagues. In Chapter 1 we highlighted the benefits of professional supervision in enabling critical reflection and reflective practice. Supervision can provide a reflective space for both social worker and supervisor (Knott and Scragg, 2016). There are many reasons for facilitating critical reflection and, by extension, reflective practice (*Community Care*, 2011a, 2012, 2013a). It is also helpful to use a 'model' of reflection, that is to say a framework or process that guides you through considering things more systematically and in ways that bring out your thoughts and emotional reactions to any particular issue. There are many different models available for social workers to use. Each has their own strengths and weaknesses. The key is to find a model that works for you. The next activity should help you with this process. Four models commonly used in education, health and social care are identified for you to explore and weigh up for how useful they are.

Activity 6.2: Models of reflection

1.   In pairs or small groups choose *one* of the models of reflection listed below to research. Original references are supplied below if needed but these models are written up and referred to widely in social work texts and are also available on the Internet.

   (a)   Atkins and Murphy's cyclical model
   (b)   Boud et al.'s triangular representation
   (c)   Gibbs' reflective cycle
   (d)   Rolfe et al.'s reflective model.

2.   Produce a poster or presentation that you can use to explain how the model works to the rest of the group. Often a diagram helps to explain the process.

3.   As a whole group discuss the strengths and weaknesses of each model and decide which model you think might be most helpful in assisting with the task of critical reflection on practice.

4.   Finally, as individuals, choose the model that you think most suits you personally and use it to reflect on the activity you have just undertaken. What have you learned?

(Continued)

(Continued)

Models of reflection

Atkins, S and Murphy, K (1993) 'Reflection: a review of the literature', *Journal of Advanced Nursing*, 18, pp. 1188–92.

Boud, D, Keogh, R and Walker, D (1985) *Reflection: Turning Experience into Learning*. London: Kogan Page.

Gibbs, G (1988) *Learning by Doing: A Guide to Teaching and Learning Methods*. Oxford: Further Education Unit.

Rolfe, G, Freshwater, D and Jasper, M (2001) *Critical Reflection in Nursing and the Helping Professions: A User's Guide*. Basingstoke: Palgrave Macmillan.

Commentary

One thing you might have noticed about the different models is that they are all 'iterative' in how they work. That is to say they involve a repeating cycle of going back over and revising earlier thoughts and impressions. We continually need to adjust our thinking depending on new discoveries, new evidence or changed perspectives. This process reflects the 'open' and 'curious' habits of mind referred to earlier. The models all also require us to turn our reflective gaze on ourselves as well, for example examining our feelings and reactions. The process of reflecting on oneself in order to expose one's subjectivity and achieve a more effective and impartial analysis is known as 'reflexivity'.

It should be noted that there are many other models that have been suggested other than the four identified above. It is also worth underlining that models of reflection are useful, but they are not for everyone. We all need to find our own way of developing critical reflection. If a certain model helps that is good but if you struggle to make them work for you, that does not matter – the important thing is to be aware of the principles behind such models.

Summary

- Critical reflection is distinguished from everyday thinking by being more analytical.
- Critical reflection involves being aware of the factors that can influence the quality of our thinking.
- Critical reflection requires emotional intelligence and developing professional habits of mind.
- Critical reflection requires the ability to see things in their full context.

- Critical reflection should not only lead to better outcomes but also outcomes that can be better justified.
- There are many tools to assist with critical reflection including reflective logs and supervision. Using a model of reflection can also be helpful.

Further reading

Community Care (2011) 'The need for more critically reflective social work', online at http://www.communitycare.co.uk/2011/04/08/the-need-for-more-critically-reflective-social-work/.

Community Care (2012) 'How reflective practice can help social workers feel "safe"', online at http://www.communitycare.co.uk/2012/08/03/how-reflective-practice-can-help-social-workers-feel-safe/.

Jones, S (2013) *Critical Learning for Social Work Students*, 2nd edition. London: Learning Matters.

Knott, C and Scragg, T (eds) (2016) *Reflective Practice in Social Work*, 4th edition. London: Learning Matters.

Rutter, L and Brown, K (2015) *Critical Thinking and Professional Judgement for Social Work*, 4th edition. London: Learning Matters.

Knowledge and evidence

The domain descriptor states that social workers need to 'identify, distinguish, evaluate and integrate multiple sources of knowledge and evidence'. Although sometimes we use the terms interchangeably and there are overlaps in meaning, knowledge and evidence are not exactly the same thing. A helpful way of making the distinction is to think about both *how* we come to know what we know and the formality of method(s) used in producing this knowledge. In our everyday lives knowledge, in the broadest sense of the word, is something we believe as 'true' regardless of the source and method used to establish it. The sources of our everyday knowledge are many and diverse. These include direct experience, our own personal system of 'logic', what other people tell us, received wisdom, formal education, the media and so on. So, for example, we might 'know' that we are a 'worrier' when it comes to air travel or that if we press certain buttons on the computer it will solve a certain problem or that Mrs Smith at number 43 is a divorcee or that a certain politician is unpopular and so on. We do not expect formal evidence for all of the things we 'know', we treat them as 'fact' until such times as we stop believing them for whatever reason. Often there are ideas we still treat as 'true', despite being presented with evidence to the contrary.

Evidence is usually taken to mean 'scientific' or more formally produced knowledge, that is to say that evidence is knowledge that comes from properly conducted research or investigations such as formal enquiries, experiments, observations, surveys and evaluations. For example, when police produce 'evidence' in court it has to be able to withstand cross-examination and attempts to discredit it. It would not survive these tests very well if it just came from a policeman's intuition or on the basis of what they were told by someone in a pub. An acceptable and checkable process of enquiry would need to be demonstrated or else it could be dismissed as just opinion or 'hearsay'. Evidence is therefore knowledge that can be verified in some way and is testable against some objective standard(s).

The same broad distinction is true in the world of social care and social work. As SCIE (2005: 3) pithily put it:

- Knowledge = evidence + practice wisdom + service user and carer experiences and wishes
- Evidence = research findings + interpretation of the findings

Evidence, in these definitions, conforms to a more tightly drawn set of criteria. SCIE propose that the 'structured enquiry' used to produce evidence makes it capable of being generalised (SCIE, 2005: 3). In Chapter 5 we introduced the study by Pawson et al. (2003) published by SCIE that identifies the five different types and quality of knowledge used in social care. According to the definition provided by SCIE above not all of it would be counted as 'evidence' in the formal sense.

Activity 6.3: Sources of knowledge and evidence

1. Either from memory or by returning to Chapter 5, list the five types of knowledge that Pawson et al. propose are used in social care.

2. Which types do you think would be specifically counted as 'evidence' using the SCIE definition? Give reasons.

3. Does this mean that more formally produced knowledge does not count as highly? Share your thoughts about this with a colleague.

Commentary

Pawson et al. identified 'organisational knowledge', 'practitioner knowledge', 'knowledge from the policy community', 'research knowledge and 'service user and carer knowledge'. Return to Chapter 5 or, better still, seek out the original text by Pawson et al. for a fuller discussion of these different types of knowledge. Those that would be counted as 'evidence' using the definition we have provided would definitely be knowledge from research and knowledge from the policy community. For these types, it should be possible to check the research methods used and the sources drawn upon. This should be able to confirm it as the objective 'structured enquiry' identified by SCIE. Organisational knowledge would also usually (but not always) come into this category. However, it depends on the organisation how explicitly they set out how their knowledge is produced.

Practitioner and service user and carer knowledge are subjective types of knowledge that are derived from personal experience. So, for example, a service user with rheumatoid arthritis will know (from experience) that their best time to get out of the house for appointments is in the afternoon. A social worker might equally 'know' that the best time to visit a particular older person is mid-morning before he or she gets tired and the effects of their medication make them drowsy. There are numerous examples in social work of such knowledge derived from experience. It is not formal evidence as such but it is useful knowledge all the same.

In response to question 3 you might have come to the conclusion that there is no obvious hierarchy of knowledge in social work. There is an appropriate place for all types of knowledge. All can be equally useful when working with individuals or families. Yes, research and policy knowledge is objective and generalisable, but not in every single case. Practitioner and service user and carer knowledge cannot be dismissed purely because it is subjective and is not derived from structured enquiry or formal investigation. That said, practitioner and service user and carer knowledge (and much organisational knowledge) is clearly limited in how far it can be generalised, if at all. All knowledge and evidence is context-specific, but knowledge derived informally and purely from personal experience is very context specific, that is to say applicable to *that* particular individual's circumstances.

Activity 6.4: Learning how to identify, distinguish, evaluate and integrate multiple sources of knowledge and evidence

The Ndefo family have been referred to the Social Care department. Both the school which the son attends and the nursery where the daughter goes have passed on their concerns about the children's well-being. Chikanso Ndefo is a 27-year-old woman of Nigerian heritage living in East London. She is a single mother with two children. Her son Boseda is aged 6 and her daughter Emiene aged 3. The children have different fathers. Chikanso does not see Boseda's father.

Mother's perspective

According to Chikanso's account she had to escape from the house where she and Boseda's father lived in North London because he was frequently violent towards her.

(Continued)

(Continued)

His family are still hostile towards her for calling the police. That is a reason she moved to a different part of London. The relationship with Emiene's father, Aboh, is more complicated. He offered her a home when she was desperate to find somewhere and was initially very caring towards both her and Boseda. However, it turned out he mainly wanted a sexual relationship. When Chikanso fell pregnant with Emiene she really wanted him to marry her and provide for her. Aboh accused her of getting pregnant to trap him and also taking advantage of his good nature. He said he would never get married to someone who was 'damaged goods' and had a 'bastard son' whom he could not bring himself to treat as his own. He occasionally makes contact with Chikanso but does not take any responsibility for raising either of her children. Although the couple still have some feelings for each other, his visits often end with a row and Aboh storming out. On one occasion the row became so heated that Aboh slapped Chikanso around the face. He was wearing a heavy ring which caused a gash across her face and cheek. He was apologetic afterwards. Chikanso says that the children never witness their rows and that, apart from needing more money, she has the situation under control and doesn't need any help from social workers. She also discloses that she saw her GP to get something to 'calm her nerves'. She was expecting some sort of tranquilisers but, in the first instance, the GP suggested that she undertook a computer-based anxiety management programme. She has not pursued this but says she feels OK now anyway. The GP confirms that Chikanso visited her and that she prescribed an online self-help anxiety management programme.

School referral

At the primary school that Boseda attends, the teachers say that he is falling behind the other children and his behaviour is difficult to manage at times. He sometimes hits out at or is aggressive towards other children. On the most recent occasion, the other child's parents insisted that something must be done. Aware that Chikanso had to flee from Boseda's father because of domestic abuse, in their referral the school states that 'Boseda's episodes of aggression could be the result of witnessing violence at home'. They also wondered whether Boseda might be displaying signs of 'disorganised attachment' because the violence she experienced might have affected Chikanso's capacity to bond with him. They have referred Boseda to an educational psychologist for an assessment of his learning needs.

Nursery referral

Staff at the nursery which Emiene attends have also expressed their concern about what goes on in the home and the impact it might have on the children. They recently observed Chikanso with a black eye and cut on her face when she brought her daughter in. Both mother and daughter looked subdued and Emiene was particularly 'clingy' when it came to her being dropped off. They added that Emiene can be quite withdrawn at times. She recently drew a picture of her house which showed her, her brother and her mother inside and a man wearing a mask on the roof. When asked to describe it Emiene had said 'That's me, "Bosa" and mummy and a naughty burglar on the roof. I don't like him. I wish he would go away.' Also aware that Chikanso had been in violent relationships, the staff took this to mean that this was her father whom she wanted to keep away.

Sue, the social worker processing the referrals, did a quick check on the NSPCC website which states that:

Children who witness domestic abuse may:

- *become aggressive*
- *display anti-social behaviour*
- *suffer from depression or anxiety*
- *not do as well at school – due to difficulties at home or disruption of moving to and from refuges.*

Source: https://www.nspcc.org.uk/preventing-abuse/child-abuse-and-neglect/domestic-abuse/signs-symptoms-effects/

For Sue this helped confirm that a full assessment needed to be carried out. She also remembers from her training that there is much published research relevant to this case. We referred to one such study by Cleaver et al. (2006) in Chapter 5. However, Sue looks out a report published by UNICEF also in 2006 that collated much of what was known at the time. See below for an extract and the supporting references contained within it.

Children who live with and are aware of violence in the home face many challenges and risks that can last throughout their lives.

There is significant risk of ever-increasing harm to the child's physical, emotional and social development. Infants and small children who are exposed to violence in the home experience so much added emotional stress that it can harm the development of their brains and impair cognitive and sensory growth.[13] Behaviour changes can include excessive irritability, sleep problems, emotional distress, fear of being alone, immature behaviour, and problems with toilet training and language development.[14] At an early age, a child's brain is becoming 'hard-wired' for later physical and emotional functioning. Exposure to domestic violence threatens that development.

(Continued)

(Continued)

As they grow, children who are exposed to violence may continue to show signs of problems. Primary-school-age children may have more trouble with school work, and show poor concentration and focus. They tend not to do as well in school. In one study, forty per cent had lower reading abilities than children from non-violent homes.[15] Personality and behavioural problems among children exposed to violence in the home can take the forms of psychosomatic illnesses, depression, suicidal tendencies, and bed-wetting.[16] Later in life, these children are at greater risk for substance abuse, juvenile pregnancy and criminal behaviour than those raised in homes without violence.[17]

Notes

13. Osofsky, Joy D., 'The Impact of Violence on Children', *The Future of Children – Domestic Violence and Children*, Vol. 9, no. 3, 1999; Koenen, K. C. et al., 'Domestic Violence is Associated with Environmental Suppression of IQ in Young Children', *Development and Psychopathology*, Vol. 15, 2003, pp. 297–311; Perry, B. D. 'The neurodevelopmental impact of violence in childhood', Chapter 18, in *Textbook of Child and Adolescent Forensic Psychiatry* (eds D. Schetky and E. P. Benedek), American Psychiatric Press, Inc., Washington, DC, pp. 221–38, 2001; James, M., 'Domestic Violence as a Form of Child Abuse: Identification and Prevention', *Issues in Child Abuse Prevention*, 1994.

14. Osofsky, Joy D., 'The Impact of Violence on Children', *The Future of Children – Domestic Violence and Children*, Vol. 9, no. 3, 1999.

15. James, M., 'Domestic Violence as a Form of Child Abuse: Identification and Prevention', *Issues in Child Abuse Prevention*, 1994.

16. Fantuzzo, John W. and Mohr, Wanda K., 'Prevalence and Effects of Child Exposure to Domestic Violence', *The Future of Children – Domestic Violence and Children*, vol. 9, no. 3, 1999; Kernic, M. A. et al., 'Behavioral Problems among Children whose Mothers are Abused by an Intimate Partner', *Child Abuse and Neglect*, Vol. 27, no. 11, 2003, pp. 1231–46.

17. Felitti, V. J. et al., 'The Relationship of Adult Health Status to Childhood Abuse and Household Dysfunction', *American Journal of Preventive Medicine*, Vol. 14, 1998, pp. 245–58; James, M., 'Domestic Violence as a Form of Child Abuse: Identification and Prevention', *Issues in Child Abuse Prevention*, 1994; Herrera, V. and McCloskey, L. 'Gender Differentials in the Risk for Delinquency among Youth Exposed to Family Violence', *Child Abuse and Neglect*, Vol. 25, no. 8, 2001, pp. 1037–51; Anda, R. F., Felitti, V. J. et al. 'Abused Boys, Battered Mothers, and Male Involvement in Teen Pregnancy', *Pediatrics*, Vol. 107, no. 2, 2001, pp. 19–27.

Source: UNICEF (2006, p. 4)

Task

In pairs or small groups:

1. From the case as presented what do you think is going on with the Ndefo family? Do you think the children are at risk?

2. Using the typology produced by Pawson et al., identify the types of 'knowledge' presented.

3. Using the distinction made between knowledge and evidence, what counts as evidence? Give reasons.

4. Evaluate the knowledge that you think is useful in deciding what to do in this case, but also explain where you would like to see more actual evidence.

5. Lastly, discuss how it is useful to analyse and integrate different types of knowledge and evidence to get the fullest possible picture of what is going on and what needs to be done.

Commentary

Question 1

Despite a lack of firm knowledge and evidence about exactly what is going on at this stage, there does seem to be conflict and disharmony in the home largely brought about by the sporadic and occasionally violent relationship between Chikanso and Aboh. Chikanso's own account confirms the violent nature of their relationship. The nursery staff have observed her facial injuries. Despite Chikanso saying that the children do not witness the rows, it would be reasonable to assume that they are affected negatively by the disharmony caused by Aboh's aggression, if only by the atmosphere of fear and tension it creates. Chikanso also refers to possible money problems and to having a problem with her nerves. This, together with what the school and nursery have observed, means that a social worker might *hypothesise* that there are several factors in the children's home situation that could be affecting their well-being and development. We will discuss further the part that hypotheses play in social work decision-making in the following section.

Question 2

Chikanso's account could be regarded as a form of service user and carer knowledge, although whether Chikanso's interpretation fully captures the 'realities' of the situation is obviously open to question. Sue drew on her own practitioner knowledge to explore the possible links between domestic violence and child development and well-being. On this basis she checked the NSPCC website which is an example of organisational knowledge (implicitly informed by research) that adds weight to her hypothesis.

Both the school and nursery pass on knowledge about the children's behaviour which has been observed by their staff, for example Boseda's aggression, Emiene's clinginess and withdrawn moods, the mother's facial injuries and the picture drawn by Emiene of her family. However, they also offer interpretations of each child's behaviour, for example about Boseda's 'disorganised attachment' and Emiene's view of her father. These interpretations can only be regarded as speculative. There is currently not enough 'evidence' to support them. To go back to the first part of this chapter, this is where we need to be 'critical', that is to say keeping an open mind, challenging assumptions, separating fact from opinion and, looking for confirmatory evidence, but also any disproving evidence – i.e. being analytical (Jones, 2013).

Lastly, the UNICEF report would count as research knowledge. This draws on a range of studies that have investigated the impact on children who live with and are aware of violence. It is worth noting the dates on the studies cited though, as they are quite old.

Questions 3 and 4

Following on from above we can see that, while there is enough known about the case at this point to cause concern, more information needs to be gathered and more evidence found in order to make important decisions about whether and how to intervene with this family. Chikanso's own account is an important starting point. From that we know that there has been domestic abuse in the past and that there continues to be. However, we only have her word for it and that includes the fact that she claims that the children have not witnessed or been affected by it. Gaining their perspectives – using age-appropriate methods – would be valuable. It might even turn out that one or both children have been abused themselves. Again, we need to keep an open mind. It is also entirely possible that Chikanso is minimising the extent of her emotional/mental problems. To have a medical opinion on this would be useful. Therefore we could be said to have relevant knowledge but it would be useful to have corroborating evidence to know exactly what we are dealing with. The knowledge provided by organisations such as the NSPCC and UNICEF is definitely relevant and should help guide thinking. However, published research can only guide or inform as it based on other studies – it cannot tell us exactly what is happening in a particular family. As respected researchers on attachment Shemmings and Shemmings (2012) state:

> *The problem is that we do not know enough from research about the connections between 'carer characteristics' – such as parental mental ill-health, or alcohol and substance misuse – and child maltreatment. They are strongly correlated, but correlation is not the same as causation.*

The fact that studies show that there are links between violence in the home and disorganised attachment and also that disorganised attachments can lead to aggressive behaviour in later life is relevant. However, it should not be taken for granted that this is necessarily the case with the Ndefo family. More careful investigation and evidence-gathering is needed, which brings us on to what was said earlier in the chapter about the need to be able to reflect *critically*.

Question 5

It is clearly imperative that social workers can not only evaluate but can also integrate different types of knowledge and evidence. To proceed on just one or even two sources of information, for example the school account, the nursery account or what Chikanso said, would not provide a very comprehensive picture. Key sources of information are missing, for example the children's perspectives and medical, psychological and other specialist opinion – even Aboh's account. All possible sources of knowledge have to be critically reflected upon, analysed, evaluated and integrated with what else is known. Only then can professionals say with some confidence that they understand what is going on in a situation like this, although what is then decided in terms of intervention is another question and you could refer back to Chapter 5 for a selection of approaches that might be effective. However, as this is a different case there might well be other approaches worth pursuing.

Constructing and testing hypotheses

Hypothesis – a supposition or proposed explanation made on the basis of limited evidence as a starting point for further investigation. (Oxford English Dictionary, 2016b)

The Domain descriptor requires social workers to be able to 'understand the need to construct hypotheses in social work practice'. The previous sections and activities will have demonstrated that to understand complex cases as fully as possible requires systematic information-gathering and thoughtful, critically reflective analysis. It will also have become apparent that the process requires constructing hypotheses on limited evidence initially but then testing and revising one's initial hypothesis as new knowledge and evidence is gathered. That is the starting point. Social workers need to be confident that the knowledge they have is both accurate and relevant. The next stage would be to gather information that can either confirm or disprove your proposed explanation. Information that could disprove your initial hypothesis is called 'counterevidence' (sometimes known as 'contra-evidence'). It is a good habit of mind to look for 'counterevidence' because often we find it hard to let go of flawed hypotheses and usually have a lot invested in just finding confirmatory evidence.

Activity 6.5: Confirming or disproving hypotheses

Let us return to the Ndefo family and hypothesise that the children's well-being is at risk from the mother's continued and abusive relationship with Aboh. What information would we need to gather to confirm the hypothesis and what information might disprove it?

Commentary

To confirm or disprove our initial hypothesis we would need to gather more knowledge about the exact nature of the relationship between Chikanso and Aboh and what happens when they are together in the home. This would need to include information collected using suitably child-friendly methods from the children (Hutton and Partridge, 2006). It would also mean gathering information from Aboh, if he could be persuaded to contribute, and from any other relevant members of networks around the family. More supportive information could be gathered from the school and nursery but this would need to be based on fact rather than speculation. A properly organised observation of Boseda might show that he is no more likely to be aggressive than any of the other children.

As well as an educational psychologist, Boseda could be referred to the GP and then to a paediatrician if needs be to investigate his learning difficulties and his aggressive behaviour. Either of these problems might turn out to be attributable to something else. To have a GP or Health Visitor's assessment of Emiene would also be useful. It would also be beneficial to have a better picture of Chikanso's mental state and health generally. It might seem unfair to Chikanso and even outrageous to propose it, but there is the possibility that she is fabricating the whole story, or at least parts of it. Maintaining an open mind means being alive to all possible explanations until they can reasonably be disproved. Only by identifying, distinguishing, evaluating and integrating multiple sources of knowledge and evidence can this be done to a professional standard. The good practice that underpins all aspects of professional decision-making in social work is exactly the same as that required for making good quality assessments, as we will see in Chapter 7.

Summary

- The knowledge used in social work can take many forms. Some of it comes from experience, some from more formal methods of enquiry.
- Evidence is knowledge that can be externally verified.

- Social workers need to be able to reflect critically upon, analyse and evaluate knowledge and evidence they have gathered for accuracy and relevance. They then need to be able to integrate it in order to obtain the fullest, most accurate picture possible.
- Social workers need to be able to identify gaps in knowledge and evidence.
- Social workers need be able to construct hypotheses based on the knowledge and evidence they have gathered. They also need to be able to test and revise their hypotheses in the light of new evidence.

Further reading

Mathews, I and Crawford, K (2011) *Evidence-based Practice in Social Work*. Exeter: Learning Matters.

NSPCC (2016) online at https://www.nspcc.org.uk/preventing-abuse/child-abuse-and-neglect/domestic-abuse/signs-symptoms-effects/.

7: Intervention and skills

- Demonstrate core communication skills and the capacity to develop them
- Demonstrate the ability to engage with people in order to build compassionate and effective relationships
- Demonstrate awareness of a range of frameworks to assess and plan intervention
- Demonstrate the basic ability to produce written documents relevant for practice
- Demonstrate initial awareness of risk and safeguarding

Introduction

As with Domain 5 this domain also covers a large range of content. Using the bullet points from the domain description as its guide, the first part of the chapter focuses on the range of communication and interpersonal skills needed in social work. This will cover verbal, non-verbal, written and symbolic forms of communication. You are invited to review the extent of the relevant skills in these areas you currently possess. This section concludes with a summary of key points. Suggestions are also made to help your development.

A key reason why social workers need a high level of communication skill is because they need to carry out assessments with a diverse range of people. Assessment is considered one of the core tasks of social work and provides the main focus for the second part of the chapter. Social workers need to be able to assess for a variety of reasons, including to assess need, to assess eligibility and to assess risk – commonly in the context of safeguarding. We therefore discuss the knowledge, values and skills needed to undertake assessments professionally. We use a case study to illustrate the stages of the assessment process using an approach provided by Milner et al. (2015). We also discuss the applicability of different models of assessment.

Lastly, once an assessment has taken place and an intervention agreed and implemented, good practice requires that progress against intended outcomes is monitored, reviewed and evaluated. Therefore we end with some practical suggestions about how social workers can evaluate interventions. The chapter will end with a summary of key points and suggestions for further reading.

The importance of communication in social work

In Chapter 1 we referred to the study 'Standards we Expect' (Harding and Beresford, 1996) which highlighted that service users and carers expect social workers to be good communicators. Many subsequent studies have backed this up. This is not just about social workers being good at delivering important information clearly or listening attentively. Good communication is also a vital component in how social workers establish their credibility, express their respect, convey their empathy, build relationships and work in partnership with service users. Trevithick (2005: 3) explains:

> *Good communication involves being able to hear how others gather and form their thoughts and feelings, and the meaning they give to particular experiences. This requires being able to establish a rapport and to form a relationship so that the information gained and experience shared can be consolidated and, hopefully, used to open up new avenues and inform future action.*

Communicating well and building good rapport with people therefore forms part of a virtuous circle. The ability to communicate effectively and the ability to form good relationships are inextricably bound up with each other.

Studies into the deaths of children who are known to social care and other services have found repeatedly that a major contributory factor was poor communication between professionals and between agencies (Reder and Duncan, 2003). Studies examining the findings from serious case reviews in adult social safeguarding have highlighted similar failings in communication between agencies (Manthorpe and Martineau, 2009). Therefore, our focus should not only be about developing effective interpersonal communication with service users and carers but developing effective inter-agency communication. We say more about inter-agency working in Chapter 8.

Social workers often think they have communicated something only to find later that it has been ignored, misinterpreted or not even seen or heard in the first place. The same can be true of information communicated to social workers. Therefore a fundamental point to grasp about any form of communication in social work is that it is a *two-way* process (*Community Care*, 2008). A message delivered is not necessarily a message received let alone understood. Therefore social workers need to check that their messages have been understood and they also have to let those with whom they are working know that they have received and understood any messages that have been communicated to them. Social workers also need to know who their audience is and what particular communication needs they might have. Messages will only be properly understood if the form or style of communication used is appropriate to the intended audience. For example, it is no use talking to a six-year-old child as one would with a lawyer and, arguably, vice versa.

With regard to the fundamental role played by communication in social work, SCIE (2016) state that:

> *Without effective communication skills social workers will be less able to:*
>
> • *Find out what service users, carers or other professionals are thinking and feeling*
>
> • *Provide the kind of information others need*

- *Interpret complex situations accurately*

- *Negotiate, mediate and intervene sensitively, authoritatively and appropriately.*

Source: https://www.scie.org.uk/assets/elearning/communicationskills/
cs01/resource/html/object1/object1_1.htm

It is suggested that you visit the web pages cited as they contain a range of useful material on all aspects of communication in social work including an interactive quiz.

Activity 7.1: Forms of communication used in social work

The Oxford English Dictionary (2016c) defines communication as:

The imparting or exchanging of information by speaking, writing, or using some other medium.

Question

1. Using the definition provided, in what different ways do social workers communicate?

Commentary

There is a bit more to the answer to this question than just restating the dictionary definition. For example, social workers certainly communicate by speaking (**verbal communication**). This can take many forms. For example, it could be face-to-face, via the telephone or computer (e.g. Skype) or it could be by using an interpreter. There are many reasons to use verbal communication in social work. It could be to conduct interviews, request information for assessments, to discuss and explain decisions and so on. Because communication is always a two-way process, to be effective verbal communication usually requires 'active listening' (Moss, 2015). The 'active' part is not only making sure that you are listening attentively but letting the person with whom you are communicating know that you are listening attentively and understanding what they are saying. Active listening is a good way of conveying respect to someone. Common examples are maintaining appropriate eye contact, nodding, paraphrasing or using paralanguage, which is the non-verbal sounds we use to let people you know we understand them such as 'ah' or 'uh-huh' (Koprowska, 2010; Lishman, 2009).

This naturally brings us to another important way in which social workers communicate and that is by using **non-verbal communication** in its many forms. These include eye contact, facial expression, body language, gesture, touch and so on. It has been estimated that non-verbal communication makes up a bigger percentage of human communication than verbal communication (Mehrabian, 1981). This makes it important for social workers to be aware of how they communicate non-verbally. Communication can be confused or complicated if there is a lack of congruence between what is being said and the body language associated with it (Koprowska, 2010; Lishman, 2009; Moss, 2015). For example, telling someone how much you understand their pain while looking at your phone undermines the sincerity of any message you are trying to convey. Also, think about how difficult it can be to assess the emotional subtleties of someone's communication just by talking to them on the phone or reading their emails. Non-verbal communication can also prove a complicating factor for a variety of cultural reasons. Not everybody is happy with direct eye contact, for example. Touching people is also open to misinterpretation and is generally considered something that social workers should think hard about before doing. Within non-verbal communication 'proxemics' is the study of how the space and distance between us influence how we communicate and 'kinesics' is the study of the way in which certain body movements and gestures – including eye contact - serve as a form of non-verbal communication (Lishman, 2009).

Activity 7.2: Experiment with non-verbal communication

With a partner try the following experiments.

Take it in turns to ask each other about something the other person enjoys doing, for example hobbies, interests or a recent holiday they might have had. Experiment having the conversation where the person finding out the information:

1. just sits completely impassively, without using any hand gestures, facial expressions or non-verbal cues such as nodding;

2. moves their chair very close to the person giving the information;

3. moves their chair a long way from the person giving the information;

4. maintains little or no eye contact and becomes preoccupied with messages on their phone or some other distraction;

5. one person stands while other sits.

Exchange views on how the discussions went.

Comment

If you took part in the activity it should have demonstrated the important part that different aspects of non-verbal communication play in our overall communication with people. For example, in scenario 1 you probably found it difficult to talk about something of interest to you when the other person is seemingly not sharing your interest nor giving any sign as to what they are thinking. In scenarios 2 and 3 most people will have found it inhibiting or challenging to have someone either too physically close to or far away from them. In scenario 4 it was probably frustrating, disconcerting and even annoying to be asked something and then not have the other person pay proper attention to what you are saying. In scenario 5, having one person stand changes the power dynamics and makes the communication experience less comfortable. As with all the other scenarios, this probably curtailed or inhibited the communication significantly and made it a lot loss satisfactory to participate in.

Social workers also use **written communication** but this can take many forms. For example, this could be through texts, emails or more formal written communication such as reports. Again, there are different conventions used in each of these examples of written communication. The style of language acceptable in a text or email may well not be suitable for other written communication such as court or panel reports, case recordings or letters. Therefore, with written communication, not only does the audience need to be considered but so do the conventions associated with the format and medium used. All communication needs to be clear, accurate and jargon free. However, written communication in social work has extra importance because, whatever form it takes, it is open to scrutiny by supervisors, managers and officials and professionals from other agencies. It is subject to Data Protection and Freedom of Information legislation and will form part of an auditable record that could be used in legal proceedings. Poor report writing, for example, not only impairs understanding and increases the risk of poor outcomes, it also embarrasses the individual social worker, their organisation and the profession generally (*Community Care*, 2015). To develop in this area see *Community Care* (2010) on 'How to write a good report'. However, we would recommend any of the texts listed below to help you improve this important communication skill. Usefully, Healy and Mulholland (2012) focus on writing skills alone.

The dictionary definition above referred to 'using some other medium' and we have already referred to 'non-verbal communication'. However, you might also have talked about more specialised forms of communication aimed at certain audiences such as British Sign Language for deaf people and systems such as Makaton, Signalong and Widgit Software for people with learning disabilities. These forms use signs and pictures but should not be confused with what writers such as Lishman (2009) call **symbolic communication**. This is a very important concept to grasp in social work. Symbolic communication includes behaviours like way that we dress or how punctual or reliable we are. For example, if we dress scruffily we are 'communicating' to people that they are not worth making an effort for. Similarly, if we repeatedly turn up late or cancel appointments we are sending a message that might interpreted by the person affected that they are not that important to us.

Finally, there are many barriers to effective communication ranging from basic problems such as our failing to listen properly but also different psychological cultural, physical and environmental factors. We cannot expand on all of these here, but both Coulshed and Orme (2012) and Moss (2015) provide good coverage of this important aspect of communication.

Activity 7.3: Communication skills audit

Task 1

Using a scale of 0–10 where 0 = 'I do not have this skill' and 10 = 'I am fully proficient in this skill', assess yourself where you are currently in relation to:

Verbal communication with:

- your peers
- people with learning disabilities
- children under the age of ten years
- via an interpreter
- people with dementia
- people with who are hearing impaired
- interviewing people
- active listening.

Non-verbal communication with:

- strangers
- proxemics and kinesics (see above) with someone of the opposite sex and from a different culture
- your verbal communication – in other words, how congruent is your verbal and non-verbal communication?

Written communication:

- case recording
- report writing
- writing the minutes of a meeting
- writing professional emails
- writing professional letters.

Symbolic communication:

- dressing appropriately for the occasion
- time-keeping and reliability.

Task 2

Reflect on your scores. Where do you need to focus your efforts in order to achieve an appropriately professional level of communication at this stage? For each area think about how you will develop the necessary skills.

Commentary

Everyone will have had their own individual scores based on factors such as your past experiences, background and personality. For some questions it might have been difficult to respond without having had the experience of knowing exactly what the task or format requires. We highlighted two particular 'verbal' skills – interviewing and active listening – to which you should pay particular attention and from which you would definitely benefit with more research and more practice (see Henderson and Mathew-Byrne, in Davies and Jones, 2016). However, they are all areas where social workers are expected to be proficient. This activity should underline that professional social work requires a broad range of competence across a range of different forms of communication.

Communication is such an important area of social work that it is impossible to do it justice in one short section. Fortunately, there are many good texts that cover this topic more thoroughly. Some are listed below and it is strongly advised that you work your way through all the different skills required. However, you cannot read your way into communicative competence. You need to practise the skills with different people (different audiences). Because communication is a two-way process you need to be able to gain feedback on how effective you are, how clear you have been, how respectful and so on. You cannot just take it for granted. The most effective communicators are usually those who are sensitive to the needs of others but also have a high degree of reflexivity, that is to say are emotionally intelligent and have the ability to look at themselves critically.

Summary

- Communication takes many forms in social work: verbal, non-verbal, written and symbolic.
- A social worker's written communication can be subject to scrutiny by the courts and other external bodies.
- Communication is a two-way process. A message delivered is not necessarily a message understood.
- Active listening is a key skill of effective communication.
- Good communication goes hand in hand with sensitivity, emotional intelligence and critical reflective practice.
- Social workers need to be aware of the needs of their audience in order to communicate appropriately and effectively.
- Many studies show that a failure to communicate effectively is disempowering for service users, impacts negatively on relationship building and can significantly add to placing service users at risk of harm.

Further reading

Community Care (2008) 'Proven practice: communicating with service users and their carers' online at: http://www.communitycare.co.uk/2008/10/15/proven-practice-communicating-with-service-users-and-their-carers/.

Community Care (2010) http://www.communitycare.co.uk/2010/07/28/how-to-write-a-good-report/.

Community Care (2015) 'Social worker criticised by judge for using jargon in court report', at http://www.communitycare.co.uk/2015/08/05/social-worker-criticised-judge-using-jargon-court-report/.

Coulshed, V and Orme, J (2012) *Social Work Practice*, 5th edition. Basingstoke: Palgrave, Chapter 4.

Davies, K and Jones, R (eds) (2016) *Skills for Social Work Practice*. Basingstoke: Palgrave.

Healy, K and Mulholland, J (2012) *Writing Skills for Social Workers*, 2nd edition. London: Sage.

Henderson, K and Mathew-Byrne, J (2016) 'Developing communication and interviewing and skills', in K Davies and R Jones (eds), *Skills for Social Work Practice.* Basingstoke: Palgrave, pp. 1–22.

Kadushin, A and Kadushin, G (1997) *The Social Work Interview: A Guide for Human Service Professionals*, 4th edition. New York: Columbia University Press.

Koprowska, J (2014) *Communication and Interpersonal Skills in Social Work*, 4th edition. Exeter: Learning Matters.

Lishman, J (2009) *Communication in Social Work*, 2nd edition. Basingstoke: Palgrave.

Mantell, A (2013) *Skills for Social Work Practice*, 2nd edition. London: Learning Matters, Chapter 7.

Mehrabian, A (1981) *Silent Messages: Implicit Communication of Emotions and Attitudes*. Belmont, CA: Wadsworth.

Moss, B (2015) *Communication Skills in Health and Social Care*, 3rd edition. London: Sage.

Trevithick, P (2005) *Social Work Skills: A Practice Handbook*, 2nd edition. Maidenhead: Open University Press, Chapters 3 and 4.

Assessment and intervention

'The process of assessment is core to social work practice', so state Coulshed and Orme (2012: 21), and just about all writers about social work would agree. It would therefore be a useful starting point to think about why that would be the case.

Activity 7.4: Why do assessments in social work?

1. Think about the various reasons why social workers carry out assessments. Who and what are they are assessing and why?

2. Why is the process of assessment so critical in social work practice?

Why social workers assess

Social workers carry out assessments for a variety of different reasons. Broadly speaking assessments can either be about assessing the needs of individuals and families, assessing people's mental capacity, assessing risks or assessing eligibility for services. There is often an overlap between these broad tasks. To a large extent the reasons for assessment are determined by the setting in which a social worker works, the service user group with whom they work and the legislation and policy that frame and guide the work of that setting. Some major examples are discussed next.

Statutory adult services

The work of statutory teams involving older people and adults with disabilities is mainly covered by the Care Act 2014. This Act states that, among other duties, local authorities must:

- **carry out an assessment** of anyone who appears to require care and support, regardless of their likely eligibility for state-funded care;
- **focus the assessment on the person's needs** and how they impact on their well-being, and the outcomes they want to achieve;
- **involve the person in the assessment** and, where appropriate, their carer or someone else they nominate;
- use the new national minimum threshold to **judge eligibility** for publicly funded care and support.

Source: SCIE http://www.scie.org.uk/care-act-2014/
assessment-and-eligibility/

Therefore, in this context, social workers have the important task of assessing the needs of 'anyone who appears to require care and support'. Then, using laid-down criteria, they need to 'judge eligibility for publicly funded care and support'. You should note the duty to involve the person in the assessment.

The Care Act 2014 covers a range of other situations where a social worker might need to carry out an assessment, for example in the area of adult safeguarding social workers need to carry out assessments to judge whether someone has been abused or is at risk of abuse. The Care Act 2014 also requires 'transition assessments' which need to be carried out when:

> . . . a child, young carer or an adult caring for a child is likely to have needs when they, or the child they care for, turns 18.

The local authority must assess them if it considers there is 'significant benefit' to the individual in doing so and arrange services as appropriate.

Finally, in relation to the Care Act 2014, it is also worth mentioning 'carer's assessments'. Carers can be eligible for support in their own right if they meet two conditions. Firstly, if the carer's needs for support arise because they are providing necessary care to an adult, and secondly if, as a result of their caring responsibilities, the carer's physical or mental health is either deteriorating or is at risk of doing so or the carer is unable to achieve any of the outcomes as specified in the [Care Act] regulations. Therefore, this is a good example of social workers needing to assess need, risk and eligibility all in the same assessment.

Mental capacity

Social workers who work in adult services might also be required to assess someone's mental capacity under the Mental Capacity Act 2005. Among other things this Act states:

- The Mental Capacity Act (MCA) 2005 applies to everyone involved in the care, treatment and support of people aged 16 and over living in England and Wales who are unable to make all or some decisions for themselves.

- The MCA is designed to protect and restore power to those vulnerable people who lack capacity.

- The MCA also supports those who have capacity and choose to plan for their future – this is everyone in the general population who is over the age of 18.

- Anyone caring for or supporting a person who may lack capacity could be involved in **assessing capacity** – follow the two-stage test.

Source: SCIE http://www.scie.org.uk/publications/ataglance/ataglance05.asp

The point of Mental Capacity assessments is to decide whether people who, because their mind is affected by illness or disability, or the effects of drugs or alcohol, have the mental capacity to make important decisions for themselves (for example, where to live or whether to have support). If they do not then social workers and others can take that decision on the basis of what is judged to be in the person's best interest.

Mental health legislation

In statutory mental health services it is common for social workers to perform the role of the Approved Mental Health Practitioner (AMHP). AMHPs have a central role to play in assessing whether there are grounds to detain mentally disordered people who meet the criteria laid down in mental health legislation. These assessments focus on assessing the risk of harm to the person or to others caused by their behaviour.

Statutory services for children and families

Various pieces of legislation guide social work children and families. The Children Act 1989 remains a very important piece of legislation in this branch of social work. For example, Section 17 of the Children Act 1989 states that 'children in need' may be assessed under this section in relation to their 'special educational needs, disabilities, as a carer, or because they have committed a crime'. Following such an assessment the local authority might then be required to provide appropriate services. Under section 47 of the Children Act 1989 local authorities, with the help of other organisations as appropriate, have a duty to make enquiries [carry out an assessment] if they 'have reasonable cause to suspect that a child is suffering, or is likely to suffer, significant harm, to enable them to decide whether they should take any action to safeguard and promote the child's welfare.'

These two sections form the main basis upon which social workers are required to either assess a child's needs or assess the risk of significant harm to a child requiring intervention. Fuller a fuller discussion of all the assessments required under the Children Act 1989 and other legislation relevant to children and families, see Working Together Online (2016) http://www.workingtogetheronline.co.uk/index.html.

Special guardianship, fostering and adoption

Other areas of children and families work require assessments. For example, social workers working in the area of fostering and adoption need to assess the suitability of special guardians and foster carers wanting to look after 'looked after' children and adopters who want to permanently adopt children who can no longer live with their biological parents. This is to ensure that the needs of the child or young person are met appropriately and that their health and well-being will be promoted in the most appropriate family setting.

Why assessment is critical

This has not been an exhaustive list of legislation by any means, but it should have demonstrated the range of reasons why social workers undertake assessments and the different service user groups involved in such assessments. Assessment is critical for several reasons. This can be because, without an assessment, people's needs might go undetected; people might not get the services to which they are entitled or the services that are most appropriate to their needs. Without an assessment people who were 'ineligible' might get services which would be wasteful of scarce resources. Finally, it could be that without a proper assessment taking place people could be placed at risk of harm – either the individual themselves or others with whom they have contact. In short, without assessments there would be no appropriate evidence base with which to inform what happens when someone with complex needs or who is at risk is referred.

The critical importance of assessment in social work has been underlined in several major reports. Parker and Bradley (2014:2) recall that:

> *The centrality of good social work assessment was emphasised by the inquiry into the death of Victoria Climbié (Laming, 2003), is further reinforced in Lord Laming's updated report (Laming, 2009), and forms an important plank within Eileen Munro's final report (Munro, 2011) in calling for higher quality assessment to improve the child protection process throughout its duration.*

Therefore, there are many reasons why assessment is a core activity in social work and this raises the question of what is required to carry out assessments to a professional standard. To a large degree the answer to this question can be found in the domains of the PCF. However, now is a good opportunity to gather our thoughts about what particular knowledge, values and skills a social worker needs in order to carry out an assessment effectively.

Activity 7.5: Assessment: knowledge, values and skills

Using the three headings: 'knowledge', 'values' and 'skills', brainstorm what you believe should most appropriately be included under each heading.

Knowledge required in assessments

Given the range of contexts in which assessments take place, it would be impossible to list all the necessary knowledge. However, you have should have included knowledge of relevant legislation and policy. For example, you cannot assess someone's eligibility for a service or their suitability for being a foster carer without knowing what the policy guidance states the specific criteria are against which you should be assessing.

A degree of subject knowledge is also important. For example, you cannot assess how well a child is being parented without having knowledge of normal child development and attachment. A social worker need not have all the specialist subject knowledge themselves but they need to know where to go for such knowledge. This relates to the skills of working collaboratively and of researching, which we will discuss in subsequent chapters. Therefore, for any assessment, a reasonable awareness of the specific knowledge pertaining to that case is important. You don't have to be an expert on dementia to assess someone with dementia but you need to be aware that expert knowledge on dementia might well be important in making the assessment and then you need to know where you can obtain it from if necessary. The same would be the case for any illness or impairment that the person you are assessing has. However, certain specific subject knowledge is definitely useful across most areas of social work. Key examples would be theories of loss and systems theory.

Values required in assessments

In essence the values required in assessments are the values of social work. That would include being anti-oppressive, anti-discriminatory, non-judgemental, person-centred, respectful, open-minded, culturally sensitive and so on. An important principle in assessment is that of working in partnership with the individual being assessed as far as possible. Certain values such as, for example, the need to respect confidentiality might need to be circumscribed by the nature of the assessment. If you are making a safeguarding assessment, information would need to be shared with other professionals as appropriate.

Skills required in assessments

We discussed the importance of being a good communicator earlier in the chapter while emphasising that communication is always a *two-way* process. Therefore, a basic assessment skill is for a social worker to clarify the purpose of the assessment, explain their role and what will happen next, and then make sure that the person understands this. Depending on the particular circumstances, a whole range of communication skills could be required but interviewing, active listening and recording skills are always essential in assessments. Observation is another skill fundamental required in most social work assessments (O'Loughlin and O'Loughlin, 2015). Observation supplements the information gathered from asking questions and other means. It is valuable in assessing interactions, relationships, moods and physical and mental health. However, it is important to evidence and record any observations as factually as possible. For example, 'Mr Smith seemed to be very angry. He spoke with a raised voice, swore several times, paced up and down and put his face very close to mine when speaking' is more informative than 'Mr Smith was angry'.

Many other important assessment skills are part of the basic skillset of social work which have been discussed in other chapters. This includes the skill of thinking analytically, reflecting critically and being able to understand things in their appropriate family, cultural and social context. To be holistic and comprehensive in our assessments normally requires the skill of working collaboratively with other agencies and professionals.

We now need to think about how best to utilise the necessary knowledge, values and skills in ways that mean that our assessments result in beneficial and productive outcomes for those concerned. It is worth reviewing the texts selected for further reading at the end of this section for various ways that have been suggested. However, here we use the widely known approach proposed by Milner et al. (2015) as a good example. They suggest the following five-stage process for exploring a situation:

1. Preparing for the task.

2. Collecting data, including perceptions of the service user, the family and other agencies of the problem and any attempted solutions.

3. Applying professional knowledge (practice wisdom as well as theory) to seek analysis, understanding or interpretation of the data.

4. Making judgements about the relationships, needs, risks, standard of care or safety, seriousness of the situation, and people's capacities and potential for coping or for change (is the progress good enough?).

5. Deciding and/or recommending what is to be done, plus how, by whom and when, and how progress will be reviewed.

Source: Milner et al. (2015), p. 2.

Activity 7.6: Assessing using a five-stage approach

George and Elsie Pocklington (1)

The older person's social care team has received a referral from the GP of George and Elsie Pocklington. The GP has described how George (78) is in the advanced stages of Parkinson 's disease and is on a prescription of levodopa to help him manage his symptoms which, in George's case, are rigidity of movement and some tremor. George's illness causes him to fall frequently. The latest fall led to George crashing into a glass-topped coffee table. When he found out, George's son, who lives some 60 miles away, sought the GP's help. The GP states that, when he visited, George had cuts and bruises but did not need hospital attention. However, the GP said that George's restricted movement is such that he now needs help with all of the activities of daily living. His wife Elsie (77) is his only carer. They live together in their own three-bedroomed terraced house. The GP thought Elsie looked very 'on edge' and under stress. The GP requested that a social worker visit to assess the situation with a view to putting in a support package.

Task 1

Given this information how would you 'prepare for the task'?

George and Elsie Pocklington (2)

As part of your preparations you ring the Pocklingtons to make an appointment to visit to carry out an assessment. You speak to Elsie Pocklington. She describes herself and her husband as a 'private couple' who like to keep themselves to themselves. Elsie is clearly stressed and seemingly bitter about having to devote so much time and energy to her husband. She tells you 'I have no life of my own now'.

Elsie says the GP talked about having carers in but that they are not keen to have strangers in the house. She wonders whether her husband might have to go into a home but clearly is in two minds about this saying 'When you marry them it is for better and for worse.' She describes her situation as 'Whereas before I was a wife, now I am just a skivvy.' When you ask about the recent fall, she tells you she finds it hard to help her husband up after his falls. She says she already had a heart problem and now has persistent backache. Elsie adds that she is also on tranquillisers prescribed for her 'bad nerves'. She tells you that she often has to leave her husband on the floor when he falls – sometimes for days. She knows it's wrong but can't see why she should 'bust a gut' lifting him up all the time. She says it would be different if her son and daughter visited a bit more often, but they both work full time and live over fifty miles away. They both visit about one weekend a month.

Task 2

Based on this phone call, you have further information but you clearly need more. If we refer to the approach suggested, we need to think more about stages 2, 3 and 4 of the assessment process. Therefore comment on the following:

2. The data already collected and what more needs to be gathered at this stage.

3. Applying professional knowledge (practice wisdom as well as theory) – what is your analysis/interpretation of the situation so far? In other words what is your hypothesis?

4. What are your judgements about the relationships, needs, risks, standard of care or safety, seriousness of the situation, and people's capacities and potential for coping or for change?

Task 1: commentary

Preparing for this task would require that you had all the correct information about the person referred and significant family members. This would include George and Elsie's dates of birth, address and contact details, as well the contact details of the son and daughter. Having the referrer's name and contact details is also necessary. You might also want to check whether there was any other relevant medical information that you needed to know. This would include whether either George or Elsie were receiving any medical treatments or other health involvements such as physiotherapy or community nursing. Preparation would also include checking to see whether the Pocklingtons were already known to your organisation and, if so, for what reason.

Generally, you would also need to know your role and that of your organisation in terms of legislation and policy. You would need to make sure that you had all the information you required in terms of forms, paperwork and leaflets to take to the assessment.

Lastly, while social workers are not expected to be medical experts it would be generally useful to find out more about Parkinson's disease, its effects and treatments. However, it would need to be borne in mind that each individual experiences a condition like Parkinson's differently.

Task 2: commentary

The first thing to highlight is that, while the stages are logically ordered, they are not always discrete. There is bound to be some going back and forth filling in gaps as new information and new questions emerge. From what Elsie tells you about her own physical and mental health and also about her leaving George on the floor when he falls, there is clearly an increased risk to both of their health, possibly to the point where you might want to consult with a supervisor about whether it should be treated as a safeguarding matter. It is worth returning to the GP to share the information you have received and also to clarify what is known about Elsie's health.

As George's only carer Elsie is an important person in this assessment. From what we know, Elsie appears to be under stress from caring for George and her health appears to be deteriorating as a consequence. The situation is having potentially serious implications for her capacity to cope and also for both her and George's health and well-being. This is borne out by research that indicates that carers of people with long-term progressive conditions such as Parkinson's suffer stress which not only affects their ability to care but also affects their own mental and physical health (Carers UK, 2015). Systems theory is useful here because it highlights how both George's and Elsie's situations are interconnected and that the health of one affects that of the other and vice versa. An understanding of theories of loss would be useful in understanding the various losses that both George and Elsie have experienced and continue to experience. They are experiencing loss of freedom, loss of mobility, loss of relationship and so on. All of these can impact upon mental health.

One might hypothesise that the situation will only continue to get worse and the risks to both parties will increase. To help assess any risks there needs to be a full exchange of information between all the appropriate health and social care services as well as family members.

It is very important to see and speak with George himself to find out at first-hand how he is, what he needs, what the risks are, how he sees the situation and what he wants to do. Also, it is only when you are able to observe George and Elsie together in their own home that you can get a better picture of their relationship and both the strengths and the risks of the situation. Preferably with the permission of the couple, you should also contact their children to gather their perspectives on the situation. Not only might they contribute more relevant information, they also might well be part of any solution decided. Lastly, you would need to check whether the Pocklingtons are getting all the benefits to which they are entitled – in this case, for example, Attendance Allowance. Not only can having a disability make life more expensive, often people can be put off seeking support because of worry about the costs involved. Maximising benefits can be a way of helping in this respect.

These are some of the main points that should have been considered in progressing from stage one through to later stages of the assessment process. Each step is designed to add more information, bring in more perspectives (particularly those of the person being referred), clarify any areas that are unclear and build a more holistic and comprehensive picture. Given the perceived risks, all of this would need to be carried out in a timely fashion. All of this is so that we can move to the final stage of deciding what is to be done, by whom, when and how.

We will discuss possible decisions or recommendations that might result from our assessment later. However, to keep our focus on the dynamics of the assessment process for a moment, it should be noted that different models have been proposed and we review a widely known typology of assessments next.

Models of assessment

In thinking about assessing George and Elsie's situation we highlighted the importance of actually going to visit and speak to them in person. The face-to-face interview is the cornerstone of most social work assessments. However, the dynamics of interviews can vary according to the model of assessment adopted. Smale et al. (1993) suggested three broad models of assessment: a procedural model, a questioning model and an exchange model. Each has its own strengths and weaknesses depending on the nature of the assessment being undertaken.

Procedural model

This model is characterised by having to follow set procedures laid down by the organisation. The questions asked are largely determined by the eligibility criteria for services. The line of questioning is designed to enable judgement to be made about access to resources. The format is therefore determined by those setting the criteria for resource allocation, not service users. Often answers are recorded in terms of a numerical score or some other type of scale rather than the service user's own words. The procedural model will usually:

- Identify a particular level of dependency and categorise service users accordingly.

- Be a service-driven rather than needs-driven process.

- Define the nature of the client's needs in the terms of the services offered.

- Ensure that the agency remains central to the definition of problems and the range of available solutions.

Questioning model

This is not dissimilar to the procedural model in that it also largely relies on pre-prepared questions. It is less governed by the need to establish eligibility and more about assessing suitability for a particular intervention, for example someone's suitability for cognitive behavioural therapy or attendance at a parenting group. With the questioning model:

- The worker is considered to have the expertise – the service user supplies the answers for the worker to process. The service user's own words are more likely to be recorded than in the procedural model.

- Information gathered outside that required to judge the suitability of the intervention is not really considered relevant.

Exchange model

As its name suggests this model is less uni-directional and more of an exchange between the parties concerned. This model assumes that people are generally 'experts by experience' in their own lives. It is also less concerned with just seeking out deficits, that is to say what a person lacks or cannot do. It tries to recognise someone's strengths and potential and is curious to know the person's own perceptions of the issue and what should be done. It assumes that the worker:

- has expertise in the process of problem-solving with others;

- understands and shares perceptions of problems and their management – does not interpret;

- negotiates desired outcomes and gets agreement about who will do what to attain the outcomes.

In reality, assessments are not always exclusively one model or the other but they might be much more like one type of model than the other two. However, the typology provided by

Smale et al. is useful because it allows us to 'take account of differentials of power'. It alerts us to how our assessment approach affects and influences the degree of partnership working and power dynamics.

Activity 7.7: An assessment model for George and Elsie

Think about which model would be most appropriate to use in the assessment of George and Elsie Pocklington. Give reasons. What features of the other two models might also be required?

Commentary

In this situation it would be useful not to go with too many predetermined questions and to try to get a much better sense of what both George and Elsie thought about the situation and also what they thought the best solution was. This suggests mainly an exchange model might be adopted. They, after all, have been living with this situation for a long time and will each have their own idea of what works and what does not. That said, because of the particular risks to which you have been alerted, as an assessor, you will need to ask about how the couple manage the activities of daily living, the falls George has had, the carer stress that you are concerned about and so on. You will also need to establish whether either George or Elsie's situation makes them eligible for a service. From the information received so far, this seems likely but would still need to be properly assessed and evidenced.

The first visit could be the first stage of an assessment process that involved more specialist assessments later such by a falls prevention professional or mental health professional. It might be more appropriate for those assessments to be structured around a questioning model but one would still expect some element of exchange about them.

What happens following assessment: interventions

It is not possible to decide what the exact outcomes of an intervention should be in the case of George and Elsie because we are too early in the assessment process. However, on the information gathered so far we can form a working hypothesis and, indeed, social workers are encouraged to do so. As we have discussed, this can always be adjusted in the light of new information. So, we need to be thinking about a range of things at this point:

1. What the main needs are.

2. What the main risks are.

3. What the strengths of the situation are.

4. What the desirable outcomes are.

5. The sorts of interventions that would help achieve the outcomes.

Activity 7.8: Deciding and/or recommending what is to be done with and for George

Using the five questions above as headings think about what you could reasonably list under each. Although George is the focus, Elsie is an important part of the situation, so you would need to include her in your thinking. Where possible, your suggestions for interventions should be realistic and refer to relevant legislation and policy.

The following is not exhaustive but indicative of the points that would feature in an assessment.

Needs

George needs help to prevent him falling. He also needs help with the activities of daily living, getting up, getting dressed and so on. He needs to have his independence, choice and dignity maintained but he also needs to be safeguarded. Elsie needs a break from the stresses of looking after George. She needs to feel less stressed and anxious. Elsie, too, needs to be able to have choice in her life and to feel independent. Both of them need practical support.

Risks

George risks serious injury by falling. Elsie's physical and mental health is at risk by the constant effort and worry of looking after George. Elsie's deteriorating mental state places George at risk from neglect or abuse – albeit from stress rather than a desire to be cruel. The marital relationship is at risk of breaking down.

Strengths

There is some strength and resilience in the extent to which Elsie is 'soldiering on'. The son and daughter visit at least once a month and the son alerted the GP with his concerns. The couple are not completely isolated. They agree to an assessment.

Desirable outcomes

1. George's falling better managed.

2. George's health and well-being safeguarded.

3. Elsie's health and well-being safeguarded.

4. Elsie feeling supported in her caring role and given the choice of a break from caring.

5. The couple to maintain their independence as far as possible.

Possible interventions according to desired outcomes

Outcome 1

This could be addressed by a visit from the local falls prevention coordinator and an occupational therapist who could both risk assess and advise on strategies to prevent falling as well as advise on adaptations to the house, assistive technology and equipment to help reduce and manage the risks.

Outcome 2

A support package to help George with the activities of daily living through a personal budget could be offered. This could be directly arranged by the local authority or could be provided via a direct payment that the couple could use to employ someone of their choosing (Age UK, 2016). The GP could refer George to specialist neurological services and to a dedicated Parkinson nurse if there was one in the area to ensure that George was on the best possible treatment regime.

Outcomes 3/4/5

Elsie's physical and mental health would benefit from further assessment by her GP. From this, it might well be that she might be helped by specialist help for her anxiety and any depression she might be experiencing. Elsie could be offered a Carers Assessment in her own right. She might benefit from a break provided by a sitting service or even a respite stay in a home for George, as long as he was willing. She also might benefit from attending a carers support group or she might want a direct payment to organise something for herself.

However, it would appear that many of Elsie's problems are bound up with her caring role. Therefore, while Elsie would potentially benefit from individual interventions, as mentioned earlier a systemic approach would treat them as a couple.

The couple could be signposted towards a national support organisation such as Parkinson's UK or Age UK who could provide information on local support. However, each locality has its own particular support organisations, so some help with 'navigation' would be useful. Lastly, George, Elsie and the son and daughter could be engaged in generating solutions from with family and other informal networks about how to provide more support in ways that are palatable to the couple. This might involve the use of more universal services such as shopping online and having it delivered, going to a choir, going on outings or other such activities. All of these could improve the couple's quality of life and promote their well-being.

Needless to say all of these interventions would need to be discussed and agreed with the parties concerned. This might not necessarily be straightforward. For example, it is thought to be on Elsie's mind that George might need to go into a care home, but this would not be a decision that could be taken without his consent. George and Elsie need to be seen as a mutually dependent couple but also individuals in their own right. Their interests might not always be exactly the same, so an important skill of social work is to strike the best balance of rights and risks that meets the range of outcomes you want to achieve.

Having assessed more thoroughly and agreed a support plan which might include all or some of the above, it is good social work practice to frequently monitor the interventions against the agreed outcomes and to formally review any support package at agreed intervals. George and Elsie need to be fully involved in the decision-making at each stage.

Moving on beyond this case, different situations require different interventions and we would refer you to the Further Reading below which not only examines assessments in more depth but also discusses a far wider range of interventions.

Summary

- The process of assessment is core to social work practice. It is usually a staged process rather than a one-off event.
- The reasons for assessment are determined by the setting in which a social worker works, the service user group with whom they work and the legislation and policy that frame and guide the work of that setting.
- Generally, assessment is essential for the effective planning and implementing of interventions.
- Assessment is critical to determine needs and matching needs to resources.
- Assessment is important in deciding about risks particularly in the context of safeguarding.
- Assessment is critical for efficient and equitable resource allocation.
- There are different models of assessment. They vary according to their exact purpose but also in the how in which they take account of differentials of power and the extent which to service users have control over the process.

Further reading

Aspinwall-Roberts, E (2012) *Assessments in Social Work with Adults*. Maidenhead: Open University Press.

Beckett, C (2010) *Assessment and Intervention in Social Work: Preparing for Practice*. London: Sage.

Coulshed, V and Orme, J (2012) *Social Work Practice*, 5th edition. Basingstoke: Palgrave.

Davies, K and Jones, R (eds) (2016) *Skills for Social Work Practice*. Basingstoke: Palgrave.

Lindsay, T (ed.) (2013) *Social Work Intervention*, 2nd edition. Exeter: Learning Matters.

Mantell, A (2013) *Skills for Social Work Practice*, 2nd edition. London: Sage.

Milner, J, Myers, S and O'Byrne, P (2015) *Assessment in Social Work*, 4th edition. Basingstoke: Palgrave.

O'Loughlin, M and O'Loughlin, S (eds) (2015) *Effective Observation in Social Work Practice*. London: Learning Matters.

Smale, G, Tuson, G, Biehal, N and Marsh, P (1993) *Empowerment, Assessment, Care Management and the Skilled Worker.* London: HMSO.

Trevithick, P (2005) *Social Work Skills: A Practice Handbook*, 2nd edition. Maidenhead: Open University Press.

Walker, S and Beckett, C (2011) *Social Work Assessment and Intervention*, 2nd edition. Lyme Regis: Russell House.

8: Contexts and organisations

Introduction

This chapter is divided into three sections. The first section looks at the various contexts in which social work takes place and which influence its practices. In this section we discuss social work in its historical context. This highlights how various social, economic, political, demographic and global factors have influenced and continue to influence the organisational context of social work over time. For example, much has changed organisationally since the creation of local authority social services departments in the 1970s. Unlike then, social work is now more likely to take place in specialist (often multi-disciplinary) teams working within a multi-agency context where many of the agencies involved increasingly operate in the independent sector.

The organisational context of social work provides the focus for the next two sections. Firstly, we use the example of a multi-disciplinary learning disability team to look at the knowledge and skills that social workers need to possess in order to work effectively in such organisational environments. In the final section we use the example of a children and families team to examine the range of agencies that collaborate with each other in that field of social work. We also explore what can be done to develop the skills and knowledge required to meet the challenges of working effectively in this context.

The contexts of social work

Social work does not take place in a vacuum. It takes place in a variety of different, interconnected and overlapping contexts. These different contexts shape social work policy and practice. The main contexts that we need to be aware of are:

- historical
- demographic
- global
- social
- economic
- political/ideological
- legislation and policy
- organisational.

As stated, the different contexts interconnect with and influence each other. For example, legislation usually reflects the political philosophy or ideology of the government of the day. However, legislation and policy also reflect global and national economic conditions, social attitudes and demographic trends pertaining at that time. The economy is affected by global, demographic and social trends and vice versa, often in complex ways. For example, at the time of writing, immigration is a much debated topic. Migration would be described as a demographic trend and is affected by a range of political, social, economic and other factors. When immigrants arrive in a country or leave a country this has economic, social and political effects. Whether you think that, on balance, these effects are good or bad, is a matter of opinion, as we know from the EU referendum debate (BBC, 2016). However, the point is that all these effects are interconnected. Whatever affects society and the economy affects social work in some way.

Legislation and policy made in response to political, social, economic and demographic conditions influences organisations in several ways. For example, it influences what organisations exist, how they are regulated, how they are run, who they are run by and also what tasks they have to perform and which services to provide.

We start by concentrating on the historical context of social work, particularly its early origins. The reason for doing this is that it helps demonstrate how the way social work is practised always reflects the values, social and economic conditions and political thinking of the day. It also helps illustrate how much social work has changed as the times have changed, although you will notice that there is also some discernible continuity over time.

Historical context of social work

Ideas about what social work is and how it should be practised are very much shaped by the various political ideological, social, economic and demographic factors that exist in any one historical period (Healy, 2005; Page and Silburn; 1999; Pierson, 2011). The roots of modern social work are various and run deep in the social history of the United Kingdom. The origins of the modern social work role can be traced back to at least the nineteenth century. During most of the nineteenth century the dominant political and economic doctrine adopted by governments was that of 'laissez-faire'. This theory was based upon the doctrine of 'individualism' in that it was believed that allowing individuals to pursue their own ends, with as little state interference as possible would achieve the best outcomes for both the economy and society. The function of the state was merely to maintain order and security and little else. It was a time of 'small government'. Although there was some limited help available from charities and the local parish, by and large people were expected to look after their own welfare needs.

A prototype for today's social work could be seen in the administration of the Poor Law and the distribution of charitable relief. Following the 1834 Poor Law it was the job of the poor law relieving officers to evaluate the cases of all persons applying for medical or poor relief from their local poor law union in order that they could authorise emergency relief or entry into the workhouse. In the charitable sector, the Charity Organisation Society (COS) was set up in 1869 to coordinate the efforts of the many and various charitable bodies working with 'destitute' individuals and families, 'Case workers' were trained to investigate thoroughly the circumstances of applicants and decide whether they were sufficiently 'deserving' to receive it. You were considered deserving if you were genuinely sick and disabled and were trying your best to get by on your own. You were deemed to be 'undeserving' if you did not lead a sufficiently moral lifestyle, for example if you were 'feckless', 'idle' or drank alcohol you would be refused support (Harris, 2008; Pierson, 2011). Above all, the COS wanted to foster the spirit of self-help and for people to lead a sober, hard-working and morally correct lifestyle (BBC, 2011).

The roots of modern social work

As the nineteenth century progressed, so did the social and health effects of industrialisation. These most notably included the growth of urban and rural poverty, increased urban squalor, growing social unrest and the spread of disease. Among other things, the need to maintain social order and need for a healthier and better educated workforce to keep Britain's economy competitive meant that, towards the end of the century, it started to become accepted that the state needed to play a larger role in combating social problems and attending to the health and well-being of the population.

You might think that the early roles described were a far cry from today's social work and, indeed, neither would have been described as 'social work' at the time. However, the roots of social work are clearly evident in both roles. For example, we see the use of casework techniques such as assessment to investigate people's home and family circumstances in order to be able to judge their eligibility for support. One of the most strikingly different aspects of the assessments carried out in those days was the underlying values and principles that guided them (see Chapter 2). This was reflected, for example, in the wish to judge moral character and to decide what was 'good' for people rather than involve them in the assessment and ask them their opinion. The client was not considered to have any 'rights' as such. The discretion of professionals and officials in deciding how deserving you were was all important. Partly because of this, to apply for poor relief of any kind was a negative, disempowering and very stigmatising experience, so much so that many people were deterred from applying.

Those early 'social work' roles were being performed at a time of laissez-faire, long before the welfare state was set up and while social sciences such as sociology and psychology were in their very infancy. Ideas about 'universal' human rights were far from developed and notions of racism, sexism or any kind of discrimination had scarcely been thought about let alone entered official discourse. Attitudes to poverty, mental ill health and disability were very much seen as primarily the individual's problem and the responsibility of the individual or their family. They were certainly not seen as the responsibility of the state. Questions of what welfare should consist of and what welfare practices should look like reflected both the attitudes and the (mainly deterrent) system of welfare at the time.

As the times and contexts have changed, so has social work (Harris, 2008). The end of the nineteenth century and the beginning of the twentieth saw the first scientific social research beginning to be undertaken. This enabled poverty and its associated disadvantages to be seen in more of its socio-economic context – that is to say not just the fault of the individual.

Changing attitudes to social welfare

Professional social work training started to be developed at the beginning of the twentieth century and was informed by the newly established and growing social sciences. These were not just psychological and sociological theories but also the new discipline of social administration (Pierson, 2011). After the First World War social work started to be influenced by Freudian psychoanalysis (Healy, 2005) and, in general, psychodynamic theories dominated social work thinking and practice for the next few decades.

After the Second World War, the welfare state in Great Britain was created on the principle that the state would look after the individual 'from the cradle to the grave', in stark contrast to before the war and even more so to the nineteenth century. This reflected the dominant ideology of the times which was 'collectivist' rather than 'individualist' and regarded welfare provision as primarily a responsibility of the state. There are several reasons for this change in thinking. They include the emergence of Keynesian economics, and the impact of the Second World War itself which fostered the need for social cohesion and more of a collectivist mindset in the population which made it more receptive to socialist and social democratic ideas. The vision of a *welfare* state was fleshed out in policy by the Beveridge Report of 1942 (Lowe, 2005). Arguably, the welfare state was a form of paternalism that, while benevolent, saw welfare 'clients' as passive recipients of services about which they had little say or choice. Use of the private sector was practically non-existent.

The creation of the 'Social Services'

No single piece of legislation was aimed at creating the personal social services as we know them today. Instead, the passing of laws such as the Children Act 1948 and the National Assistance Act 1948 led to the creation of various services and job roles that were mostly undertaken in a patchwork of different departments of local government and the newly created NHS. These roles included local authority welfare department workers, child care officers, mental health workers, probation officers, family case workers, case workers for invalid children and almoners working in hospitals and other health services. They each had their own specific training and practice. However, practice of this period was generally characterised by a paternalistic attitude towards clients, the segregation of people according to their 'handicap' or problem and the use of institutional rather than community-based solutions in most cases.

In 1968 the publication of the *Report of the Committee on Local Authority and Allied Personal Social Services* (known as the Seebohm Report) led to the Local Authority Social Services Act 1970 being passed and, from that, we see the creation of the first social services departments (Harris, 2008; Pierson, 2011). This was very much a landmark in the history of social work because for the first time it created a 'single door' through which children, families and adults who were 'vulnerable' for various reasons could apply for help. As Harris (2008: 10) explains:

> As social services departments were being established in local authorities, at the national level, the British Association of Social Workers (1970) and the Central Council for Education and Training in Social Work (1971) were also set up and new legislation (e.g. the 1969 Children and Young Persons Act and the 1970 Chronically Sick and Disabled Persons Act) was ready for the Social Services departments to implement. After 1971, the dominant form of social work was provided in these generic local authority social services departments.

The bringing together of various roles and functions into 'universal' social services departments run by local authorities had various effects. For example, it helped reduce the stigma of seeking help and, as a consequence, increased the demand for services. Also, with so many different workers coming together from different backgrounds and specialisms, it stimulated debates about what the role of professional social work should be and what training was required to practise effectively.

This brief account has intended to put the origins of the personal social services in its historical context. The challenge from now on is to understand the current context(s) from in which social work takes place. Space does not permit an exhaustive discussion of all the changes that have taken place since the 1970s up to the present. However, to stimulate thought and to fill in some important gaps try the following activity.

Activity 8.1: The impact on social work of the 'New Right'/ Thatcherism in the 1980s and 1990s and New Labour/ modernisation in the 1990s and 2000s

1. For background information you will need to use the article by Harris (2008) and other suitable texts such as Lymbery and Postle (2007), Pierson (2011) or Lowe (2005) to cover these periods.

2. Investigate the main political, ideological, social and demographic factors that impacted on social work in the decades since local social service departments were set up in the 1970s.

3. List them as bullet points and be prepared to exchange ideas with another.

Commentary

Over recent decades there have been major changes in the contexts in which social work takes place. Some particularly noteworthy ones are discussed below. Note that, because they are often interconnected, many factors could be included under more than one heading.

Demographic

People are living longer. More and more of us are living into our eighties, nineties and beyond. This has many social and economic implications but perhaps the biggest impact for social work is the challenge of supporting increasing numbers of older people and their carers through later life, which is the period in the life course in which illness and disability are most likely to occur. Another demographic trend (linked to globalisation) is the increased levels of immigration from all over the world. This is for various reasons. Some immigration is to do with refugees escaping various forms of oppression; other immigration is due to economic reasons. That is to say, people come to the UK because they want to have a better quality of life or they move for reasons of employment. This, too, has many social and economic implications. One that affects social work is that society is now much more culturally and ethnically diverse. However, the social work workforce has reflected this trend and has also become more socially diverse. Both of these trends present challenges to practising in ways that are culturally sensitive, anti-discriminatory and anti-racist and that promote human rights.

Global

As mentioned above we are living in times of increased global migration for different reasons. In recent years conflict in the Middle East has led to a massive rise in the number of refugees travelling to Europe. However, increased migration is just one manifestation of globalisation. Events or changes in the global economy also impact on Britain in different ways. For example, the banking crisis of 2007–8, which originated in the USA, meant that the British economy went into recession affecting public finances and causing a significant deficit. Successive British governments have pursued cuts in public spending in order to bring the deficit down. As social work is largely sourced by public funds such as taxation this has resulted in significant cutbacks in resources. This has meant that while the demand for social work support has risen the resources needed to meet demand have been cut (Jordan and Drakeford, 2012).

Social

As mentioned earlier, society is now more diverse. However, in addition, in recent decades, partly due to economic challenges but also government policies, we have seen increased social inequalities and rising levels of poverty in Britain (Backwith, 2015). This creates many challenges for social work because it increases demand for a whole range of services, from support for socially deprived families through to supporting growing numbers of people with mental ill health. That said, since the 1970s, we have become a more socially liberal society and a society more concerned with human rights and the need to combat discrimination of all kinds (see the section on 'legislation and policy' below for more on this). Society has changed in many other ways over recent decades. We have become a more consumerist and individualist society (Cunningham and Cunningham, 2012). We have seen the rise of 'participationism' across all areas of society, that is to say members of the public wanting more say in matters that concern them, whether that be reflected in consumer surveys, public consultations, sitting on boards and panels or other forms of involvement in decision-making.

Economic

The biggest change in terms of the government economic policy since the 1970s came with the election of Margaret Thatcher in 1979. It should be seen as part of a wider global phenomenon but Thatcherism in economics (also known as neo-liberalism) favours market rather than state-run approaches to running the economy. It brought in the idea of privatisation and the ethos of business into the public sector. So, for example, what were state-run monopolies (such as British Gas and British Telecom) were sold off to private investors and more competition between providers was encouraged. The idea was to create choice and drive down costs through the use of competition. The intention was to promote 'consumerism' by giving power to the consumer to shop around between services, thereby forcing service providers to be more responsive and offer more choice and better value for money. However, whether this has actually happened in all sectors is more of a moot point.

The most obvious examples of neo-liberalism in social work might be the fact that most care provision these days, such as care homes of varying kinds and other services such as home care and fostering agencies, are now run by private companies or non-profit organisations – not the local authority which would have been the case in the 1970s.

Political/ideological

As discussed above under 'economic', one of the biggest political changes since the 1970s has been the replacement of social democratic values by neo-liberal ones. This is a complex area that is easily oversimplified; however, the core of the idea centres on shifting (or outsourcing) many of the functions of the public sector to the private sector, reducing government spending, promoting free trade and markets and the deregulation of business and markets as far as possible (see Crouch (2011) for a fuller discussion of this important political and economic trend). Two other effects of neo-liberalism have had a noticeable impact on public services. The first is managerialism which gave more organisational power to managers in order to curb the power of professionals and run services on a more business like footing.

The second is 'consumerism' where users of services have increasingly been encouraged to see themselves as 'customers' rather than clients or patients.

Since the 1970s we have seen a move away from class-based politics and the rise of identity politics and 'new social movements' (Macionis, 2017). This had created challenges for the two mainstream political parties as people are less likely to vote for them based on class allegiance alone. Instead people now campaign about other aspects of their identity. Examples of this are gay rights, the green movement, Black Lives Matter, the SNP in Scotland and so on. In recent decades politicians and the public have identified a democratic deficit – where traditional political structures and process are not regarded as representing the electorate adequately. Attempts to deal with this are more devolution of powers to local levels which also links to the rise of 'participationism' described above.

When New Labour governments were in power they promoted the idea of 'modernisation'. Among other things this was about pursuing 'joined up' government (see the section which follows), increasing accessibility of services (often by making them digital) and concentrating on 'what works' which, for New Labour, meant continuing the privatisation of public services through various means.

Legislation and policy

As discussed in previous chapters much legislation and policy has impacted upon social work. The 1970s saw the passing of legislation such as the Sex Discrimination Act 1975 and the Race Relations Act 1976 designed to end discrimination and promote equality. However, these and other pieces of social legislation have now been consolidated in the Human Rights Act 1998 and the Equality Act 2010.

The passing of the Children Act 1989 and the NHS and Community Act 1990 was significant for social work because, together, these two Acts paved the way for generic social services departments to be split into separate children's and adults' services. The NHS and Community Act 1990 also introduced the idea of a 'quasi-markets' in health and social care (Page and Silburn, 1999). However, since then, much legislation and policy focused on social work has been about ensuring that different agencies work together around the citizen/service-user rather than work separately in 'silos'. The project of integrating services and ensuring collaboration between different agencies has not always been easy to achieve. For example, aware that health and social care services were very badly coordinated, the New Labour Secretary of State for Health at the time, Frank Dobson, observed that it was as if there was a 'Berlin Wall' between the two sectors (Dobson, 1999). The main thrust of New Labour's plan for modernising government was to make it more 'joined up'. This policy goal has been adopted by successive governments and can be seen enshrined in policies such as *Working Together to Safeguard Children* (HM Government, 2015) and the Care Act 2014 (Quinney and Hafford-Letchfield, 2012).

Organisational

Policy directed at social care and social work has placed great emphasis on integrating services, promoting collaboration and partnership between organisations in order to provide more seamless and person-centred services. However, at the same time there has been a greater fragmentation of the social care sector generally. Whereas in the 1970s social work and social care was almost exclusively provided by local government and health services by the NHS, today this is not the case. Since the 1990s the role of state organisations has changed from providing services directly to commissioning services from the independent sector. This explains why services today are more fragmented and delivered by a range of different types of state-run, private and independent sector agencies. Therefore, for this reason alone, the challenges and tensions faced in working collaboratively are not insignificant, although as we will discuss later problems of inter-agency working can arise out of professional rivalries and 'silo' mentalities (Quinney and Hafford-Letchfield, 2012; Weinstein et al., 2003).

Social work organisations have been transformed by the impact of managerialism and consumerism. Consumerism has provided 'consumers' with more opportunities to complain and comment on the quality of services. Managerialism has meant that organisations have focused more on outputs (for example, the number of reviews carried out per annum) rather than processes building up effective relationships. Although attempts have been made to restore a greater degree of professional judgement in social work (see, for example, the Munro Report, 2011) the work of many public sector organisations is still regulated and inspected against externally set performance measures.

The introduction of both managerialism and consumerism into organisations can be seen as attempts to improve accountability, ensure quality of services and, in the case of managerialism, keep a lid on costs. Another significant change to the way social work organisations have been run since the 1970s has been the introduction of independent regulation. Currently, the Care Quality Commission inspects and regulates health and social care provision and Ofsted children's services. Therefore, social workers in organisations are accountable in four ways: to their profession (see Chapter 1), to the management of their employing organisation, to their service users and to industry regulators.

As will now be obvious, getting to grips with the various contexts of social work and all their impacts is a huge topic. Much more could be said, but we need to move on to examine other parts of the domain. We therefore conclude this section with a summary of key points and suggestions for further reading.

Summary

- Social work takes place in a variety of different, interconnected and overlapping contexts.
- The rise in immigration and people living longer are part of the demographic context.
- Britain is a now a more culturally and ethnically diverse society. However, in recent years, Britain has become a more unequal society and poverty is increasing.
- Public finances are running historically high deficits.
- Demand for social work is increasing while resources are diminishing.
- People want more say in and control over decision-making that affects their lives.
- Since the 1980s neo-liberal ideas have become dominant. These favour smaller government, a bigger private sector, a more marketised economy and free trade.
- Offshoots of neo-liberalism are the introduction of managerialism and consumerism into public-sector organisations.
- Legislation and policy has directed health, social and other related services to pool their resources, to work more collaboratively to provide 'joined up' services and to integrate provision in some cases.
- Social workers in organisations are accountable in four ways: to their profession, to the management of their employing organisation, to their service users and to regulators.

Further reading on social work contexts

Backwith, D (2015) *Social Work, Poverty and Social Exclusion.* Maidenhead: Open University Press.

BBC (2011) online at http://www.bbc.co.uk/history/british/victorians/bsurface_01.shtml.

BBC (2016) online at 'Immigration: threat or opportunity?' online at: http://www.bbc.co.uk/news/uk-politics-eu-referendum-36548750.

Crouch, C (2011) *The Strange Non-Death of Neoliberalism.* Cambridge: Polity.

Bubb, S (2014) *Winterbourne View – Time for Change,* a report by the Transforming Care and Commissioning Steering Group, chaired by Sir Stephen Bubb, November.

Cunningham, J and Cunningham, S (2012) *Social Policy and Social Work: An Introduction.* London: Learning Matters.

Guardian (2010) 'A brief history of social work', online at: https://www.theguardian.com/society/2010/nov/11/social-work-interviews-archive.

Harris, J (2008) 'State social work: constructing the present from moments in the past', *British Journal of Social Work*, 38 (4): 662–79.

Healy, K (2005) *Social Work Theories in Context.* Basingstoke: Palgrave.

Hill, A (2010) *Working in Statutory Contexts*. Cambridge: Polity Press.

Jordan, B and Drakeford, M (2012) *Social Work and Social Policy under Austerity*. Basingstoke: Palgrave Macmillan.

Lowe, R (2005) *The Welfare State in Britain since 1945*. Basingstoke: Palgrave.

Lymbery, M and Postle, K (eds) (2007) *Social Work: A Companion to Learning*. London: Sage.

Macionis, J (ed.) (2017) *Sociology*, 16th edition. Harlow: Pearson.

Page, R and Silburn, R (1999) *British Social Welfare in the Twentieth Century*. Basingstoke: Palgrave.

Payne, M (2005) *The Origins of Social Work*. Basingstoke: Palgrave.

Pierson, J (2011) *Understanding Social Work: History and Context*. Maidenhead: Open University Press.

Williams, P and Evans, M (2013) *Social Work with People with Learning Difficulties*, 3rd edition. London: Learning Matters.

Operate effectively within own organisational frameworks and contribute to the development of services and organisations

We have seen that social workers in organisations must work within multiple contexts, each with their own particular demands and pressures, and that they must also work to multiple and changing agendas. It is therefore quite a challenge to keep up to date and to be able to work effectively.

Activity 8.2

Lisa is newly qualified social worker. She is keen to get a job working with adults with learning disabilities and spots the following advertisement.

North Wieldshire Adult Learning Disabilities Service

Who are we?

We are an integrated team consisting of social workers, community nurses, community team assistants, carer's development worker and administrative

(Continued)

(Continued)

staff. All of our services are supported by friendly, professional and knowledgeable staff who are motivated to support and care for adults with learning disabilities.

What do we do?

We provide a specialist service to adults who are 18 years old and over, have a formal learning disabilities diagnosis and who live in North Wieldshire. The team can offer support and advice with specialist health care need.

Your role

- You will manage a small caseload and have the ability to effectively prioritise work in relation to risk and deadlines.
- You will carry out assessments and implement and review person-centred support plans for adults with a learning disability.
- You will also need to have a good working knowledge of adults with a learning disability and safeguarding adults at risk experience.

Lisa applies and is offered an interview. From advice given to her from her university tutor she believes that she will be asked the following questions.

1. Tell us about the current context in which work with adults with learning disabilities takes place? Can you tell us what you believe are the current issues relating to working with adults with a learning disability?

2. What do you think you need to work effectively in this team?

3. How do you think you would contribute to the development of the service?

Task

How would you advise Lisa to answer these questions satisfactorily?

Commentary

As has been explained, contexts change so to be too specific at the time of writing risks out-of-date comments. That said, in answer to the first question it would be useful to have a sense of the recent as well as the current policy landscape. For example, moving people with learning disabilities out of large institutions has been a policy goal since before the NHS and

Community Care Act 1990 was implemented in 1993. This policy and practice goal has been given impetus by the 'personalisation' agenda which promoted the use of personal budgets (Williams and Evans, 2013) and the Care Act 2014. The fact that this policy had not been fully achieved was highlighted by the Bubb Report (2014) which investigated the abuse filmed by the BBC *Panorama* programme at the Winterbourne View care home.

Legislation and policy encourages the involvement of carers in deciding support plans. In this area of social work applicants would do well to be aware of the *Valuing People* initiative and its updates (DH, 2001, 2008, 2010). They all point towards a more person-centred approach based upon human rights, inclusion and a social model of disability, indicating that social workers need to work not only in partnership with service users but also with other agencies such as health, housing and employment organisations. Legislation such as the Mental Capacity Act 2005 and Care Act 2014 allows for the use of advocacy to ensure that the person's voice is heard and rights protected. Social workers must therefore also work effectively with and alongside advocates.

Unfortunately, the economic context is such that resources cannot match the demand for support for people with learning disabilities whatever their level of need (Guardian, 2015a, 2015b).

For perhaps more complex reasons, reports indicate that equality of access and the uptake of services for black and minority ethnic people with learning disabilities is not being achieved (Foundation for People with Learning Disabilities, 2012). So a realistic answer to the first question would to talk about the more personalised, inclusive and rights-based approach embedded in recent legislation and policy but acknowledge that challenges still remain in achieving this because of economic and other factors. Social workers need to be aware of the emotional stresses on them and others that are associated with working within constrained resources and manage this appropriately using supervision and other methods (see Chapter 1).

In answer to questions 2 and 3, to work effectively in that environment and contribute to the development of the service, you would need to have a clear understanding of your own role as well as that of other workers in the team. You would need to be a good communicator and a good team worker, and to be able to work to the shared values set out by your own professional body and embedded in policy on learning disability. You should not only be committed to your own professional development but also that of the team. You can do this by joint working, actively participating in team meetings, group supervision and study groups as well as organising and participating in team training. There would be many relevant topics for training for this team, including safeguarding, mental capacity and working with carers/relatives. Lastly, a service such as the one in the advertisement would require good links with a range of local organisations. Therefore outreach and networking skills are also vital. For good coverage of a range of skills relevant to working in a statutory social work organisation see Hill (2010).

Operating effectively within multi-agency and inter-professional partnerships and settings

We now extend the discussion to look beyond working within our organisation to working effectively with other agencies, organisations and professionals. As always, we need to think about the meaning of key terms and concepts. In their curriculum guide written for the College of Social Work, Thomas and Baron (2012: 1) explain that:

> It is important to distinguish between 'inter' as in inter-professional and inter-agency and 'multi' as in multi-professional or multi-agency. Multi tends to be used when a range of services are provided by professionals from different agencies and, although they may communicate and share information with each other in the support of service users and their families, they may not necessarily work actively together at a strategic level to plan and deliver integrated services (despite the crucial importance of this). The terms inter-professional and inter-agency imply that some active thinking and planning has taken place, not only about what services are needed, but also about how the services and professionals can work effectively together (often referred to as co-configuration), including working with service users and carers.

Activity 8.3: Terminology

Make sure that you are clear about the similarities and distinctions made between the ways in which the prefixes 'inter' and multi' are used in this context. Provide examples of each to demonstrate your understanding of how they differ.

Commentary

There are many terms used to describe the situation when more than one party works to provide services for people in need. The Domain descriptor refers to 'multi-agency and inter-professional partnerships and settings', so the least we should be able to do is to understand the similarities and differences between 'multi-agency' and 'inter-professional'. As Thomas and Baron (2012) indicate the basic similarity is that both refer to situations where a 'range of services are provided by professionals from different agencies'. However, they highlight that 'interprofessional and inter-agency imply that some active thinking and planning has taken place'. This suggests that when 'inter' is used as a prefix it means that rather than just operating alongside each other and coming together over specific cases, services have been more actively strategically coordinated and organised. So, for example, when social care, the local NHS, the Department of Work and Pensions and possibly a credit union or food bank work together to help a family struggling with poverty, mental health and safeguarding issues, this would most appropriately be an example of multi-agency working. They are working together communicating and exchanging information but not necessarily working to a laid down partnership agreement. There might even be some fundamental differences in perspective on what should happen with certain agencies at odds with each other.

Inter-professional partnerships can be illustrated by the work of entities like a local Health and Wellbeing Board which formally brings together leaders from local organisations that have a strong influence on health and well-being, including the commissioning of health, social care and public health services. Its focus is on planning the right services for and securing the best possible health and well-being outcomes for all those resident in a specific locality. It is a fine distinction and one that sometimes can be blurred anyway (see, for example, the function of Multi-Agency Safeguarding Hubs (MASH) (Home Office, 2014). However, language is always important and, at the very least, it should make you think about the different ways that agencies and professionals can work together and to be clear what is meant when certain phrases are used. That said, if we are sometimes confused think about how much more confusing it is for service users. Quinney and Hafford-Letchfield (2012, p. 5) provide a fuller discussion of terminological issues in this area.

Activity 8.4: Multi-agency and inter-professional working – why do it?

Task

With a partner or in a small group, think about and be prepared to feedback on:

1. The reasons why social workers both operate in multi-agency settings and participate in inter-professional partnerships?

2. What do you think are the advantages to the service user and what, if any, are the disadvantages of such practices?

Commentary

Two reasons we might suggest to begin with are to do with the nature of professional social work itself. Firstly, it is a major part of social work's professional vision to work holistically with people in their social context. Secondly, the nature of the problems and issues faced by service users is often multi-dimensional and complex. So, if you are committed to working holistically with people who often have complex problems, while understanding them in their individual, family, social and economic context, this will need all the relevant aspects of their situation to be taken into account. This might include their education or employment, their finances, their health, their housing, their sexuality and their faith. Consequently, working holistically with people with complex problems inevitably means working with other agencies and service providers. The more complex the issue the less likely that a single agency could meet all of someone's needs.

You might have suggested other reasons. For example, service users often expect that public services 'join up' and speak to each other. They don't necessarily want to have to present themselves to a range of different agencies (assuming they even know of their existence) and have to repeat their stories multiple times only to be shunted off somewhere else. It is time-consuming and frustrating. There are important exceptions to this view where, for example, abusive parents deliberately give different versions of events to different professionals to hide the reality of what is really going on. And situations like these, of course, provide a compelling reason why agencies should work closely together as has been recognised in policy.

Finally, on the subject of policy, there is an accumulated weight of policy guidance that directs social workers to work together collaboratively with other agencies and other professionals to provide services that are 'person-centred'. Policy on all major social work agendas, be it safeguarding children or adults, the personalisation agenda, the Care Act 2014, domestic abuse, mental health, hospital discharges and end-of-life care all advocate that services be person-centred and that agencies work in partnership to both safeguard and promote the health and well-being of individuals and families (see Morris, 2008). Therefore there is a range of reasons why social workers need to know how to operate effectively in multi-agency and inter-professional contexts. These include professional reasons, responding to the expectations of service users and adhering to policy guidance. Some would propose that, over and above the reasons discussed here, it is more financially efficient as it enables 'synergy' and cuts down on the duplication of effort (Meads and Ashcroft, 2005). Services that are well coordinated and 'joined up' in terms of both planning and execution *should* be to the advantage of service users.

You might have considered that, despite the obvious advantages, there are also potential disadvantages to multi and inter-agency working. For one, it can be time-consuming and working together has not always been shown to be effective in producing better outcomes (Quinney and Hafford-Letchfield, 2012). Also, while service users do not necessarily want to experience services that are uncoordinated, they do not necessarily like the idea of their personal information being shared around a range of organisations and judgments being made about them – especially when not involved.

Activity 8.5: Operating effectively within multi-agency and inter-professional contexts

Joel is a newly qualified social worker who has just joined a children and families safeguarding team (the same team in which he undertook his final-year placement). As part of the terms of his Assessed Year in Employment (ASYE), Joel is required to attend a CPD module at his local university which focuses on making the transition from student to social worker. His first assignment requires him to undertake the following task:

ASYE Assignment 1

1. Use a spider diagram to map all the agencies and organisations with whom your team ordinarily works. Put those that you work with most closely near the centre of the diagram and those worked with least closely further out.
2. Identify as many different ways as you can in which you can develop your working relationships with the various agencies and organisations identified on your map in order to make them more effective.
3. Reflect on the first two activities. What are the challenges that need to be overcome?

Imagine you were in Joel's position. What do you think would be reasonable answers for each of the three assignments?

Commentary

With regard to assignment 1, given that it is a children and families safeguarding team one would expect that professionals and agencies such as nurseries and schools, education welfare officers, school nurses, health visitors, GPs, mental health workers, domestic violence workers, advocates, the police and, probably, housing would be located close to the centre. Possibly also identified but located further out from the centre might be educational psychologists, welfare rights advisors, Sure Start, fostering agencies, women's refuges, paediatric services, the Probation service, the Department of Work and Pensions, speech and language therapists and a range of local voluntary and community organisations that might provide different types of support. This is not an exhaustive list but includes most of the main players.

The number and diversity of potential involvements reflects the wide range of issues that need to be tackled in such teams. These include potential problems around child development, education, physical and mental health, finances, housing and protection from harm. The more diverse the community within which a social worker operates, the greater the number of community organisations there are to find out about and with whom to engage. The challenges of working effectively with such diversity of agencies and professionals are therefore not inconsiderable.

With regard to assignment 2, a useful approach to developing good working relationships generally is to be clear and confident about your own role, to be a good communicator, to have good networking skills and to display a healthy curiosity about and respect for the roles played by others. Jumping to conclusions about, say, the way police or GPs work or thinking that you know what others do when you actually do not acts as a barrier to effective multi-agency working.

There are activities that you can do to build relationships, fill in gaps in knowledge and build networks of expertise (Morris, 2008; Quinney and Hafford-Letchfield, 2012). These might commonly include the following.

Networking

Networking is as much a state of mind as it is undertaking certain activities and can take many forms (Hughes and Wearing, 2013). Essentially, it is about identifying and seizing opportunities to engage with and build rapport with other people with shared interests. It can take place either through specifically planned events such as conferences, training or coffee mornings and open days or more informally by spending time before and after meetings getting to know other workers and professionals. More generally, networking is a valuable way of learning about and engaging with the communities in which you work.

Attending case conferences/meetings

The focus of these meetings is to share knowledge and make decisions about a particular case. They are a critical meeting point between different workers, professionals and service users. Before participating in such meetings it is recommended that you attend a few as an observer. This is a good way of finding out more about the role of others and how communication works between the different agencies and professionals. It is interesting to observe group dynamics and think about issues of power, especially when service users are involved. When it is your actual case always make sure that you are fully prepared in advance in order to project the appropriate level of professionalism and to do the best for the service user involved.

Attending liaison meetings

Liaison meetings differ from case meetings in that they do not focus on just one case. They are usually held at regular intervals such as bi-monthly and are a coming together of professionals from a local area whose work overlaps. While cases in common might be discussed, liaison meetings are used to flag up and improve any issues that affect the effectiveness of inter-professional working such as communication sharing between agencies. They take time and effort to start and keep going but are definitely a worthwhile contribution to effective multi-agency working. If liaison meetings do not exist and you feel there is a need for them, consider setting one up yourself.

Participating in multi-disciplinary supervision

Multi-disciplinary supervision can be issue-based but tends to be more case-focused. It is based on the desire to develop critical reflection, evidence-informed practice and inter-professional learning. Usually a particular case is selected for critical discussion and participants share their perspectives. Multi-disciplinary supervision sessions take time and preparation and are not always easy to organise for logistical reasons. They more commonly take place in settings where professionals already work together in an integrated team environment such as mental health teams either in the community or located in a hospital.

Organising and participating in joint training and attending multi-disciplinary conferences

It has been recognised in many areas of practice – safeguarding is a good example – that there are benefits from organising training events that are multi-agency and inter-professional. This means that they not only might have teaching input from different professionals and disciplines but also that attendees come from different occupational and professional backgrounds. If organised properly (for example, by creating an interactive teaching environment) this can help break down barriers, facilitate networking and broaden people's perspectives, enhancing the chances of improved collaborative working once the training is over. Joint training can take place in-house or in different educational establishments. Increasingly such training involves service users in both the design and delivery of courses. Look out for multi-agency conferences organised by organisations such as Community Care (http://www.communitycare.co.uk/live/) and be prepared to put your networking skills to the test.

Joint visits

Joint visits are a very obvious sign of collaborative working. Joint visits have many advantages for both professionals and service users alike. They bring two sources of knowledge and skillsets to a situation, they can avoid service users having to tell their story twice to two separate professionals and they can enable a better informed assessment as both workers would have been present together. On the more negative side, joint visiting ties up two professionals' time and service users can also feel overwhelmed and inhibited when visited by two workers. Therefore making joint visits effective requires that they are based on a shared philosophy of care, are well-planned and, as far as possible, have the consent of the service user.

Work shadowing

Work shadowing tends to be associated with new and inexperienced workers following a more experienced worker in order to learn the job. While this is a major reason for work shadowing it need not just be regarded as an activity for new workers. It is an excellent way to learn about other job roles and organisational cultures and how other agencies operate generally. Services that are committed to multi-agency and inter-professional working should be open to different workers learning about each other's roles and challenges in this way. It is a good way of breaking down barriers between occupational groups and helps with networking.

Finally, with regard to assignment 3, there are several potential challenges to developing multi-agency and inter-professional working. We have already alluded to some of these. Obviously, finding the time to disengage from front-line activities is always challenging. Another challenge is dealing with professional 'tribalism' or stereotyping. That is to say, if you undertake any collaborative activity with your mind full of negative stereotypes about other workers, for example believing that all nurses are interested in is giving people injections and that all nursery workers are pleasant but incapable of critical thought, then you will probably find ways of having these views reinforced. The same applies to negative stereotypes you might have about GPs, the police and so on. Suspicion breeds suspicion. The key to operating effectively within multi-agency and inter-professional contexts is about seeing the value that working with others can bring rather than seeing them as threats or as 'part of the problem'. Be aware that other professions are more than capable of pigeon holing social workers negatively. Part of the professional challenge of social work is to counteract this kind of attitude.

We have identified a variety of ways of working collaboratively and learning from others in a social work setting. Some are more formal than others but all are useful if undertaken with a critical but open frame of mind. It is worth noting that the domain descriptor refers to the contribution played by carers, volunteers and foster carers and it is important to be inclusive rather than exclusive when it comes to learning about and from the perspective of others involved in social work.

Summary

- The organisational context of social work is affected by multiple agendas and contexts.
- Contemporary social work mainly takes place in specialist teams working within a multi-agency context where many of the agencies involved increasingly operate in the independent sector.
- Multi-agency and inter-professional partnership working can take many different forms in different settings.
- To be effective in any of these settings, social workers need to be good communicators and networkers.
- There are many ways of contributing towards the effective operation of multi-agency and inter-professional partnership working. These include developing networks of expertise and common interests, joint working and participating in multi-disciplinary supervision and study groups as well as participating in inter-professional education and multi-agency training.

Further reading

Cameron, A, Lart, R, Bostock, L and Coomber, C (2012) *Factors that Promote and Hinder Joint and Integrated Working Between Health and Social Care Services*, Research Briefing 41. London: SCIE.

Gov.uk (2014) online at https://www.gov.uk/government/news/working-together-to-safeguard-children-multi-agency-safeguarding-hubs.

Healy, K (2005) *Social Work Theories in Context*. Basingstoke: Palgrave.

Hill, A (2010) *Working in Statutory Contexts*. Cambridge: Polity Press.

HM Government (2015) *Working Together to Safeguard Children: A Guide to Inter-agency Working to Safeguard and Promote the Welfare of Children*. London: TSO.

Hughes, M and Wearing, M (2013) *Organisations and Management in Social Work*, 2nd edition. London: Sage.

Littlechild, B and Smith, R (eds) (2012) *A Handbook for Interprofessional Practice in the Human Services: Learning to Work Together*. Harlow: Pearson.

Meads, G and Ashcroft, J (2005) *The Case for Interprofessional Collaboration in Health and Social Care*. Oxford: Blackwell.

Morris, K (2008) *Social Work and Multi-agency Working: Making a Difference*. Bristol: Policy Press.

Nevo, I and Slonim-Nevo, V (2011) 'The myth of evidence-based practice: towards evidence-informed practice', *British Journal of Social Work*, 41 (6), pp. 1176–97.

Pollard, K, Thomas, J and Miers, M (2010) *Understanding Interprofessional Working in Health and Social Care Theory and Practice*. Basingstoke: Palgrave Macmillan.

Quinney, A and Hafford-Letchfield, T (2012) *Interprofessional Social Work*. London: Learning Matters.

Thomas, J and Baron, S (2012) *Curriculum Guide – Interprofessional and Inter-agency Collaboration*. London: College of Social Work.

Weinstein, J, Whittington, C and Leiba, C (eds) (2003) *Collaboration in Social Work Practice*. London: Jessica Kingsley.

9: Professional leadership

Achieving a Social Work Degree

This chapter will help you develop skills in the following domain of the Professional Capabilities Framework:

> **Professional leadership:** *Take responsibility for the professional learning and development of others through supervision, mentoring, assessing, research, teaching, leadership and management*

Currently, the Professional Capability Framework (BASW, 2015) states about this domain that:

> *The social work profession evolves through the contribution of its members in activities such as practice research, supervision, assessment of practice, teaching and management. An individual's contribution will gain influence when undertaken as part of a learning, practice-focused organisation. Learning may be facilitated with a wide range of people including social work colleagues, service users and carers, volunteers, foster carers and other professionals. (BASW, Professional Capability Framework – Readiness for Practice Capabilities)*

The domain statement goes on to say that, at the point of going out on their first practice placement, social work students need to be able to:

- Demonstrate awareness of the importance of professional leadership in social work

Introduction

Domain 9 can often, on an initial look, seem to be beyond the capabilities of social work students, especially at the beginning of their course. However, on closer examination, once the key concept of 'professional leadership' is unpacked and broken down into its different skills, it becomes eminently achievable at whatever level of social work practice it takes place. Therefore the first part of the chapter aims to explain and demystify 'leadership' in general. It breaks it down into its constituent parts. We then move on to discuss what professional leadership consists of and, specifically, what it might look like from the perspective of a social work student in terms of activities that can be undertaken and what knowledge and skills demonstrated.

As signalled in the domain descriptor, an important part of professional leadership in social work is taking 'responsibility for the professional learning a development of others'. In the second part of the chapter we focus on relevant activities that social workers and social work students can undertake to meet this goal. These are specifically: practice research, supervision (especially peer supervision) and assessment of practice. Both sections include activities to help develop your learning and conclude with a summary of key points and suggestions for further reading.

Professional leadership

As a student of social work you might well think that professional leadership is not your concern at the moment and that matters of leadership are really best left to more experienced workers or managers. However, while it is true that social work managers and experienced qualified social workers need to demonstrate professional leadership, everyone involved in professional social work needs to engage with the concept of what leadership means and embrace it fully. It is the only way that the *profession* of social work will continue to develop. To be able to take the lead in certain key areas is therefore a professional requirement which applies as much to social work students as it does to directors of social services. We will look at what these areas are as the chapter continues but before we discuss in more detail what professional leadership means in the context of social work, it will be useful to reflect more deeply about what we understand by the concept of leadership more generally.

Activity 9.1: Thoughts about leadership – what is it and what does it involve?

Task 1

Think about times in your life when you were a leader in some shape or form. What did you do and what did it involve?

(Continued)

(Continued)

Task 2

Using the task above as a starting point, share your thoughts with a colleague and jot down your ideas about the following questions:

- What is 'leadership'?
- What do leaders do?
- What are the qualities of an effective leader?
- Where do you think leadership figures in social work?

Commentary

Hopefully, everyone could think of some examples where they were a leader, whether it be in situations within the family, with friends, on holiday or at work. However, some of you might have thought you are not and never have been and never will be a leader. You might think that, for whatever reason, you are one of life's followers. That suggests a view of leadership that assumes that leaders are only born not made and that, whatever leadership is, it comes from within and that we do not all necessarily have it in us. However, in case you become too pessimistic about achieving this domain, you need to know that that is just one view of leadership. What leadership is exactly is a contested concept and can be interpreted in many ways. The important thing to grasp is that effective leadership does not depend on the possession of personal charisma or other heroic qualities (Grint, 2005).

Dictionary definitions seldom do justice to the diverse ideas about what leadership involves. For example, the Oxford Dictionary defines leadership as:

> *The action of leading a group of people or an organization, or the ability to do this.*
> (*en.oxforddictionaries.com/definition/leadership*)

What do leaders do?

This doesn't take us a great deal further and it really rests on what you understand by 'leading'. It is worth pointing out at this stage that, despite some overlaps, being a leader is not the same as being a manager. Not all leaders are managers and the fact is that not all managers are leaders. So, turning to what you might have said in response to the question about what leaders do, there are many activities or roles you could have identified. For example, at different times, leaders use initiative, they show moral courage, they create a vision for themselves and for others of what needs to be done, they organise, they help produce change where it is needed, they take control of situations, they demonstrate creativity and generate ideas, they educate, they suggest improvements and they make sure that things get done. At times leaders impose their will on others but if that is all they did then that would be dictatorship rather than leadership. An important aspect of leadership involves carrying people along with you. This means that effective leaders are generally respectful, inclusive and considerate of the needs of those they seek to lead. This brings us on to the question about the qualities of a leader.

Leadership qualities

As suggested earlier, you might have said that leaders need to have personal 'charisma' that sets them apart from those around them and it is certainly true that some leaders do possess this quality. However, we have all found ourselves in groups or in situations where the leader (it could have been us) might not have necessarily been hugely charismatic but, nevertheless, possessed other qualities that helped them lead effectively. Good leadership qualities include being able to use one's initiative, being analytical, being thoughtful, being able to establish appropriate goals and creating a vision of how to achieve them, being a good communicator, being considerate of and attentive to the needs of others and being comfortable with responsibility. This list of attributes is not exhaustive nor is it essential that effective leaders display all of these qualities all of the time, but it serves to illustrate that there need not be any great mystique about leadership. The role when practised effectively rests on embracing certain values such as the need to lead on the basis of inclusion, respect and consent. It can be broken down into its constituent parts and learned. Consequently, most of us can lead in certain circumstances. And this brings us onto the final question which asks about the role of leadership in social work.

Leadership in social work

Professional leadership in social work is not just the preserve of managers. Since the recommendations of the Social Work Reform Board were accepted, all qualified social workers (and social work students) are now expected to demonstrate professional leadership (*Community Care*, 2011). However, many students and qualified social workers struggle with what this means. Interestingly, there are very few social work texts that include 'leadership' in their index and fewer still that focus on this as a topic in its own right. This can make finding suitable examples difficult. However, emerging insights into what form professional leadership should take can be found in several recent policy statements on social work. For example, in addition to the Professional Capabilities Framework, social workers now need to practise in accordance with the different 'Knowledge and Skills Statements' that have been published in recent years (Department for Education 2014; Department of Health, 2015). For example, the *Knowledge and Skills Statement for Social Workers in Adult Services* (Department of Health, 2015) includes the following statement, under the heading of 'Professional ethics and leadership':

Social workers should be able to explain their role to stakeholders, particularly health and community partners, and challenge partners constructively to effect multi-agency working. They should contribute to developing awareness of personalisation and outcome-based approaches to improving people's lives. Social workers should be able to demonstrate the principles of social work through professional judgement, decision-making and actions within a framework of professional accountability. They should be able to work collaboratively to manage effectively the sometimes competing interests of service users, their families and their carers ensuring that the needs of all parties are appropriately balanced, but that where children are involved, the children's interests are always paramount. They should be able to acknowledge the inherent tensions where there is a dual role of care and control, they should be able to meet eligible needs within limited resources and they should be able to manage the emotions and expectations of service users and carers. They should be able to identify potential deprivations of liberty and understand the process for assessing and authorising these in individuals' best interests. They should feedback the views and experiences of clients and their colleagues to contribute to the continued improvement of services, policies and procedures within the organisation. They must be able to recognise and address poor practice and systemic failings which put people at risk, whether in their own organisation or the organisations and institutions with which they are working, making appropriate use of whistle-blowing procedures. (Department of Health, 2015, para. 10)

Activity 9.2: Translating leadership into practice

- Make sure that you read the paragraph above quoting from the Knowledge and Skills Statement carefully.
- Think about what it is asking practitioners to do and paraphrase it for yourself so that you understand it.
- Does it require you to be a manager, possess great personal charisma or have many years of experience?

Commentary

Among other things, the Knowledge and Skills Statement sees leadership in terms of explaining their role to others, demonstrating the principles of social work through professional judgement, working towards improved multi-agency working working collaboratively, recognising problems, acknowledging tensions and conflicts, and being able to recognise and address poor practice. It mentions other things as well, but everything specified should be well within the capabilities of a professional social worker working at any level in the context of adult social work. While one would naturally expect one's leadership to improve with time, especially as one's confidence grows, it definitely does not require having years of experience, being in a managerial role or possessing 'special' charismatic leadership qualities.

Taking responsibility for the professional learning and development of others

Although aimed at qualified social workers, the leadership tasks mentioned in the Knowledge and Skills Statement should be something social work students could also aspire to and demonstrate when they have the opportunity. If we focus on what social work students should be able to demonstrate at the point of entering practice, the domain descriptor outlines the requirement that you need to take 'responsibility for the professional learning and development of others'. This might appear daunting but the activity below will help you think about ways in which this can be done.

Activity 9.3

Sarah-Jane is a student doing her first placement at the Dunsford Young People's Project. This is a service run by a local housing association which provides support and accommodation to young people aged 16–21 who are either homeless or at risk of homelessness and who need support to achieve independent living. There are currently four male and three female residents who have diverse histories and backgrounds. The male residents comprise two Afghan asylum-seekers, Abdul aged 19 and Karim 18. They have very little English and are often out of the hostel most of the day with no one really knowing where they go. John (aged 20) has various mental health problems and a history of school exclusion. He is unemployed. He has recently been caught sniffing glue and has been given a caution. He spends most of the day sitting alone in the 'communal' room watching TV. Aaron (17) has a background of sexual abuse by his stepfather and a history of self-harm. He is enrolled at the local FE college but rarely attends. He spends most of his time alone in his room. The female residents comprise Gulnaz, a Kurdish woman of 19 who has fled honour-based violence; Keeley (18) who fled the family home after being raped by a relative and has recently had an abortion; and Samira, another 18-year-old who suffers from severe anxiety. She also has trichotillomania, a kind of compulsive hair pulling disorder. As with the other female residents she spends most of the time in her room. When the residents come into contact with each other (which is not very often) they hardly communicate. To Sarah-Jane the Project seems to be just a temporary 'bolt-hole' for the young people residing there. The atmosphere lacks warmth and homeliness. It seems that despite efforts from some of the staff the residents are all drifting rather aimlessly.

None of the staff, including the manager, have any specific social work qualifications. The manager has told her that, because of their various needs and

(Continued)

(Continued)

the lack of resources, it feels as though the Project has just become a 'holding pen' for the youngsters. It becomes clear to Sarah-Jane that the staff group are not only not dealing very well with the needs of the residents but also with their own frustrations. Staff morale seems to be low. Attendance at meetings is poor. More and more the young people are being left to their own devices, which is not helping meet the aims of the Project. This is reflected in the individual support plans which have very little of use contained in them and are seldom up to date.

When she meets with her Practice Educator, Sarah-Jane shares her own frustrations. She feels there is so much more that could be done. She really wants to put the theories and ideas she has learned at university into practice. She is also aware that she needs evidence to cover all the domains of the PCF but is not sure where this is going to come from. The Practitioner Educator assures Sarah-Jane that the opportunities are definitely there for her but that she needs to use her initiative and be creative.

Task

- What are your thoughts and feelings about Sarah-Jane's situation?
- What, if anything, do you think she could do not only to improve her own situation but also that of the residents and the staff?
- Reflect on your answers to questions one and two and how they might relate to the need to demonstrate professional leadership and taking responsibility for the professional learning and development of others.

Commentary

Hopefully, your response to Sarah-Jane's situation was not just one of despair and resignation in the belief that she is, after all, 'just' a student' and therefore is not a position to do anything. In social work we can often find ourselves in what look like unpromising situations. However, by taking responsibility, by using creativity and initiative as her Practice Educator suggests, things can, more often than not, be turned round. If Sarah-Jane simply shrugged and accepted the situation passively then things would almost certainly not improve for any one. Her needs would not be met and, perhaps more importantly, the needs of the service users would not be met either. The fact that she is 'just' a student should not stop Sarah-Jane from taking responsibility for making things better.

What Sarah-Jane might do

The more appropriate approach for Sarah-Jane to take would be to identify the issues in the hostel that would actually benefit from improvement and work from there rather than try to start from her need to cover the domains. For example, an obvious issue is that of improving the overall ambience of the Project, making it more homely and improving the level of social interaction among the residents and staff. With these goals in mind, it would be an idea to try to involve the residents in some form of common activity to help bring them and the staff together. In terms of skills it would involve communicating and relationship building with the residents about their interests, backgrounds and strengths and not just focusing on their 'problems' (see Chapter 7). It would also involve joint planning and undertaking research into what would work best to achieve this goal. One idea worth trying could be preparing a meal. It might be interesting to base it around an Afghan or Kurdish recipe which would help educate others about the cultural heritage of those particular residents and give Abdul and Karim a sense of being included and valued. This activity could help demonstrate social work values around inclusion and diversity (see previous chapters). Therefore we can see that taking the lead on one task could not only improve the quality of life of both residents and staff but can also evidence different domains of the Professional Capabilities Framework.

If Sarah-Jane wanted to assist the staff to meet the needs of individuals better she could speak to them about what knowledge and skills they feel they needed to develop. Given the diverse backgrounds of the residents this would probably generate several topics, ranging from the needs of asylum seekers, honour-based violence and different aspects of mental illness to self-harm and trichotillomania. Depending upon what the priorities were considered to be, Sarah-Jane could do some research to find possible guest speakers or other resources that could form the basis of a staff training event. By taking the lead on such an activity, Sarah-Jane would be contributing directly to the professional learning and development of others. This should have a beneficial effect on the residents concerned as their particular situations would be better understood.

If Sarah-Jane wanted to focus more directly on the residents as individuals she could devise a questionnaire about what they liked and disliked about the project, what they would like to change, what would improve their lives and so on. She could either leave them to complete it on their own or she could make appointments to see them face to face. Whatever method was used, it would provide valuable insights into what needed to be done to make things better.

Putting professional leadership into practice

As regards the third question, the important point to note is that Sarah-Jane does not need to be an expert on any of the areas identified by staff or residents. However, by using her initiative and communicating with the staff she can nevertheless help improve their knowledge and skills in areas that need development. The same applies to attempting to reach out to the residents and seek their views. Essentially, the professional leadership challenge is about not settling for situations that are less than satisfactory but thinking creatively about what can be done and creating opportunities to learn and to change things for the better. They might not all work out exactly as planned but as long no one is made worse off in the attempt then there is no reason why such strategies cannot be used.

Conclusion

The domain descriptor states that, at the point of going out on their first practice placement, social work students need to be able to 'demonstrate awareness of the importance of professional leadership in social work'. In this section, we have set out to demystify 'leadership' and show that we are all capable of being leaders in certain situations. We have also discussed why demonstrating professional leadership is important. In Activity 9.3 we have seen how, even in what can appear the most unpromising of situations, social work students can still demonstrate professional leadership and take responsibility for the learning of others. A summary of key points follows together with suggestions for further reading. Professional learning is an important theme of this domain and in the next section we explore different learning activities in more depth.

Summary

- Everyone involved in professional social work at all levels needs to engage with the concept of what leadership means and practise accordingly.
- Professional leadership does not require having years of experience, being in a managerial role or possessing charismatic leadership qualities.
- Professional leadership can involve a range of activities including: using initiative, showing moral courage, creating a vision of what needs to be done and helping to get it done, organising, producing change, taking control of situations, demonstrating creativity and generating ideas, and taking responsibility for the learning of others.

Further reading

Community Care (2011) 'Developing leadership among all practitioners', online at http://www.communitycare.co.uk/2011/09/22/developing-leadership-among-all-practitioners/.

Davies, K and Jones, R (eds) (2016) *Skills for Social Work Practice*. Basingstoke: Palgrave.

Department for Education (2014) *Knowledge and Skills Statement for Approved Child and Family Practitioners*. London: Department for Education.

Department for Education (2015) *Knowledge and Skills Statement for Approved Child and Family Practitioners*. London: Department for Education.

Department of Health (2015) *Knowledge and Skills Statement for Social Workers in Adult Services*. London: Department of Health.

Grint, K (2005) *Leadership: Limits and Possibilities*. Basingstoke: Palgrave.

Holroyd, J and Brown, K (2016) 'Self-leadership', R Field and K Brown (eds), *Effective Leadership, Management and Supervision in Health and Social Care*, 2nd edition. London: Sage, pp. 25–41.

Lawler, J (2007) 'Leadership in social work: a case of caveat emptor?', *British Journal of Social Work*, 37 (1), pp. 123–41.

McKitterick, B (2015) *Self-Leadership in Social Work: Reflections from Practice*. Bristol: Policy Press.

McLaughlin, H (2012) *Understanding Social Work Research*, 2nd edition. London: Sage.

Parker, J and Doel, M (eds) (2013) *Professional Social Work*. London: Learning Matters.

Professional learning activities

There is a range of learning activities highlighted in the domain descriptor: practice research, supervision, assessment of practice, teaching and management. In this section we are going to focus in more depth on those specific activities that are most likely to be undertaken by social work students. Following a discussion of each activity you will be invited to think about how you might apply them to your own practice.

According to Uggerhøj (2011), p. 50:

> *The basic foundation of practice research is building theory from practice (not only from academia). The approach is based on a combination of research methodology, field research and practical experience.*

This captures well recent trends in social work research. Practice research links to two other types of research that have become popular in social work: *action research* and *participatory research* (Gomm, 2009; McLaughlin, 2012). Action research is based on the idea that you make what you believe to be a beneficial change (for example in practice) and then study its effects. Participatory (sometimes called participative) research aims to break down the traditional distinction between the researcher and the 'researched'. In participatory research the subjects of the research are treated as partners in devising, planning, designing and carrying out research projects. Taken all together these approaches to research in social work could be said to be more 'democratic' and more pragmatic or practice-focused than theoretical.

Alongside this, as we discussed in Chapter 6, there has been the emergence in social work of evidence-based (now more commonly referred to as 'evidence-informed') practice (Nevo and Slonim-Nevo, 2011). This has led to people from different professional backgrounds and service users collaborating on different research projects. Good examples of this happening on a national scale are 'Research in Practice' (RiP) which supports 'professionals from across children's services to embed evidence into their day-to-day practice' (https://www.rip.org.uk/) and

'Research in Practice for Adults' which 'brings together academic research, practice expertise and the experiences of people accessing services to enable professionals across the sector to make evidence-informed decisions about the design and delivery of adults' services' (https://www.ripfa. org.uk). It would be useful to see if your university or college has organisational membership of either of these organisations because, if so, it would not only provide a good source of evidence to assist your learning in many important areas of social work but would also give you a much better insight into various types of practice research studies.

However, there is nothing to stop any social worker undertaking their own primary research, whatever area they work in. You do not need to be part of a specific research organisation. However, in order for the findings that you produce to meet the required professional standards, any research would need to be carried out in accordance with accepted research methods and also within recognised ethical procedures. There is a range of different methods used to gather and analyse data in social work. As it is a requirement of the Professional Capabilities Framework to be research minded (see Chapters 5 and 6), most social work courses require students to undertake research in some form, usually in their final year. However, to find out about different types of research design, different research methods, ethical considerations and the specific skills required to conduct research properly, there are many good texts available that explain all these aspects of research. A selection of these is listed at the end of this section.

Activity 9.4

Firstly, read the article from Andrew Errington, a professional lead for social work at an NHS trust, published in *Community Care*.

How we're building a social work research culture that's rooted in practice

I don't have any research background whatsoever, especially as my social work training was via a diploma rather than a master's route. However, I have always been professionally curious, wanting to keep up-to-date with developments and best practice.

I was always the social worker who would be found reading his copy of *Community Care* and keeping copies of interesting articles. My role as Professional Head of Social Work at Staffordshire and Stoke-on-Trent Partnership NHS Trust has allowed me the opportunity to try and grow this curiosity among our social workers.

'Growing support for evidence-based practice'

You may well hear a lot of negative feedback about social work in NHS settings, but you can also find fantastic opportunities to harness some of the positive strengths in these settings. One thing I've really noticed is the well-established research cultures in the NHS and how this can directly benefit our profession.

I firmly believe we will start to see the growth of social work research in organisations the coming year. There is growing national support for evidence-based practice – for examples, just look at the annual report from Lyn Romeo, the chief social worker for adults, the College of Social Work's strategy; and the recent addition of the Social Care Elf site to disseminate research findings.

Finding out where to start

In my first year as professional lead, I wanted to develop a body of social work knowledge and evidence-based practice. I see this as key if we're to deliver against the standards for employers for social workers in England.

My first challenge was knowing where to start. I was fortunate that our trust already had a research strategy. The organisation wanted to become recognised as a research centre of excellence. This helped me to get strategic support and infrastructure. A little bit of self-directed learning and I found a SCIE knowledge review on 'Improving the use of research in social care practice'. It had examples of developing a whole systems approach to improve the use of research and had useful tips such as ensuring research is accessible and comprehensible.

Putting the building blocks in place

For me, another priority was ensuring that it is practice that starts to ask the questions about research by building the capability and capacity to get involved. So in Staffordshire we invited practitioners to join a workshop to consider how we should develop a culture of research in the trust. This shaped the development of an action plan that includes the following building blocks:

- Providing access to social work journals via the trust's library services and NHS Athens;
- Purchasing an online research resource providing regular updates on policy and best practice;

(Continued)

(Continued)

- Supporting a trust social worker to secure a research fellowship (the first social worker on an NHS Fellowship in the West Midlands);
- Securing funding via the national institute for health research for a part-time social work research facilitator;
- Providing evidence-based practice training;
- Re-establishing links with local higher education institutions as research partners and encouraging practitioners to support teaching programmes;
- Including the requirement for research and evidence-based practice in our workforce planning project for social work;
- Discussions with local partners about re-establishing a making research count regional network.

Being involved in research

We are now starting to participate in research and development activity. This includes supporting a project led by researchers at Birmingham University to facilitate better joint working between adult social workers and GPs. The aim is for this to make an impact for general practice-social work relationships in general and to develop training resources. It is timely work given a recent report on the benefits of GPs and social workers partnering up.

We are also working with Staffordshire County Council, one of five local authorities participating in research regarding models of safeguarding. This research by the social care workforce research unit is investigating the potential value of different models of adult safeguarding within local authorities' adult services departments. The research will provide guidance on implementation, outcomes and costs of different models of safeguarding practice.

Our trust has started our research journey and moved from research awareness and consciousness, to more participation and being active in social work research. Our profession needs to get back in touch with its evidence base. It is going to be crucial as we move into ever more integrated settings and start to see a diversifying range of social care provision. As social workers and social work employees we must recognise and support the need to promote and engage in research.

Source: *Community Care*, 11 February 2015, at http://www. communitycare.co.uk/2015/02/11/building-social-work-research-culture-thats-rooted-practice/

> **To think about**
>
> 1. What do you think are the strongpoints of the strategy that Andrew Errington took?
>
> 2. What are the advantages of the approach described in this scenario for the services concerned?
>
> 3. Are there any suggestions that you might make to add to the research evidence?

Commentary

Andrew Errington states that he is 'professionally curious' which is always a good starting point for any practice research. He is obviously happy to use his initiative and try things out. He is aware of his own limitations as a researcher so he first does his 'homework' by, for example, accessing relevant materials from SCIE. He also seeks out expert research assistance by, for example, re-establishing links with higher education institutions. Building up research partnerships among different professionals helps ensure a 'whole systems' approach. This ensures that as many relevant perspectives as possible are included in contributing towards and using the research. Importantly, Errington wants to develop a body of social work knowledge that is evidence-based, accessible and comprehensible.

The advantages for services are very much linked to the approach taken. The research aims to make an impact on real issues that have arisen from discussions between professionals about changes needed in practice. The research should then produce evidence that is directly relevant to the needs of the services. If the subsequent findings are not only relevant but also accessible and comprehensible, they have a much better chance of being adopted and embedded in practice.

Interestingly, Andrew Errington does not talk about capturing the experiences and perspectives of service users as part of his research strategy. This is very important in social work as we have seen in previous chapters. Therefore, the most obvious suggestion would be to ensure that the research undertaken in Staffordshire incorporates the perspectives of service users at all stages of the research process.

Further reading on research in social work

Engel, R and Schutt, R (2016) *The Practice of Research in Social Work*, 4th edition. Thousand Oaks, CA: Sage.

Hardwick, L and Worsley, A (2011) *Doing Social Work Research*. London: Sage.

McLaughlin, H (2012) *Understanding Social Work Research*, 2nd edition. London: Sage.

National Elf Service, online at https://www.nationalelfservice.net/social-care/.

Research in Practice, online at https://www.rip.org.uk/.

Research in Practice for Adults, online at https://www.ripfa.org.uk/.

Uggerhøj, L (2011) 'Theorizing practice research in social work', *Social Work and Social Sciences Review*, 15 (1), pp. 49–73.

Webber, N (2014) *Applying Research Evidence in Social Work Practice*. Basingstoke: Palgrave.

Whittaker, A (2012) *Research Skills for Social Work*, 2nd edition. London: Sage.

Supervision and assessment of practice

The domain descriptor indicates a variety of ways in which professional leadership can be evidenced. Without wanting to downplay the importance of either teaching or management during a social worker's professional career, at the pre-qualification stage of your professional development it is probably most appropriate to concentrate on supervision and assessment of practice as learning activities.

Supervision

The consideration of supervision actually brings us full circle. As we know, the focus of Domain 1 of the Professional Capabilities Framework is 'professionalism' including 'professional development'. In Chapter 1 we cited Laming (2003) who described supervision as 'the cornerstone of good social work practice'. Among other references McKitterick (2012) was recommended as useful reading in this particular topic. So, for one thing, it would be worth reacquainting yourself with what was said about supervision in that chapter and following up the references provided. In that earlier discussion it was made clear that both supervisor *and* supervisee need to take responsibility for making supervision an effective learning process. Therefore effective supervision involves critical reflection on what issues you think need to be discussed beforehand, preparing properly in terms of, for example, having up-to-date case records and other relevant information at hand, setting a relevant and meaningful agenda, being honest and respectful with each other, recording key points accurately and formulating realistic action plans. The other important point is that supervision needs to be regular with adequate time set aside.

The fact that you, as the supervisee, need to take, at least, equal responsibility with your supervisor for putting issues on the agenda means that supervision can demonstrate professional leadership in the development of others. In raising a particular issue or an area of learning for oneself you could well be flagging up a more general need for professional development on that issue or topic within the team – and also potentially for your supervisor. Lots of concepts in social work, for example 'mental capacity' or 'significant harm', are complex and open to different interpretations. Therefore, by sharing your own struggles to understand and put them into practice you are helping other professionals to reflect upon these issues in the search for clarity.

Social workers and social work students can demonstrate leadership in how to use supervision in other ways. One common way is through peer supervision. This is more than just the informal discussions that colleagues have about their cases on a day-to-day basis, although that is a useful way of developing practice wisdom. Peer supervision is a formal process whereby social workers and/or social work students meet, reflect upon and discuss particular cases (often complex or problematic ones) and share their different perspectives with a view to improving their practice by developing knowledge and skills.

Megele (2011b) states that 'peer supervision requires supervisees to be self-directed learners'. Therefore, it is not only a very rewarding learning activity for yourself and others, it provides a good demonstration of your ability to use initiative and of professional leadership generally. Nevertheless, to be effective peer supervision needs to be properly organised. This should be relatively straightforward to do as the following activity should demonstrate.

Activity 9.5: Peer supervision

Elsie is an MA Social Work doing her first placement in a large 'community hub' which serves people with learning disabilities. Also placed at the hub are two BA Social Work students from Elsie's university and another person who is doing a City & Guilds Level Four qualification 'Personalisation in Health and Social Care'. Elsie proposes to them that they should arrange to do some peer supervision sessions to help them develop their knowledge, values and skills and they all agree. Elsie's Practice Educator thinks this is a good idea as well and suggests to Elsie that it could provide evidence for Domain 9 in Elsie's practice portfolio.

Task

Imagine that you are Elsie. What do you think needs to be done in order that the sessions run smoothly, everyone learns and has a positive experience from participation?

Commentary

You need to make sure that everyone can participate as fully as possible. Therefore an important first step would be to agree how often and how long the sessions will be as well on what days and where they will take place. Without making them too formal, you also need to reach an agreement on how the sessions will be structured. If you try to make it up as you go along it almost certainly won't work and it will waste people's time. It is often the case that for each session a different person takes responsibility for choosing the topic or issue. Once you have an initial list of topics to get you going it is a good idea to let participants know in advance what they will be discussing as far as possible so that they have the opportunity to familiarise themselves with the case and prepare accordingly. The person choosing the topic needs to have a clear idea of what they want to get out of the session. Ideally, someone should keep minutes of key learning and action points. Needless to say the normal rules of supervision should be observed. For example, information shared in the session should remain confidential at all times and any notes should be kept securely. Megele (*ibid*), writing in *Community Care*, provides a thoughtful set of guidelines that should be of use. Her advice includes the following:

- **Regularity and attendance.** Peer supervision sessions should be regular and long enough to ensure everyone has a chance to participate. Appoint a facilitator for the group, either fixed or by rotation, who can take charge of the diary and alert members to any changes, as well as directing the sessions. Ideally, social workers should prioritise peer supervision sessions over competing commitments.

- **Structure.** Supervision sessions should be structured to prevent them from degenerating into gossip, chat or gripe. A clear framework or agenda will make it easier to enforce boundaries and uphold the quality of the supervision. This also allows for the use of structured supervision tools such as: analysis of both positive and challenging incidents, issues, dilemmas and experiences; structured questioning; and the sharing of practice and feedback.

- **Provide a safe and supportive environment.** Treat everyone in the group equally regardless of age, experience, knowledge and professional background. The effectiveness of peer supervision is directly related to the degree to which supervisees feel safe to share their experiences. Admitting incompetence is difficult in a competitive environment. Supervision sessions should be non-competitive, non-judgemental and supportive. Any existing power imbalances must be checked and promptly addressed.

- **Critical reflection.** It is important to achieve consistent high-quality supervision by sticking to the process, being candid and intuitive in your responses, balancing positive and negative feedback, avoiding lecturing and advice giving, and most of all remembering that the purpose of the group is to promote critical reflection. Supervisees should be given time to draw on their own reflective abilities.

- **Self-directedness.** Peer supervision requires supervisees to be self-directed learners, determining their own needs and choosing appropriate tools for their development. The space and the group should be dedicated to one supervisee and his or her needs at a time, without straying into other members' needs.

- **No 'post-mortems'.** After the end of each session, there should be no further discussion of the issue either in or out of the group. This is an essential ground rule that establishes clear boundaries and prevents supervision material from leaking into other places and processes.

Source: Claudia Megele 'How to . . . supervise your peers',
Community Care, 30 August 2011)

Arranging peer supervision is a useful exercise in its own right. However, it will also allow you to demonstrate professional leadership in several different ways. But, as we have seen, in order to get the most from it, it does repay time and thought in preparing for it properly. Also, there is nothing to stop you inviting Practice Educators if you feel it is appropriate.

Assessment of practice

All of the discussion of assessment so far in this book has focused on assessments undertaken by social workers in relation to the needs of and potential risks faced by service users and/or carers. However, students of social work will be only too aware that social work practice can also be the focus of assessment. On qualifying or post-qualifying courses this usually happens in a formal way in the context of undertaking assignments or meeting the requirements of the practice portfolio. This is called summative assessment because it comes at the end of the process of learning. However, you will probably have had formative assessments at some point in the learning process. These assessments do not count towards the final grade but are aimed at finding out how you are doing. They are called 'formative' because they provide the teacher with the opportunity to offer constructive feedback on the student's progress and the student with a sense of whether they are on the right track or not and what they need to work on. In the world of professional practice social workers can also give each other formative feedback as a way of developing learning. Assessment of practice used in this way would be more than the informal feedback colleagues might give each other after, say, a joint visit when one colleague might say 'you were great there mate' or 'you seemed a bit nervous in there today'. To make assessment of practice more beneficial it is a good idea for the person being assessed to be clear what it is they want feedback on and why. The following activity provides an example of how assessment of practice can be used. Your task is to think of more.

Activity 9.6: Assessment of practice

Ben is a Newly Qualified Social Worker (NQSW) who works in adult services. He has just completed a mandatory two-day course on the Mental Capacity

(Continued)

(Continued)

Act 2005. Ben is anxious that he remember everything so he asks Doreen, a more experienced colleague, to accompany him on his first Mental Capacity Assessment. He is particularly keen to know whether he has fully understood the five key principles (SCIE, online at http://www.scie.org.uk/mca/) and can put them into practice. So he asks Doreen specifically to have this in mind as she observes his practice.

Task

Can you think of other examples where social work colleagues could assess and give constructive feedback on each other's practice?

Commentary

Colleagues can assess each other's practice in many situations. It could be on visits of various types or it could be looking at chairing skills in meetings, giving feedback on presentations or assessing courtroom skills. There are also many opportunities to assess written practice such as commenting on reports of different kinds, panel applications, case records and so on. As discussed earlier, it works better if the person asking for feedback identifies the specific areas upon which they want you to comment. As the assessor, you not only need to explain where you think there is room for improvement, but also praise examples of good practice giving reasons. The 'sandwich method' of giving assessment feedback is widely used to give a mixture of constructive criticism and positive feedback (see Kelly, 2010, for more details).

Conclusion

This chapter has been about how to demonstrate professional leadership, taking responsibility for one's own learning and also facilitating the development of others in social work. The domain descriptor lists a range of activities that can support these goals. However, some such as mentoring and teaching are more appropriately undertaken by more experienced social workers and managers. Therefore, as this book is mainly aimed at students at the stage of getting ready to practice, we have focused on three learning activities: practice research, supervision and assessment of practice, in which both social work students and less experienced social workers can participate and make a real contribution. A common thread throughout the chapter has been that to be effective in this domain involves critical reflection, taking responsibility, demonstrating initiative, being creative and suggesting and making changes where they are needed.

Summary

- Practice research is a way that social workers, together with other professionals and service users, can focus on questions that are relevant to social work and build the evidence base to inform and improve practice. It draws on research methodology, field research and practical experience.
- Supervision assists with critical reflection and improves practice by, among other things, developing knowledge and skills.
- Peer supervision requires supervisees to be self-directed learners. It is a good way for social workers not only to further their own professional development but also that of others.
- Assessment of practice can take many forms. It enables professionals to provide constructive feedback to their colleagues on an identified area or areas of their practice.

Further reading

Dicken, C and van Graan, D (2016) 'Reflective practice skills', in K. Davies and R. Jones (eds), *Skills for Social Work Practice*. Basingstoke: Palgrave, pp. 145–8.

Fenge, L-A and Field, R (2016) 'Supervision', in R Field and K Brown (eds), *Effective Leadership, Management and Supervision in Health and Social Care*, 2nd edition. London: Sage, pp. 61–75.

Field, R and Brown, K (eds) (2016) *Effective Leadership, Management and Supervision in Health and Social Care*, 2nd edition. London: Sage.

Hall, B (2013) 'Skills for self-management', in A Mantell (ed.), *Skills for Social Work Practice*, 2nd edition. London: Learning Matters, pp. 53–68.

Howe, K and Gray, I (2013) *Effective Supervision in Social Work*. London: Learning Matters.

Knott, C and Scragg, T (2016) *Reflective Practice in Social Work*, 4th edition. London: Learning Matters.

Lawler, J and Bilson, A (2010) *Social Work Management and Leadership: Managing Complexity with Creativity*. London: Routledge.

McKitterick, B (2012) *Supervision*. Maidenhead: Community Care/Open University Press.

Mantell, A (2013) *Skills for Social Work Practice*, 2nd edition. London: Sage.

Oko, J (2011) *Using and Understanding Theory in Social Work*, 2nd edition. London: Learning Matters.

SCIE (2013) 'Effective supervision in a variety of settings', SCIE Guide 50, at http://www.scie.org.uk/publications/guides/guide50/.

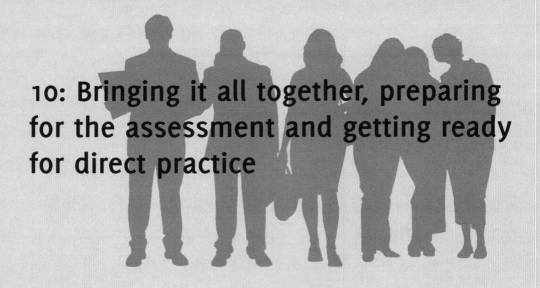

10: Bringing it all together, preparing for the assessment and getting ready for direct practice

Achieving a Social Work Degree

This chapter will help you to bring the domains of the Professional Capabilities Framework together.

Introduction

In each of the previous chapters, we have focused on the nine domains of the Professional Capabilities Framework in turn with the purpose of 'unpacking' each specific domain in order to understand it better. However, in practice, it is not a good idea to treat the domains of the Professional Capabilities Framework in isolation from each other. The domains need to be integrated around the overarching theme of professionalism, as the title of the framework suggests. Therefore, in this final chapter, the first section engages with the challenge of bringing the content from the nine domains together. After all, service users and others with whom we work are not really interested in different domains – all they want from us, the social worker, is for us to act professionally. With this in mind, we use an activity to get you to think how the domains can be linked together and how the knowledge, values and skills embedded therein can be synthesised in practice. This is followed up with an illustrative case study which aims to demonstrate the domains of the Professional Capabilities Framework coming together in practice.

The next part of the chapter is about preparing for the practical assessment. Not all universities or colleges assess readiness for direct practice in exactly the same way. However, whatever format is used, they all need to cover the basic requirements of the PCF one way or another.

For illustrative purposes we include a commonly used format as an example with which to ensure that you are orientated to what the assessment process is seeking. This will help you do yourself justice, demonstrate the domains and pass the assessment at the first attempt.

The final section assumes that you have been successful and looks forward to your first practice placement where you will need to achieve the PCF at the next level. In this section we highlight what the PCF expects of you and suggest good, professional habits to acquire that will help you build on what you have learned and develop the necessary knowledge, skills and values needed to complete your Practice Portfolio successfully. This section should provide you with plenty of useful points to discuss in your first meeting with your Practice Educator and should get you off to a good start.

Bringing it all together

In the preceding chapters we have looked at each of the domains of the Professional Capabilities Framework. However, as has been stated, they need to be integrated and incorporated into practice. The following activity will help you test your understanding of the key points of the domains. It will also encourage you to gather your thoughts about how everything can be brought together in practice situations.

Activity 10.1

In pairs:

1. From memory list the main headings or topics of the nine domains of the PCF (try to list them in the correct order).

2. Against each heading/topic write down what you think are the key points to remember for each domain.

3. Now go back through the chapters and remind yourself what each domain is about in more depth.

4. Reflecting on questions 1–3, what would you say are the *three* most important skills or qualities that a social worker should possess in order to be able to demonstrate the full range of professional capabilities in practice?

Commentary

Your answers for questions 1 and 2 will provide a useful reminder of how well you have grasped the PCF and understood what it requires of you at this stage. Your response to the third task should have made you aware of where you are confident in what you know and where you need to go back over what we have covered. It is perfectly normal not to have grasped everything at this stage. The main thing is to have a reasonably clear sense of where you need to develop your knowledge, values and skills.

As far as what you were asked in question 4, all the capabilities set out in the PCF are important. However, we need to incorporate them all in the way that we practise. This requires finding ways to makes connections between and synthesising the various areas of knowledge, values and skills laid out in the PCF. There is no one single, correct answer to this question, but a reasonable case could be made for the following.

Communication

In many ways communication in its various forms is the key to effective social work practice. Unless we can communicate effectively with others, whether it be verbally, in writing or in other formats, we cannot build relationships, conduct interviews, carry out assessments, provide information, express empathy, make case records, write reports or carry out any of the core activities that constitute professional social work. We may have the required knowledge, we may have the required values but unless we can communicate all of this effectively with a range of diverse audiences, we are unlikely to be effective in social work. Social work is a people profession. It is about relationships and interactions – see Chapter 7 for a reminder about the importance of communication. However, two key points worth repeating here are that communication is always a two-way process and that a message delivered is not necessarily a message understood.

Values and ethics

We can have good knowledge of the law and relevant policy; we can also be proficient in our grasp of psychology, sociology and human development as well as theories of social work interventions. We might well be good communicators in the sense that we have the technical skills for giving and receiving information to a range of audiences. However, we would not be practising social work to the required professional standard unless our practice is thoroughly grounded in social work values and ethics as discussed in Chapter 2, but also covered in Chapters 3 and 4. If we were ignorant about how ethics and values underpinned social work, we might well (among other things) have problems in working in ways that are anti-discriminatory and anti-oppressive, that respect difference and human rights, that are culturally sensitive, and that respect professional boundaries and the importance of confidentiality. All of these approaches are fundamental to professional social work practice and underline that social work is not simply a technical activity but is a moral and ethical activity. As was discussed in previous chapters, professionalism requires us to ensure that there is congruence between our personal values and the professional values and ethics of social work.

Critical reflection/emotional intelligence

How people experience social work is through the way that we communicate, the decisions that we make and the plans that we put in place. Throughout these processes, how we are as human beings, makes a big difference to the way that this impacts on people. Consequently, we need to have a good level of self-knowledge about how we come across to others. We need to be aware of how our thoughts, values and feelings impact on the interactions that we have with people and on the assessments and decisions that we make. Therefore, we need to be able to expose and examine the various intuitions, prejudices, biases and gut feelings that are bound to affect all aspects of our practice. This requires us to have the ability to think critically about ourselves (reflexivity). This was discussed in Chapters 1 and 6 where we introduced different models of reflection.

However, the ability to reflect critically in social work is essential for reasons other than the need to focus on ourselves. Reflecting critically and with emotional intelligence also enables us to better understand service users' emotions, behaviour and situations. It helps give us a sense of perspective and to place things in their full context. To be able to reflect critically enables us to take a step back, to be able to hypothesise and to be analytical rather than to be driven purely by intuition or impulse. To be able to reflect critically enables us to be clearer about what knowledge we already have and what further knowledge we need to gather, how to sift and sort evidence objectively and also how to synthesise different types of knowledge in order to make informed and reasoned judgements. Critical reflection and emotional intelligence also enable us to maintain our well-being, manage stress, avoid burn out and to develop both as people and professionally. All of this relates to the discussions that we had in Chapters 5, 6 and 8 and is also an important dimension of professional leadership as discussed in Chapter 9.

In conclusion, there is no single correct answer to the question that you were asked in Activity 10.1. You could have made a good case for other skills or qualities that help social workers bring together the different domains of the PCF. However, for the reasons argued above, it would definitely be advisable for you to strive to develop your communication skills, your ethics and values and your critical reflection skills. If you can do this, it will be easier to demonstrate the PCF in its entirety. The following activity aims to illustrate how this can work. It should also make you think more generally about how the various domains overlap and can be brought together.

Activity 10.2

It is two weeks before Christmas and Katherine has just started her first placement at a supported housing project for people with severe and long-term mental illness. She has never worked with this service user group before and is struggling

(Continued)

(Continued)

to know how to make relationships and to find a role for herself. She discusses the situation with her Practice Educator (PE). Fearing that she will not do a very good job of gathering evidence for her practice portfolio in this environment, Katherine tells her PE that she doesn't have anything to offer the residents and suggests that, as she has discovered that many of the residents have illnesses such as schizophrenia and bi-polar depressive disorder, maybe she should take some time away from the placement to go to the library and read up on these conditions. Katherine's PE advises her that, while having that knowledge would be relevant to the placement, she should not to absent herself from the placement at this early stage. Instead, she reminds Katherine that the project is not a psychiatric hospital. Its main aims are to promote the residents' well-being, to support people to live independently and to foster social skills where possible. She encourages Katherine to reflect upon what strengths that she already possesses that could help meet the aims of the project.

Katherine accepts that having medical knowledge about mental illness is not the immediate priority. It is much more about making connections and building relationships with people. As a keen baker she decides that she will use her talents in this area to organise a Christmas party for the residents and use her baking skills to make cakes for it. Thinking about it some more, she decides that maybe she should seek the views of project workers and, particularly, the residents about the idea of having party. On further reflection, Katherine then thinks that, assuming they want one, she should seek their views about their dietary needs and what she should bake. After more reflection and discussing it with staff members, Katherine decides to involve any residents who want to participate in deciding what food they want at the party and also in the process of buying the ingredients and doing the cooking with her support. When it was put to them most of the residents thought having a party was a good idea. It took quite a bit of time and effort to prepare for and organise but it was a success. The residents were clearly pleased to have been involved and to have made a contribution. For those who did not want to participate directly, Katherine offered them a choice of cakes to have when they wanted them. In the process Katherine had started to find out more about what the other people were like and was able to start building relationships. Overall, although there was still a lot to learn, she was much happier about her role at the project. Katherine's PE praised her for her ability to listen, to use supervision, to reflect appropriately and to use her initiative. She suggested that Katherine use this experience to write critical reflection on practice for her practice portfolio. She particularly wanted Katherine to reflect upon why she was so anxious to leave the placement and go to the library.

Task

1. What are your thoughts about this situation? How did Katherine use communication skills, social work ethics and values and critical reflection skills to produce beneficial outcomes for the service users and, at the same time, evidence for her portfolio?

2. Identify the domains that could be said to be evidenced in some way by Katherine organising the Christmas party in the way that she did.

Commentary

It is not uncommon for social work students to feel 'lost' and lacking in both knowledge and skills when they start a placement. Katherine's first reaction was to seek permission to go to the library in order to build up her knowledge about the various residents' illnesses. This would also have had the effect of removing her from a difficult and anxiety-provoking social situation. However, having communicated this with her Practice Educator, she accepted that a bigger priority at that stage was to overcome her anxiety and start to get know the residents as individuals. Baking for a Christmas party was both a good use of her talents and a 'natural' way of getting to know people. The more she reflected on the situation the more she recalled what she had been learning on the course about the importance of involving service users in decisions that affect them and to offer them choices. She also remembered about not treating everyone as if they had the same needs and not to make people feel excluded if they didn't want to participate in that particular activity. This way they would not be discriminated against. A Christmas party provided a good opportunity for Katherine to communicate with both the residents and staff, seek their views and also get to know them a bit better. Even if they had rejected the idea, it was a good ice-breaking exercise.

In this instance Katherine needed to communicate, she needed to reflect critically both on her own situation and on the situation of the staff and residents, she needed to involve people in decisions that affected them, offer choice, promote inclusion and ensure that any special needs were acknowledged. By doing this she went some way in evidencing Domain 1 (Professionalism), Domain 2 (Values and ethics), Domain 3 (Diversity), Domain 5 (Knowledge), Domain 6 (Critical reflection and analysis), Domain 7 (Intervention and skills), Domain 8 (Contexts and organisations) and Domain 9 (Professional leadership). It would be fair to say that all of these domains would need more evidence generated over the course of the placement and that one activity did not allow all the domains to be covered.

A key point about this scenario is that it demonstrates that portfolio building (and therefore meeting the domains) is more successful when you consider what would be an appropriate activity for the placement and its service users rather than thinking about how you might garner domain evidence purely to have a complete portfolio. If you take the latter path the tasks that you undertake are likely to be artificial and harder to integrate around the concept of professionalism. In this scenario the original idea came from Katherine but, by utilising social work values and using reflection and communication and skills, it very quickly became something that involved the project.

Summary

- The overarching theme of the PCF is professionalism.
- The different domains should not be treated in isolation from each other – you need to integrate them in your practice.
- This means that you need to become very familiar with what each domain requires of you and make sure you can see how the domains overlap and relate to each other.
- If you can communicate effectively, practise in line with social work values and ethics and reflect critically on what you are doing, you will have a good basis for professional practice.

Passing the Readiness for Direct Practice Assessment

This section follows on very appropriately from the key points made above because you will have to put them into practice in the Readiness for Direct Practice Assessment. The assessment requires you to demonstrate that, before you can go and practise directly with service users in real-life situations, you have to be able to demonstrate the requirements of the PCF at the appropriate level and to be able to practise accordingly. As you will be aware, if you cannot demonstrate the appropriate capability, you will not be able to start your first placement.

Although working to the same assessment framework, different higher education institutions (HEIs) have their own methods of assessing readiness for direct practice. Therefore it will not be possible to be specific about the assessment situation that every student is likely to face. However, most HEIs base their assessment around a role play and associated activities such as reflection and report writing. HEIs need to be able to satisfy themselves that, you have the basics of practice in place. This includes, for example, that you can:

- engage and communicate effectively and respectfully with another person;
- practise according to social work values and ethics (specifically including anti-discriminatory and anti-oppressive practice);

- make an initial assessment of someone's needs and strengths (helping them to tell their story in their own words);

- make an initial assessment of risks in a potential safeguarding situation;

- reflect critically;

- record accurately (clearly separating fact from opinion);

- demonstrate awareness of professional boundaries and of your professional responsibilities generally;

- demonstrate an awareness of limitations to your knowledge and that you can seek help appropriately;

- practise safely.

The list above is not exhaustive but you will see that a key part of the Readiness for Direct Practice Assessment is obviously about demonstrating what social work knowledge, skills and values you have learned. However, it is also about ensuring, as the latter bullet points indicate, that you recognise that you are at an early stage of your social work career and that you are aware of your limitations and therefore know when to seek help or check things out with someone more senior. Consequently, in any role play situation, it is important not to make unrealistic promises, pretend that you know more than you do or feel that you need to demonstrate great expertise or analytical insights. If you need to check something with your supervisor it is better to state this rather than give a misleading impression to the service user. Also, do not feel compelled to rush into making great judgements or analyses about what is going on. Focus on letting the person tell their own story. Do not ask leading questions and concentrate on making sure you establish the facts accurately. Save any hypothesising or analysis until later once you have had time to reflect critically on the situation and can discuss it with your supervisor.

In the following activity we provide an example of an assessment format which an HEI might use. It will encourage you to think more about what a typical assessment panel (comprising teachers, practitioners and service users) is actually looking for. If you look at things from the assessors' perspective it can often make it easier to think about what you need to do to demonstrate your capabilities.

Activity 10.3

For their Readiness for Direct Practice Assessment, Eddington College have organised the assessment into three parts. Firstly, they have hired actors to play the part of somebody who has safeguarding concerns about an elderly relative and is seeking help from a duty social worker in an adult social care team. Students will

(Continued)

(Continued)

be required to play the part of the duty social worker whose job it is to gather basic details and to start collecting information about the person's situation, including any perceived risks. This information will form the basis of an initial assessment. The role play will last for a maximum of 15 minutes. Secondly, the students will be required to write up a brief case summary of the encounter highlighting the salient points. Lastly, the student will be asked to attend an oral 'viva' (interview) in which they will be asked to reflect critically on their experience.

Task

Taken all together, the three parts of the assessment need to evidence all the domains in some way. Imagine that you are designing the questions and checklists for each of the three activities. Indicate what you would be looking for students to demonstrate as a minimum in the first two parts (role play and case record) and what questions might you use to guide the reflective viva?

Commentary

It would be very easy for assessors to simply use the domains as they are written in the PCF either as checklists or for questions. However, as this book has demonstrated, not only do the different domains need to be interpreted in order to make sense in practice, they also overlap with each other in many instances. This is why it is useful to be able to link the domains together and integrate them. As we have discussed there is no single way of doing this – it can be done in different ways. However, below we have included examples of the checklists and questions used in real-life assessments. They are not perfect in that they do not contain every single element of every domain. However, given that the purpose of the exercise is to assess the basics of professional practice in a relatively short period of time, they are fit for purpose. Take a look, compare them to what you have produced and think about how you would might adapt or improve them so that if you were an assessor you had a good enough set of questions to meet the requirements without making the whole process too laborious, repetitive, time-consuming and artificial.

Exemplars of assessment materials

Role-play observation checklist

Has the student:		
• Introduced themselves clearly?	Yes / No	Comment:
• Given a clear summary of the conversation at the end?	Yes / No	

Has the student:		
• Behaved in a professional manner	Yes / No	Comment:
• Demonstrated awareness of their role and the role of their supervisor?	Yes / No	Comment:
• Demonstrated awareness of social work values, and of anti-discriminatory and anti-oppressive practice?	Yes / No	Comment:
• Identified the risk factors in the scenario?	Yes / No	Comment:
• Identified the strengths of the service user and their social and physical environment?	Yes / No	Comment:
• Demonstrated adequate communication skills, been attentive and shown respect?	Yes / No	Comment:
• Overall, have they demonstrated safe practice?	Yes / No	Comment:
Any other observations/comments		

Guiding questions for the assessment panel during the reflective viva

Overall, the panel is looking for basic skills in critical reflection and emotional intelligence and an ability to demonstrate social work values.

	Comments:
• How do you feel the role-play went overall?	
• What parts were you satisfied with?	
• What might you change if you were doing it again?	
• What was your emotional reaction to hearing about the situation the service user was in and how did you deal with any feelings?	
• Can you name at least one human right that you feel was at risk in what you heard in the role-play?	
• What legislative and/or policy framework might be applicable in the scenario you heard about?	

Criteria for assessing the case report

Overall, the panel is looking for the basic ability to write a professional quality, reliable (and therefore safe) record of the interview.

Did the record/report contain:	Comments
• Accurate contact details – names, addresses, etc.?	
• An accurate, coherent and well-set out description of the case?	
• Any risks and strengths that were identified in the scenario?	
• Any action points where appropriate?	
Any other observations/comments	

By looking at the assessments from the assessors' point of view, hopefully, it has highlighted the fact that to pass you need to actually *demonstrate* the capabilities in a 'real-life' practice scenario in ways that can be observed and assessed by others who do not know you. It is worth looking at it as one might the driving test. Certainly, theoretical knowledge is required but on its own it is not sufficient. You actually need to be able to drive a vehicle safely and competently on the road according to the relevant traffic laws and the Highway Code.

The question therefore arises of how to perform at your best on the day. This brings us back to the theme of self-management. Below we provide some tips on how to avoid common pitfalls and ensure that you can do yourself justice.

Key points for a successful assessment: interview

Relax

Take the assessment seriously but do not take it so seriously that you become too nervous or stressed. Assessors want to see someone who can engage professionally with a stranger and put them at their ease. This will not be possible if you are overcome with nerves. Don't forget to greet the person with a professional smile, not a nervous grin or anxious frown! First impressions are important so practise your professional greeting face and self-introduction in front of a mirror. Think about what you wear as well. It should project professionalism without being overly formal.

Don't rush . . . but don't get lost in aimless chitchat

Under pressure it is sometimes tempting to go straight into trying to find out what the 'problem' is ('So, why are you here?') while forgetting to introduce yourself and your role, and asking the other person's name and how they like to be addressed. You also need to briefly explain about confidentiality and its limits, any other procedures and processes relevant to the interview and also what will happen next. However, you cannot spend limitless time engaged in small talk without getting to the point of why they are there. Once introductions and explanations are over, a good first question would be something like 'So, would you like to tell me what has brought you along to the social care team today?' Then with appropriate prompting and some direction let the person tell the story in their own way.

Avoid leading questions and unnecessary interpretations

Avoid making leading or interpretative statements such as 'that must have made you very angry' or 'maybe it goes back to a resentment that she developed in her childhood'. At this stage you are primarily focused on getting the facts of the situation as accurately as possible. If the other person expresses an opinion, you can reflect it back to them: 'So you are saying that your sister can't be trusted to look after the money', and then record it accurately.

Clarify, check and summarise

Do not wait until the end of the whole interview to try to summarise what you have been told. Do this at appropriate intervals and don't forget it is OK to ask clarifying or checking questions such as 'Have I heard you correctly, you are saying . . .?' Make sure that you get the facts straight and the key reasons why they require input from a social worker. Often direct quotes are useful. For example, 'the referrer said that his mother was "at the end of her tether"'.

Take notes but explain why and don't look down all the time

It is important to have an accurate record of what is said. Therefore it is obviously helpful to take notes. If you do this you need to look down. However, you also need to remember to look up and make eye contact. Do not forget the importance of non-verbal communication such as eye contact and nodding in communicating active listening and encouraging someone to talk.

Avoid jargon

Telling someone that you will need to pass this on to the 'MARAC' or that you need to complete a 'SOC 301' will not help with communication. Keep your interactions in plain English. Again, it is useful to check out not only whether you have understood them but also whether they have understood you.

Remember it is OK not to know everything

Do not pretend to be somebody that you are not. You are role-playing as yourself, a student social worker. Therefore it is perfectly acceptable to explain that, once you have gathered the information, you will need to share it with your supervisor and check things as necessary. It is also acceptable in these circumstances to explain to people that 'I don't actually know that right now, I will need to check that with my supervisor but I will get back to you with an answer by . . .' (which is all the more reason to get contact details at the start).

Key points for a successful assessment: written component

- **Write in plain English that is grammatically correct and has accurate spellings.** Avoid writing in note form or jargon and using slang or colloquialisms. Write in the first person and keep sentences to a reasonable length (15–20 words).

- **If you are not working to a pre-designed format, use appropriate subheadings to structure your record or report.** If you use a pre-designed form you should complete it using the boxes provided. However, if you are starting with a blank document you need to create your own format using appropriate headings. Headings that are commonly used are:

  - name, address and contact details;

  - date of birth, gender, marital status;

  - composition of household;

  - referrer's name, address and contact details;

  - other professional involvements (e.g. GP);

  - background and reason(s) for referral;

  - specific risks identified;

  - action to be taken.

If you follow this kind of structure you will know whether you have everything covered and also what you might need to find out in a follow-up phone call or visit. Record the date and time and include your name, role and signature.

Remember the basics of good communication: the reader must be able to easily understand the details of who is involved, what has happened and what was discussed.

Key points for a successful assessment: reflective component

The reflective element of the assessment is important for different reasons. Firstly, social work students need to be able to demonstrate that they are self-aware enough to be able to critique their own practice and identify any areas for future development. As we have discussed, this does not mean that you need to be negative about yourself all the time. You need to be able to identify those parts of the assessment where you felt you did well (your strengths) as well as those parts that you think could have gone better (areas for development). In each case you need to be able to provide reasons why you come to that view. You can't just say 'I really messed up in there' and leave it at that. It is more professional to explain which part, in particular, you were not happy with and explain why. But then you also need to be able to say where you think you did well and also explain why.

Nobody is perfect therefore it would only be normal to make some mistakes in the assessment. However, if you can assure your assessors that you are aware of what they are, why you made them and what you would do again differently, you can often retrieve the situation and still pass. That is as long as there have not been too many mistakes and the mistakes have not been too major. Major mistakes would include, for example, being overtly discriminatory or completely misunderstanding why the person was seeking help. However, if, for example, you felt that you had rushed the interview too much at the beginning because of your nerves, but that you were aware of this and that you know how you would manage it better if you had to do it again, this would show that you have a promising level of self-awareness. It demonstrates that you can look at yourself critically and adjust your practice accordingly. Assessors would see that as a good example of your developing professionalism.

You also need to be able to reflect on the emotional impact that any given situation has had on you. You need to be able think what the reasons for this are and how this might affect both your thinking and practice as a social worker. So, for example, if you found it hard to hear about another person's situation because it reminded you of a similar situation in your own family, it is good to be able to recognise and articulate this. This will help you disentangle your feelings and not fall into the trap of over-identification. Therefore, as we have discussed in various parts of the book, the ability to reflect critically on oneself and one's own practice is a fundamental characteristic of professionalism in social work. It is this quality that assessors are looking for as much as relevant knowledge of the law or of different social work theories.

Making a success of your first placement

Let us assume that you have taken on all the necessary lessons and that you have been able to satisfactorily demonstrate your readiness for direct practice. The next stage will be actually starting your first practice placement. This stage of your course is beyond the specific focus of this book which is to make sure that you are actually ready for direct practice. In this respect a selection of references specifically on social work placements is listed at the end of this section. However, because the learning process over the whole of the course is designed to be continuous and progressive with each stage preparing you for the next, it is a good idea to begin making the links between this part of the course and what follows before we conclude. Therefore, in this final section, we will briefly look ahead to what is required of you in your first placement and what you can do to help develop your learning and achieve the domains at the next level.

The Professional Capability Framework makes the following statement about what you should be able to do by the end of the first placement:

By the end of the first placement:

Students should demonstrate effective use of knowledge, skills and commitment to core values in social work in a given setting in predominantly less complex situations, with supervision and support. They will have demonstrated the capacity to work with people and situations where there may not be simple clear-cut solutions.

Parts of this statement should look familiar by now. However, fully unpacking what this means in practice will be easier and will make more sense when you are placed in a specific practice environment. This stage of your professional social work development will be the joint responsibility of your Practice Educator, your lecturers and tutors, an on-site supervisor if you need one and, of course most importantly, yourself.

HEIs usually require you to identify your relevant past experience, learning styles and any specific learning needs together with what you hope to achieve from the placement and share this information with your Practice Educator at the beginning of the placement. The format will be specific to the particular HEI. Before their first placement, social work students can undertake a range of useful preparatory activities (see *Community Care*, 2013b; Lomax et al., 2010; Mathews et al., 2014 for examples). Whatever else you do, as we have seen throughout this book, it is fundamental to become fully acquainted with the domains of the PCF. This way, you can take responsibility for your own learning and start to identify in which areas you have already built up knowledge and in which areas you still need to develop your learning.

Activity 10.4: Mapping where you are on the PCF

In Activity 10.1 you were set the task of reminding yourself what each of the domains required. Now, for each of the nine domains, ask yourself the following questions:

1. At the moment have I got any evidence that demonstrates this capability? Explain your answer.

2. What don't I understand about this domain?

3. What further knowledge, skills and values do I need to develop to demonstrate this capability in practice?

Using Domain 4 as an example, we suggest how a typical first-year MA Social Work student might approach this task. To remind you Domain 4 states:

> *Rights, justice and economic well-being: Advance human rights and promote social justice and economic well-being.*
>
> *Social workers recognise the fundamental principles of human rights and equality, and that these are protected in national and international law, conventions and policies. They ensure these principles underpin their practice. Social workers understand the importance of using and contributing to case law and applying these rights in their own practice. They understand the effects of oppression, discrimination and poverty.*
>
> *Understand the principles of rights, justice and economic well-being, and their significance for social work practice.*

Evidence I have already got

I don't have anything from actual practice yet but I have gained an understanding of many of the underpinning concepts of this domain from the modules and skills days on the course and by completing assignments. However, I learned about the Human Rights Act 1998 and the Equality Act 2010 and how they relate to social work in the module 'Knowledge, Values and Skills for Professional Social Work' and also in the relevant ARDP skills days. We also covered the meaning of oppression and looked at different types of discrimination in the module 'Well-being Across the Life Course' as well as in the relevant ARDP skills days. As part of the module assignment we needed to choose a specific group in society and do a presentation explaining

(Continued)

(Continued)

how their well-being might be affected by poverty and other factors such as discrimination. Our group chose homeless people. For this we got a Distinction. So I have developed theoretical knowledge on this Domain which I need to be able to put into practice.

What don't I understand about this domain?

I'm not sure when it says 'Social workers understand the importance of using and contributing to case law'. I also need to read more about different ideas about justice and its significance for social work practice.

What further knowledge, skills and values do I need to develop to demonstrate this capability in practice?

Some of this domain is quite abstract and I need to work out what promoting justice and economic well-being looks like in practice and what skills are needed. If it is relevant in my placement I also need to get a sense of what using and contributing to case law might mean in practice. I suppose overall I need to understand more about the different ways in which discrimination, oppression, injustice and poverty affects people in the real world and what social workers can do about it.

Commentary

Hopefully you found the activity a useful exercise. It should give you plenty to discuss with your Practice Educator when you first meet to talk about your placement. Your Practice Educator knows that you are just beginning your journey through to professional qualification and will not expect you to have understood everything. However, they will find it useful to have a clear sense of what you are confident about and what you do not understand. It helps them help you if they know where you are stuck or where you don't 'get' something. It also helps them if you can explain where and how you covered the relevant 'theory' on the course.

In Chapter 1 and throughout this book generally, we have highlighted that reflecting critically on one's self (reflexivity) is a good habit of mind to get into throughout your professional career. As a professional social worker you never stop learning, and you yourself are almost certainly the best judge of what you need to learn and, as important, how you learn. When you qualify you should know that the HCPC expects social workers to take responsibility for their continuing professional development (CPD) as a condition of their registration as professional social workers.

The time period from passing your Readiness for Direct Practice Assessment to commencing your first practice placement will vary depending on where you are studying. However long it takes, it is important not to 'go off the boil' in terms of developing and maintaining good professional habits. The specific texts that are listed below provide much relevant advice and many good suggestions on how you can best prepare for your placement and make it a success. Your college or university will also carry out its own placement preparation sessions.

However, this chapter has been about 'bringing it all together' in terms of getting ready for direct practice, we therefore conclude with some, by now, familiar messages:

- In social work *you* as a person are the main tool of your trade. *You* are what social work looks like to service users, carers and other professionals. Ask others to give you feedback on how you come across verbally, non-verbally in writing and so forth. Consider using videos to study yourself.

- Continue to be critically reflective. Use a tool such a reflective log or diary to jot down thoughts, feelings or any other issues that you need to think about or work on in order to understand better. Use supervision discussions either with peers, a supervisor or people with more experience to examine your thoughts and feelings.

- Keep the PCF alive in your mind. Continue to think about how the domains overlap and link with each other. Whatever you do on your course, be thinking about how it relates to the different domains. Get into the habit of mapping what you have done or what you have learned to the PCF on a regular basis.

- Keep an open mind, put things into context and be research minded. In other words don't just take things at face value or accept the first thing somebody says as 'true'. It might only be part of the picture or completely wrong. Try to think both analytically and systemically. Be prepared to admit what you don't know. Be curious. Actively seek out evidence to confirm or disprove a hypothesis. Make sure that the evidence passes the normal quality tests and be prepared to change your mind in the light of contradictory evidence.

Further reading

Community Care (2013) 'Ten things you can do to make your social work practice placement a success', online at http://www.communitycare.co.uk/2013/11/21/ten-things-can-make-social-work-practice-placement-success/.

Doel, M (2009) *Social Work Placements: A Traveller's Guide* (Student Social Work). London: Routledge.

Jones, S (2015) *Social Work Practice Placements: Critical and Reflective Approaches*. London: Sage.

Lomax, R, Jones, K, Leigh, S and Gay, C (2010) *Surviving Your Social Work Placement*. Basingstoke: Palgrave.

Mathews, I, Simpson, D and Crawford, K (2014) *Your Social Work Practice Placement: From Start to Finish*. London: Sage.

References

ACAS (2014) *The Equality Act 2010 – Guidance for Employers*. London: ACAS.

Age UK (2016) online at http://www.ageuk.org.uk/home-and-care/help-at-home/self-directed-support/making-care-personalised/.

Backwith, D (2015) *Social Work, Poverty and Social Exclusion*. Maidenhead: Open University Press.

Banks, S (2012) *Ethics and Values in Social Work*, 4th edition. Basingstoke: Palgrave.

Barclay, P (1982) *Social Workers: Their Role and Tasks*. London: National Institute for Social Work.

Barnard, A, Horner, N and Wild, J (eds) (2008) *The Value Base of Social Work and Social Care*. Maidenhead: Open University Press.

BASW (2012) *The Code of Ethics for Social Work: Statement of Principles*. Birmingham: BASW.

BASW (2015) online at https://www.basw.co.uk/pcf/PCF09ReadinessForPractice Capabilities.pdf.

BBC (2011) online at http://www.bbc.co.uk/history/british/victorians/bsurface_01.shtml.

BBC (2016) online at 'Immigration: threat or opportunity?' online at: http://www.bbc.co.uk/news/uk-politics-eu-referendum-36548750.

Beckett, C (2006) *Essential Theory for Social Work Practice*. London: Sage.

Beckett, C (2010) *Assessment and Intervention in Social Work: Preparing for Practice*. London: Sage.

Beckett, C and Maynard, A (2005) *Values and Ethics in Social Work: An Introduction*. London: Sage.

Bell, L and Hafford-Letchfield, T (2015) *Ethics, Values and Social Work Practice*. London: McGraw-Hill.

Braye, S and Preston-Shoot, M (2010) *Practising Social Work Law*, 3rd edition. Basingstoke: Palgrave Macmillan.

Bubb, S (2014) *Winterbourne View – Time for Change*, report by the Transforming Care and Commissioning Steering Group, chaired by Sir Stephen Bubb, November.

Burke, B (2013) 'Anti-oppressive practice', in M. Davies (ed.), *The Blackwell Companion to Social Work*, 4th edition. Oxford: Wiley-Blackwell, pp. 414–16.

Carers UK (2015) *State of Caring 2015*. London: Carers UK.

Cleaver, H, Nicholson, D, Tarr, S and Cleaver, D (2006) 'Executive summary', *The Response of Child Protection Practices and Procedures to Children Exposed to Domestic Violence or Parental Substance Misuse*. London: Department for Education and Skills.

Cocker, C and Hafford-Letchfield, T (eds) (2014) *Rethinking Anti-Discriminatory and Anti-Oppressive Theories for Social Work Practice*. Basingstoke: Palgrave.

Comartin, E and González-Prendes, A (2011) 'Dissonance between personal and professional values: resolution of an ethical dilemma', *Journal of Social Work Values and Ethics*, 8 (2), p. 11.

Community Care (2008) 'Proven practice: communicating with service users and their carers', online at: http://www.communitycare.co.uk/2008/10/15/proven-practice-communicating-with-service-users-and-their-carers/.

Community Care (2010) online at http://www.communitycare.co.uk/2010/07/28/how-to-write-a-good-report/.

Community Care (2011a) 'The need for more critically reflective social work', http://www.communitycare.co.uk/2011/04/08/the-need-for-more-critically-reflective-social-work/.

Community Care (2011b) 'Developing leadership among all practitioners', online at http://www.communitycare.co.uk/2011/09/22/developing-leadership-among-all-practitioners/.

Community Care (2012) 'How reflective practice can help social workers feel "safe"', http://www.communitycare.co.uk/2012/08/03/how-reflective-practice-can-help-social-workers-feel-safe/.

Community Care (2013a) 'Social workers need reflective practice to make personalisation work', http://www.communitycare.co.uk/2013/06/25/social-workers-need-reflective-practice-to-make-personalisation-work/.

Community Care (2013b) 'Ten things you can do to make your social work practice placement a success', online at http://www.communitycare.co.uk/2013/11/21/ten-things-can-make-social-work-practice-placement-success/.

Community Care (2015) 'Social worker criticised by judge for using jargon in court report', online at http://www.communitycare.co.uk/2015/08/05/social-worker-criticised-judge-using-jargon-court-report/.

Cormier, S, Nurius, PS and Osborn, CJ (2009) *Interviewing and Change Strategies for Helpers: Fundamental Skills and Cognitive-Behavioral Interventions*, 6th edition. Belmont, CA: Brooks/Cole.

Coulshed, V and Orme, J (2012) *Social Work Practice*, 5th edition. Basingstoke: Palgrave.

Crouch, C (2011) *The Strange Non-Death of Neoliberalism*. Cambridge: Polity.

Cunningham, J and Cunningham, S (2008) *Sociology and Social Work*, 2nd edition. London: Learning Matters.

Cunningham, J and Cunningham, S (2012) *Social Policy and Social Work: An Introduction*. London: Learning Matters.

Dalrymple, J and Burke, B (2006) *Anti-oppressive Practice*, 2nd edition. New York: McGraw-Hill Education.

Davies, K and Jones, R (eds) (2016) *Skills for Social Work Practice*. Basingstoke: Palgrave.

Davies, M (1981) *The Essential Social Worker: A Guide to Positive Practice*. London: Heinemann.

Department for Education (2014) *Knowledge and Skills Statement for Approved Child and Family Practitioners.* London: Department for Education.

Department of Health (2014) *Care and Support Statutory Guidance Issued under the Care Act 2014, June 2014.* London: DoH.

Department of Health (2015) *Knowledge and Skills Statement for Social Workers in Adult Services.* London: Department of Health.

DH (2001) *Valuing People: A New Strategy for Learning Disability for the 21st Century.* London: Department of Health.

DH (2008) *Valuing People Now*. London: Department of Health.

DH (2010) *Valuing People Now: Summary Report March 2009 – September 2010.* London: Department of Health.

Dobson, F (1999) *Hansard*, 297 (7 July), Column 642.

Dunk-West, P (2013) *How to Be a Social Worker.* Basingstoke: Palgrave.

Epstein, RM and Hundert, EM (2002) 'Defining and assessing professional competence', *Journal of American Medical Association (JAMA)*, 287(2), pp. 226–35.

Equality and Human Rights Commission (2015) *Equality Act 2010, Guidance for Service Users: Your Rights to Equality from Healthcare and Social Care Services*, Vol. 4, online at https://www.equalityhumanrights.com/sites/default/files/equalityguidance-healthcare-socialcare-2015_0.pdf.

Fleming, ND (2001) *Teaching and Learning Styles: VARK Strategies*. Christchurch, NZ: ND Fleming.

Foundation for People with Learning Disabilities (2012) http://www.learningdisabilities.org.uk/help-information/learning-disability-a-z/e/employment-careers/.

Gaine, C (ed.) (2010) *Equality and Diversity in Social Work Practice*. Exeter: Learning Matters.

Gardner, A (2014) *Personalisation in Social Work*, 2nd edition. Exeter: Learning Matters.

General Social Care Council (GSCC) (2011) *Professional Boundaries Guidance for Social Workers*. London: GSCC.

Gomm, R (2009) *Key Concepts in Social Research Methods*. Basingstoke: Palgrave.

Grint, K (2005) *Leadership: Limits and Possibilities*. Basingstoke: Palgrave.

Guardian (2010) online at https://www.theguardian.com/society/2010/sep/01/scope-warns-cuts-disabled-people.

Guardian (2015) 'Poverty premiums: why it costs so much more to be poor', online at https://www.theguardian.com/public-leaders-network/2015/nov/10/poverty-premium-costs-poor-energy-phone-tariffs-councils.

Guardian (2015a) 'Cutting employment support for learning disabled people is a false economy', online at https://www.theguardian.com/society/2015/may/05/learning-disability-employment-support-cut-false-economy-benefits.

Guardian (2015b) 'Disabled people's rights threatened by government cuts, campaigners warn', online at https://www.theguardian.com/society/2015/jun/17/learning-disabilities-rights-threatened-government-cuts-brian-rix-mencap.

Guardian (2016) online at https://www.theguardian.com/books/2016/apr/13/rachel-dolezal-signs-publishing-deal-book-race-black-white.

Hall, B and Scragg, T (2012) *Social Work with Older People: Approaches to Person-centred Practice*. Maidenhead: Open University Press.

Harding, T and Beresford, P (1996) *The Standards We Expect: What Service Users and Carers Want from Social Services Workers*. London: NISW.

Harris, J (2008) State Social Work: Constructing the Present from Moments in the Past, *British Journal of Social Work*, 38 (4): 662–79.

Health and Care Professions Council (HCPC) (2012a) *Standards of Proficiency for Social Workers*. London: HCPC.

Health and Care Professions Council (HCPC) (2012b) *Guidance on Conduct and Ethics for Students*. London: HCPC.

Health and Care Professions Council (HCPC) (2016) *Standards of Conduct, Performance and Ethics*. London: HCPC.

Healy, K (2005) *Social Work Theories in Context*. Basingstoke: Palgrave.

Healy, K and Mulholland, J (2012) *Writing Skills for Social Workers*, 2nd edition. London: Sage.

Hill, A (2010) *Working in Statutory Contexts*. Cambridge: Polity Press.

HM Government (2007) *Putting People First*. London: HM Government.

HM Government (2015) *Working Together to Safeguard Children A Guide to Inter-agency Working to Safeguard and Promote the Welfare of Children*. London: TSO.

HM Treasury (2003) *Every Child Matters*, Cm 5860. Norwich: TSO.

Home Office (2014) *Multi Agency Working and Information Sharing Project, Final Report*. London: Home Office.

Honey, P and Mumford, A (1992) *The Manual of Learning Styles*, 3rd edition. Maidenhead: Peter Honey.

Horner, N (2012) *What Is Social Work?*, 4th edition. London: Learning Matters.

Howe, D. (2008) *The Emotionally Intelligent Social Worker*. Basingstoke: Palgrave, pp. 106–9.

Hughes, M and Wearing, M (2013) *Organisations and Management in Social Work*, 2nd edn. London: Sage.

Hutton, A and Partridge, K (2006) *Say it Your Own Way*. Essex: Barnardo's and Department for Education and Science.

Ife, J (2001) *Human Rights and Social Work: Towards Rights-Based Practice*. Cambridge: Cambridge University Press.

Johns, R (2014) *Using the Law in Social Work*, 6th edition. London: Sage/Learning Matters.

Jones, S (2013) *Critical Learning for Social Work Students*, 2nd edition. London: Learning Matters.

Jordan, B and Drakeford, M (2012) *Social Work and Social Policy Under Austerity.* Basingstoke: Palgrave Macmillan.

Kelly, R (2010) 'How To give feedback: the simple 3-step sandwich method', online at http://robdkelly.com/blog/communication/the-sandwich-method-of-feedback/.

Knott, C and Scragg, T (eds) (2016) *Reflective Practice in Social Work*, 4th edition. London: Learning Matters.

Koprowska, J (2010) *Communication and Interpersonal Skills in Social Work*, 4th edition. London: Learning Matters.

Laming, H (2003) *The Victoria Climbié Inquiry Report*, Cm 5730. London: TSO.

Laming, H (2009) *The Protection of Children in England: A Progress Report*, HC 330. London: TSO.

Lishman, J (2009) *Communication in Social Work*, 2nd edition. Basingstoke: Palgrave.

Lomax, R, Jones, K, Leigh, S and Gay, C (2010) *Surviving your Social Work Placement*. Basingstoke: Palgrave.

Lowe, R (2005) *The Welfare State in Britain since 1945*. Basingstoke: Palgrave.

Lymbery, M (2005) *Social Work with Older People: Context, Policy and Practice*. London: Sage.

Lymbery, M and Postle, K (eds) (2007) *Social Work: A Companion to Learning*. London: Sage.

Macionis, J (ed.) (2017) *Sociology*, 16th edn. Harlow: Pearson.

McKitterick, B (2012) *Supervision*. Maidenhead: Community Care/Open University Press.

McLaughlin, H (2012) *Understanding Social Work Research*, 2nd edition. London: Sage.

Manthorpe, J and Martineau, S (2009) *Serious Case Reviews in Adult Safeguarding*. London: Social Care Workforce Research Unit, King's College London.

Mathews, I (2009) *Social Work and Spirituality*. Exeter: Learning Matters.

Mathews, I and Crawford, K (2010) *Evidence-based Practice in Social Work*. Exeter: Learning Matters.

Mathews, I, Simpson, D and Crawford, K (2014) *Your Social Work Practice Placement: From Start to Finish*. London: Sage.

Meads, G and Ashcroft, J (2005) *The Case for Interprofessional Collaboration in Health and Social Care*. Oxford: Blackwell.

Megele, C (2011a) 'How to . . . sustain emotional resilience', online at http://www.communitycare.co.uk/2011/02/02/how-to-sustain-emotional-resilience/.

Megele, C (2011b) 'How to . . . supervise your peers', *Community Care*, online at http://www.communitycare.co.uk/2011/08/30/how-to-supervise-your-peers/.

Mehrabian, A (1981) *Silent Messages: Implicit Communication of Emotions and Attitudes*. Belmont, CA: Wadsworth.

Milner, J, Myers, S and O'Byrne, P (2015) *Assessment in Social Work*, 4th edition. Basingstoke: Palgrave.

Morris, K (2008) *Social Work and Multi-agency Working: Making a Difference*. Bristol: Policy Press.

Moss, B (2015) *Communication Skills in Health and Social Care*, 3rd edition. London: Sage.

Munro, E (2011) *The Munro Review of Child Protection. Final Report: A Child Centred Approach*, Cm 8062. London: TSO.

Nevo, I and Slonim-Nevo, V (2011) 'The myth of evidence-based practice: towards evidence-informed practice', *British Journal of Social Work*, 41 (6), pp. 1176–97.

O'Loughlin, M and O'Loughlin, S (eds) (2015) *Effective Observation in Social Work Practice*. London: Learning Matters.

O'Sullivan, T (2011) *Decision Making in Social Work*, 2nd edition. Basingstoke: Palgrave.

Oxford English Dictionary (2016a) online at http://www.oxforddictionaries.com/definition/english/right.

Oxford English Dictionary (2016b) online at http://www.oxforddictionaries.com/definition/english/hypothesis.

Oxford English Dictionary (2016c) online at http://www.oxforddictionaries.com/definition/english/communication.

Page, R and Silburn, R (1999) *British Social Welfare in the Twentieth Century*. Basingstoke: Palgrave.

Parker, J and Bradley, G (2014) *Social Work Practice*, 4th edition. London: Learning Matters/Sage.

Parker, J and Doel, M (eds) (2013) *Professional Social Work*. London: Learning Matters.

Parrott, L (2014) *Values and Ethics in Social Work Practice*, 3rd edition. London: Sage/Learning Matters.

Pawson, R, Boaz, A, Grayson, L, Long, A and Barnes, C (2003) *Types and Quality of Knowledge in Social Care*. London: Social Care Institute for Excellence.

Payne, S (2012) *Mental Health, Poverty and Social Exclusion*, Conceptual Note No. 9. University of Bristol, PSE UK.

Pierson, J (2011) *Understanding Social Work: History and Context*. Maidenhead: Open University Press.

Preston-Shoot, M (2014) *Making Good Decisions: Law for Social Work Practice*. Basingstoke: Palgrave Macmillan.

Quinney, A and Hafford-Letchfield, T (2012) *Interprofessional Social Work*. London: Learning Matters.

Reder, P and Duncan, S (2003) 'Understanding communication in child protection networks', *Child Abuse Review*, 12 (2), pp. 82–100.

Rutter, L and Brown, K (2015) *Critical Thinking and Professional Judgement for Social Work*, 4th edition. London: Learning Matters/Sage.

Schön, D. (1983) *The Reflective Practitioner: How Professionals Think in Action*. London: Temple Smith.

SCIE (2016) online at https://www.scie.org.uk/assets/elearning/communicationskills/cs01/resource/html/object1/object1_1.htm.

Seebohm Report (1968) Report of the Committee on Local Authority and Allied Personal Social Services. London: HMSO.

Seymour, C and Seymour, R (2013) *Practical Child Law for Social Workers*. London: Sage/Learning Matters.

Shemmings, D. and Shemmings, Y. (2012) 'Indicators of disorganised attachment in children', *Community Care*, 12 March.

Sheppard, M (1995) 'Social work, social science and practice wisdom', *British Journal of Social Work*, 25 (3), pp. 265–93.

Smale, G, Tuson, G, Biehal, N and Marsh, P (1993) *Empowerment, Assessment, Care Management and the Skilled Worker*. London: HMSO.

Smith, R (2008) *Social Work and Power.* Basingstoke: Palgrave.

Smith, R (2014) 'Ageism in the NHS may mean elderly trauma patients suffer worse care: doctors', *Telegraph*, 23 September, online at: http://www.telegraph.co.uk/news/health/news/11113843/Ageism-in-the-NHS-may-mean-elderly-trauma-patients-suffer-worse-care-doctors.html.

Social Care Institute for Excellence (SCIE) (2005) *Developing the Evidence Base for Social Work and Social Care Practice*, Using Knowledge in Social Care Report 10. London: SCIE.

Social Care Institute for Excellence (SCIE) (2016) 'Research Mindedness', available online at: http://www.scie.org.uk/publications/researchmindedness/whyrm/.

Taylor, B (2013) *Professional Decision Making and Risk in Social Work*, 2nd edition. London: Sage.

Thomas, J and Baron, S (2012) *Curriculum Guide – Interprofessional and Inter-agency Collaboration*. London: College of Social Work.

Thompson, N (1993) *Anti-discriminatory Practice.* London: Macmillan.

Thompson, N (2011) *Promoting Equality: Working with Diversity and Difference*, 3rd edition. Basingstoke: Palgrave.

Thompson, N and Thompson, S (2008) *The Social Work Companion.* Basingstoke: Palgrave.

Trevithick, P (2005) *Social Work Skills: A Practice Handbook*, 2nd edition. Maidenhead: Open University Press.

Uggerhøj, L (2011) 'Theorizing practice research in social work', *Social Work and Social Sciences Review*, 15 (1), pp. 49–73.

UN General Assembly (1989) *UN Convention on the Rights of the Child*, 20 November, United Nations, Treaty Series, Vol. 1577.

UNICEF (2006) *Behind Closed Doors – The Impact of Domestic Violence on Children.* New York: UNICEF.

Weinstein, J, Whittington, C and Leiba, C (eds) (2003) *Collaboration in Social Work Practice.* London: Jessica Kingsley.

Wilkins, D and Boahen, G (2013) *Critical Analysis Skills for Social Workers.* Maidenhead: Open University Press.

Williams, P and Evans, M (2013) *Social Work with People with Learning Difficulties*, 3rd edition. Exeter: Learning Matters.

Younge, G (2005) 'We can choose our identity, but sometimes it also chooses us', *Guardian*, 21 January 2005, online at https://www.theguardian.com/uk/2005/jan/21/islamandbritain.comment7.

Index